Streetsmart Guide to

Valuing a Stock

Streetsmart Guide to Valuing a Stock

The Savvy Investor's Key to Beating the Market

Gary Gray, Patrick J. Cusatis, and J. Randall Woolridge

McGraw-Hill

New York   San Francisco   Washington, D.C.   Auckland   Bogotá
Caracas   Lisbon   London   Madrid   Mexico City   Milan
Montreal   New Delhi   San Juan   Singapore
Sydney   Tokyo   Toronto

Library of Congress Cataloging-in-Publication Data

Gray, Gary
    Streetsmart guide to valuing a stock : the savvy investor's key to
  beating the market / by Gary Gray, Patrick Cusatis, Randall Woolridge.
      p.   cm.
    ISBN 0-07-134527-2
    1. Corporations—Valuation.   2. Stocks—Prices.   I. Gray, Gary,
  1950–   . II. Cusatis, Patrick.   III. Title.
  HG4028.V3W66   1999
  332.63'221—dc21   98-50428
                                                         CIP

McGraw-Hill

A Division of The McGraw·Hill Companies

1 2 3 4 5 6 7 8 9 0 DOC/DOC 9 0 3 2 1 0 9 8

ISBN 0-07-134527-2

The sponsoring editor for this book was Roger Marsh, the editing supervisor was John M. Morriss, and the production supervisor was Suzanne
W. B. Rapcavage. It was set in Utopia by North Market Street Graphics.

Printed and bound by R. R. Donnelley & Sons Company.

McGraw-Hill books are available at special quantity discounts to use as
premiums and sales promotions, or for use in corporate training programs. For more information, please write to the Director of Special Sales,
McGraw-Hill, 11 West 19th Street, New York, NY 10011. Or contact your
local bookstore.

 This book is printed on recycled, acid-free paper containing a
minimum of 50% recycled de-inked fiber.

To Katie O'Toole, a great writer, a terrific editor,
and a wonderful wife and mother.

G.G.

To my wife, Deborah, and my parents.

P.J.C.

To my daughters, Jillian, Ainsley, and Ginger.

J.R.W.

Contents

Preface

S *treetsmart Guide to Valuing a Stock* is a how-to book that provides you with the tools to make money in the stock market. The book's focus is on *stock valuation*—an area of great interest to many investors but understood by few.

When you have finished this hands-on, easy-to-use guide, you will have learned how to:

- Analyze a stock's value

- Spot undervalued or overvalued stocks for buying and selling opportunities

- Estimate important valuation inputs such as revenue growth, operating margin, and cost of capital

- Find valuation inputs on free Internet Web sites

- Develop a spreadsheet to value a stock

- Manipulate valuation inputs to see immediately how changes affect a stock's value

This book is for all those who *mistakenly think* they have to be stock market gurus to value stocks like the pros. All the tools you need to value stocks using the discounted cash flow valuation method are outlined in the chapters that follow. All that is required is a bit of patience, practice, and persistence.

You don't need an MBA to understand the book's concepts. The goal of the book is to give stock market participants—*individual investors, investment club members, stockbrokers, SEC staffers, corporate managers, directors of corporate boards, and ordinary people who want to learn about stock valuation*—a simple, quantitative approach for estimating stock values. Our model is a recipe for valuing common stock and increasing investment profits.

In the book we describe how you can use Excel or Lotus to write a spreadsheet to value stocks with a minimum number of inputs. If you don't feel like writing the program yourself, we'll direct you on how to tap into the Internet to get valuation software easily and cheaply. We show you how a valuation program works by using the common stock of AT&T, McDonald's, Intel, Microsoft, and Consolidated Edison as examples.

While we cannot guarantee that this book will help you outperform Wall Street analysts, it will explain how many of them value a stock. Using your own insights and assumptions, you will find bargains that the Wall Street professionals have missed. After all, a couple of back-yard astronomers discovered one of the century's brightest comets. Alan Hale and Tom Bopp were searching the same sky as NASA's rocket scientists.

If you're technologically challenged, not to worry. You don't need a computer or an Internet connection to use the discounted free cash flow method to value stocks. You can easily replicate any calculation in this book using arithmetic and a piece of paper. In Chapters 4 and 5 we describe how to calculate and estimate, *longhand,* a company's free cash flow and cost of capital—these are the essential ingredients of stock valuation. In Chapter 6 we show you how and where to get the information that you need for serious valuations. This book will help you learn about valuing stock even if spreadsheets and computers are too intimidating for your personal tastes.

Our goal is to teach you about stock valuation with a simple and powerful valuation model. This book will make you a better informed, more intelligent, more profitable investor and will help you to understand why stocks like Microsoft, Intel, and Consolidated Edison trade at their market price levels. To keep things simple, we scaled back on the use of complex equations, and relegated discussions of finance theory to appendices. Our valuation approach revolves around some very simple calculations that use only addition, subtraction, multiplication, and division—no calculus, differential equations, or advanced math. So let's begin by taking our initial plunge into stock valuation.

Good luck, tight lines, and happy valuations!

Gary Gray
Patrick J. Cusatis
J. Randall Woolridge

Acknowledgments

T his book was conceived and outlined on our recent trip to Spain. The concepts underlying stock valuation crystallized only as real livestock (6 fighting bulls and 12 to 15 steers) attempted to run over us on the narrow, crowded streets of Pamplona.

Integral to the book's progress were the discussions, over many fine meals with our friends in Pamplona, of its structure and international appeal. Ana Vizcay and Eduardo Iriso, Maria Jesus Ruiz de Azua and Emilio Goicoechea, Luiz Arguelles and Merche Amezgaray, Jose Maria Marco and Carmela Garraleta, Maria Josefa Vizcay and Hector Ortiz, and Manolo Asiain: We thank you for your hospitality and friendship over the years.

Many readers reviewed various parts of this book. We'd like to thank finance professor Russ Ezzell and management professor Charles Snow for their peer review and helpful suggestions, and Blake Hallinan for his research efforts. We'd also like to thank merchant bankers Scott Perper of First Union Capital Partners and Rusty Lewis of Transcore; derivatives specialists Patrick Mooney of UPR, Mark Hattier of Neuman, and Dave Eckhart of IMAGE; investment bankers Gerry Fallon of Key Bank and Buck Landry and Mark McBryde of Stephens; securities law expert Steve Huff of Kutak Rock; Web masters Joe and Jen Cusatis of Intelligent Data Management; Robert Frick of *Kiplinger's Magazine;* and noted Washington bureaucrat David Seltzer for their professional and careful review and help.

Especially helpful to us were the review and comments from our friends from investment clubs and the general investing public—Ann Barton, Lassie MacDonald, Sarah Ezzell, Barbara Snow, and John Nichols.

The input of the members of the Spruce Creek Rod & Investment Club is appreciated. Those members include John Wilson, Nick Rozsman, Manny Puello, Rick Simonsen, Kevin Dunphy, Constantin Nelson, Charlie Barkman, Dean Nelson, and Uncle Bob.

The helpful comments from the members of Berks Investment Group, especially Mark Hullinger and Natalie Zimmerman, are much appreciated, as well as the expertise of Michael Amato of Lehman Brothers.

As always, the input of the members of the Aspen Ski Institute, whose motto is "Saluting 20 years of mediocrity on and off the slopes," is important to us. Those members include John H. Foote IV, Tom (the Doc) Carroll, Bob Jones, and Bill McLucas, along with the previously mentioned Messrs. Seltzer, Mooney, Eckhart, Fallon, Hattier, Perper, and Lewis.

Many thanks to all of the people at McGraw-Hill who brought this book to publication, particularly: Roger Marsh, acquisitions editor; John Morriss, editing supervisor; and Suzanne Rapcavage, production supervisor.

A special thank you to Katie O'Toole, whose writing and editing skills are greatly appreciated, and whose suggestions for levity and lightening up of the material were fully accepted.

Empower Yourself with Information!

Measure Your Bungee Cord!

With today's stock market on a bungee cord, you could become just another gawking spectator—stunned by a 544-point plummet of the Dow Jones Industrial Average on one day (October 27, 1997) and thrilled by a 337-point bounce on the next (October 28, 1997). Or you could participate in the market and dive in and experience the excitement for yourself. If you were to consult the Delphic Oracle of the 1990s, Oprah would probably say, "Go for it, but empower yourself first!"

To survive in today's stock market, you need to empower yourself with information so that you've properly measured the length of your bungee cord. You don't want to be the jumper who goes **Splat!** because your cord is too long and you've severely misjudged stock valuation levels.

Some of the questions you might want to ask before taking the plunge are: Do underlying economic conditions change fast enough to justify the current level of stock price volatility? Has the dart board approach become an investor's best method for choosing stocks? Or has the stock market become a pastime for financial thrill seekers?

You may know that a stock's price is influenced by the company's revenue growth rate, operating profit margin, and earnings, along with inflation and interest rates. You may not understand how all these factors are interrelated. Maybe you're wondering:

- How does the market come up with a stock price?

- What's driving today's lofty stock market valuations?

- Why does a stock price react so violently to small quarterly earnings surprises?

- Why and how do interest rate changes affect a stock's value?

- And how can you make money by reading this book?

We answer these questions, introduce you to an easy-to-use approach for stock valuation, and teach you how to value common stock without pain, anxiety, or alchemy.

The Focus of the Book

The focus of the book is to show you how to value the common stock of most corporations by using a small set of cash flow and interest rate numbers. Our goals are to demystify the stock valuation process, make stock valuation easier to understand, and show you how to make money in the stock market by purchasing "undervalued" stocks and selling "overvalued" stocks.

How do we accomplish these goals? We explain what corporate cash flow measures are important, how they are related, and how they, along with interest rates, influence a stock's value. This book helps you put into perspective the various pieces of the stock valuation puzzle to see the big picture. It makes a seemingly complex world easier to understand.

If you're familiar with the stock market, using the valuation approach will be relatively easy, and previously confusing concepts will fall into place. If you're a relative newcomer to the market and are unfamiliar with investing concepts and jargon, you will need to read certain sections several times to understand them. Hang in there! It will be worth your investment of time and should compound quickly into investment profits.

Our valuation approach uses a discounted cash flow (DCF) method to value stocks. The DCF approach is a technique that is employed by investors and traders to value all types of financial instruments, such as U.S. government bonds, preferred stocks, corporate bonds, and mortgage-backed securities. Investment bankers use DCF models to value mergers and acquisition (M&A) targets, leveraged buyout transactions (LBOs), and initial public offerings (IPOs) of stock. DCF is Wall Street's preferred valuation method.

DCF is also the valuation approach that's favored by Main Street. Corporations from Maine to California, use DCF techniques to analyze virtually all capital budgeting and investment decisions. Corporate managers who read this book will immediately understand how their operating and financing decisions will affect their company's stock value and the managers' real bottom lines—**the value of their stock options.**

Most inputs for the valuation approach come from corporate annual and quarterly reports and can be found easily on the Internet (Chapter 6 points and clicks you in that direction) or in the corporation's published financial statements. In today's information-friendly environment, financial information flows quickly. To make information readily available to investors, most corporations have their own Internet Web sites on which they file their annual and quarterly reports. Also, the Securities and Exchange Commission (SEC) allows users to download various corporate financial reports through its EDGAR database, available at its Internet Web site address (http://www.sec.gov/).

In addition, reams of corporate financial information are accessible through computer information services like America Online (http://www.aol.com/) and the Microsoft Network (http://www.msn.com/). These services, which charge a monthly fee to subscribers, allow free access to some Web sites that otherwise carry a fee. A tremendous amount of corporate and investment information is available through on-line financial Web sites such as Morningstar, Hoover's, Value Line, the Motley Fool, Wall Street Research Net, and Standard & Poor's Information Service. Some of these services are free and some involve subscription and payment of fees. A list of Web site addresses appears in Appendix A.

The Four-Step DCF Approach to Valuation

The DCF method that we use follows a four-step approach to valuation:

1. We develop a set of future free cash flows for a corporation according to expectations about the company's revenue growth, net operating profit margin, cash income tax rates, and fixed and working capital requirements.

2. We estimate a discount rate for the cash flows of the corporation, taking into account the expected timing and potential risks of those cash flows.

3. We discount the resulting cash flow estimates and total them to calculate value for the corporation as a whole.

4. We reduce that total corporate value by the amount of debt, preferred stock, and other claims of the corporation and divide that amount by the number of shares outstanding to get the per share *intrinsic value* of the corporation's common stock.

We compare this per share intrinsic value with the stock's observed market price to determine which stocks are undervalued or overvalued by the market and which stocks to buy, sell, or hold.

This valuation procedure sounds a lot more complicated than it is. In this book we describe how you can do these calculations easily, using addition, multiplication, subtraction, and division. If you have a computer, the spreadsheet software that we teach you to develop in Chapter 8 does the work for you in a nanosecond—so don't be intimidated. If you don't want to write a spreadsheet, we show you how and where you can purchase the computer software called ValuePro 2000, which we have developed and use in the book. Information is power and with power comes money!

The book gives you the concepts and information that you need to *buy low and sell high*. The DCF valuation approach also allows you to play what-if games to see how a change in growth, profits, or interest rates affects a stock's value.

The DCF Stock Valuation Process

There are a number of questions that you should answer before you invest in a stock. Do you understand the company's business? What is the growth potential of the industry in which the company operates and how is the company positioned? Who are its competitors? What is the quality and stability of the company's management? Let's assume that you've answered these questions to your satisfaction. How does this book help you?

What this book and the spreadsheet software that we describe give you are the tools and the guidance that you need to estimate the intrinsic value of a company's stock. If you like the company, its products, and its prospects, you can use our valuation approach to help decide if the company is undervalued, overvalued, or fairly valued. Even the stock of the most well-run company is a poor investment if its price is higher than its discounted expected cash flows justify.

*An investment decision should be based on **price versus value.*** If your analysis shows that a stock is greatly undervalued—take the plunge and buy! If it's overvalued, you can sell the stock if you own it; or if you don't, you can patiently follow its price and acquire it if it moves to a more attractive price. The DCF valuation approach empowers you with the information that you need to time your buy and sell decisions carefully.

The value of any financial investment (stock, bond, mortgage, money market account, etc.) equals the present value of its expected future cash flows, discounted for the risk and timing of those cash flows. This is a basic belief underlying the theory of finance. It's so basic and important that it warrants more description. It may be helpful for us all to get on the same page with some valuation-related definitions.

Some Helpful Definitions Relating to Valuation

Expected cash flows are the most likely cash payments that you can expect (not *hope*) to receive from an investment, such as a stock or bond, or that you are expected to pay on an obligation such as a loan or a mortgage. Below we examine a simple example relating to the valuation of a home mortgage.

To *discount* means simply to multiply a number by less than 1.0. The *discount rate* that you should use in any valuation will depend upon the *timing* of the expected cash flows and the *risks* associated with receiving the expected cash flows. The discount rate is a function of both time and risk: discount rate = f (time, risk). The discount rate should **increase with increasing default risk** (e.g., a loan to your brother-in-law) and **decrease with lower default risk** (e.g., U.S. Treasury Bonds) associated with the expected cash payment.

Similar to the discount rate, the *discount factor* takes into account both the *discount rate* and the *timing* of the expected cash flow. The discount factor is a function of both the discount rate and time: discount factor = f (discount rate, time). For example, the discount factor for a 1-year cash flow, whose discount rate is 6%, is simply equal to 1 divided by 1.06, which in equation form looks like this: $1/1.06 = .9434$. The discount factor for a 2-year cash flow, whose discount rate is also 6%, is equal to $1/1.06 = .9434$, that amount divided again by $1.06 = .9434/1.06 = .8900$. This process for a 3-year cash flow continues with a third division by 1.06. The discount factor *decreases* with increasing time to the expected payment of a cash flow and *decreases* with an increasing discount rate.

The value of an investment, known as the *present value (PV)*, is found by taking the *sum of the expected cash flows multiplied by their respective discount factors.* For example, using a 6% discount rate, a discount factor of .9434, and an expected $100 cash flow in 1 year, the present value of that cash flow is $100 times .9434: $100 \times (.9434) = $94.34. Using a 6% discount rate, a $100 cash flow expected in 2 years, and a discount factor of .8900, the present value of that cash flow is $100 \times (.8900) = $89.00. The value of the investment is the sum of the present values of all the expected cash flows. The present value of the two cash flows described above is PV = $94.34 + $89.00 = $183.34.

Your Mortgage: An Analogy for Valuation

To better understand the valuation process, consider a home mortgage. You want to purchase a new house, so you go to the bank and get a $100,000, 30-year mortgage at 8%. The payments on your mortgage would be $734 a month for 360 months, as shown in Exhibit 1-1.

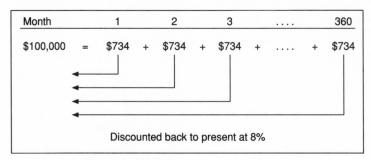

EXHIBIT 1-1 The Valuation Process

The $734 monthly payments are the *expected cash flows* that the bank receives on the mortgage. Over the life of the mortgage (assuming that you don't prepay), you will pay a total of $264,240 ($734 × 360 months) to the bank. The $100,000 mortgage amount represents the value to the bank of the 360-monthly payments of $734 discounted using a rate of 8%. This is called the *present value* of the mortgage.

Your 8% mortgage rate represents the *discount rate,* or *yield,* that the bank requires to lend you money. The discount rate is a function of the general level of interest rates in the economy (as represented by the interest rates on comparable-maturity U.S. Treasury Bonds), plus a *risk premium* for the bank to compensate for the possibility that you may not repay the loan. U.S. Treasury Bonds are considered *riskless* because Uncle Sam can always print more money to repay its loans.

The present value to the bank of the series of the 360 monthly payments of $734 discounted at a rate of 8% equals $100,000. The interest or discount rate that the bank requires on your mortgage depends very significantly upon the market interest rate at the time you get your loan. Consider these two scenarios:

1. If interest rates rise, the bank will increase its lending rates on new loans to compensate for the higher market interest rates. For example, if interest rates rise 1% (also known as 100 basis points), the present value of your 360 mortgage payments of $734 (discounted now at 9%) is only $91,223. Any new mortgage from the bank would have to have monthly payments increased to $805 (a monthly payment difference of $71) so that its present value, discounted at 9%, would equal $100,000.

2. If interest rates fall, the bank will decrease its lending rates on new loans to compensate for the lower market interest rates. For example, if interest rates fall 1%, the present value of your 360 mortgage payments of $734 (discounted now at 7%) is $110,326. A new mortgage from the bank would have to have monthly payments decreased to $665 (a monthly payment difference of $69) so that its present value, discounted at 7%, would equal $100,000.

Now for the major insight of this section: The basic valuation procedure used to value a stock is the same as that used by a bank when granting a mortgage. **The *stock's value* is the present value of the expected future cash flows to stockholders discounted at the appropriate rates, as adjusted for risk and the timing of expected cash flows.**

Stock Valuation—Art, Science, or Hocus-Pocus?

The economics underlying the movements and price levels of the stock market are a mystery to most people. At the end of trading each day, stock analysts on CNN, CNBC, and other financial news networks attribute *stock price movements* to any number of factors: government reports on consumer or wholesale prices; changes in interest rates and the bond market; the increasingly bullish or bearish sentiment of investors; statements by Federal Reserve Chairman Alan Greenspan; or company earnings reports exceeding or falling short of expectations.

For many market players, what determines *absolute stock price levels* seems to be even more puzzling. Why is the Dow Jones Industrial Average at 10001? Why does McDonald's sell for $80 per share? Is stock valuation art, science, or hocus-pocus?

In this book, we focus on the **art** and **science** of stock valuation. We contend that over time stock prices will gravitate to their underlying intrinsic values. This observation is consistent with the beliefs of renowned investors like Warren Buffett and Peter Lynch. The valuation of common stock is no different from the valuation of any other asset. Asset valuation—be it a financial, real, or human asset—is a generic exercise.

The economic value of any asset is simply the total of the cash flows that you expect to receive from the asset, discounted back to the present at a rate that reflects both the time value of money and the degree of risk or uncertainty associated with those expected cash flows. Future cash flows for common stocks can come from dividends, from the sale or merger of a company (e.g., Yahoo's offer for the stock of Geocities.com), from repurchase of stock by the company (e.g., Microsoft and Intel have large share repurchase programs), or from the sale of the stock at market prices.

The DCF valuation approach applies to all assets: financial assets such as bonds, mortgages, and stock; real assets such as buildings and real estate; and human assets such as a college education and the economic value of a person's life. (We're not getting metaphysical—but many jurisdictions use the DCF valuation technique to determine the "economic value" of a life in a wrongful death case.) For financial assets with fixed income or fixed payments such as bonds and mortgages, it's relatively simple to apply the DCF approach. Applying this approach to common stocks or an individual's life is considerably more difficult. How we overcome these stock valuation difficulties unfolds in the chapters that follow.

Stock Valuation Approaches: Where Does DCF Fit?

A number of investment techniques and philosophies are practiced by stock market participants. These philosophies range from the conservative "buy-and-hold companies you know" strategy of many individual investors (such as Warren Buffett and Peter Lynch), to the aggressive long/short, "risk-neutral" strategies (the recent collapse of Long Term Capital Management has shown that there are no completely risk-neutral investment strategies) employed by sophisticated hedge fund managers playing the international markets (such as John Meriwether and George Soros).

In general terms, the different stock market investment and valuation strategies can be classified as fitting into one of three camps—*fundamental analysis, technical analysis,* and *modern portfolio theory (MPT)*. The three philosophies have different beliefs about the relationship between the stock prices that we observe in the markets and underlying intrinsic stock values.[1] Those beliefs are summarized in Exhibit 1-2.

An example of fundamental analysis is the valuation procedure we use in this book—discounted cash flow analysis. According to this approach, the intrinsic value of a company's stock is determined by the company's current and future operating and financial performance. Fundamental analysts use other approaches to assess intrinsic value as well—primarily *target stock price* and *relative valuation—* which are discussed below. To assess a company's prospects, fundamental analysts evaluate overall economic, industry, and company data in arriving at an estimate of a stock's intrinsic value. The assumption underlying fundamental analysis is that a company's stock price over time will gravitate to its intrinsic value.

How to Value a Share?			
	Technical Analysis	**Fundamental Analysis**	**Portfolio Theory**
What Drives Stock Prices?	Psychology Technical Cosmic	Earnings Dividends	Risk & Return
How to Value A Share?	Trends Waves Factors	Forecast Dividends & Earnings	Risk & Return
Relationship Between Value and Prices?	P ≠ V	P will Eventually Equal Value	P = V

EXHIBIT 1-2   Valuation Strategies

Technical analysts believe that stock price movements are influenced primarily by changes in investor or market psychology. True technicians are not concerned with a company's balance sheet and income statement. Instead, they believe that stock prices reflect the greed versus fear mentality of investors. Thus, there is no necessary relationship between a stock's price and its underlying intrinsic value.

The followers of modern portfolio theory believe that competitive forces in the stock market result in stock prices that *always reflect* underlying intrinsic values. In MPT terminology, the market is efficient because new information is very quickly incorporated into stock prices and there **never** are any undervalued or overvalued stocks.

Fundamental Analysis[1]

The more famous advocates of fundamental analysis include investors like Benjamin Graham, Warren Buffett, and Peter Lynch; and Wall Street strategists like Abby Joseph Cohen of Goldman Sachs, Charles Clough of Merrill Lynch, and Marshall Acuff of Smith Barney/Salomon Brothers. The virtues of fundamental analysis are espoused on the Internet by the Motley Fool (http://www.fool.com/), Stock Valuation with Sense (http://www.stocksense.com/), and Value Investing (http://www.cyberramp.net/~investor).

The majority of Wall Street's analysts primarily use fundamental valuation techniques to base their buy/sell recommendations and to estimate a company's *value*. In this analytic style, value is a function of revenue, growth, earnings, dividends, cash flows, profit margins, risk, interest rates, and other factors. Most Wall Street fundamental stock analysts assess a company's stock price versus value using one or more of following three methods:

Target Stock Price Analysis. A very popular technique is to construct a model of the firm's expected performance to forecast future earnings per share (EPS). This figure is then combined with a projected price/earnings (P/E) ratio to arrive at a "target stock price." A typical target stock price analysis would conclude in this manner: "With a 1999 EPS estimate of $3, and assuming a market P/E ratio of 25, our target stock price for McDonald's is $75 per share. Given the current price of $65, we recommend buying the stock."

Relative Value Analysis. Relative value measures are often used in conjunction with the target stock price approach. Relative value analysis employs a measure of value—most commonly the P/E ratio—for a company and similar stocks and its industry peers. Relative value measures other than price/earnings ratios include price/book value (P/BV), price/sales (P/S), and the price/earnings/growth (PEG) ratios as yardsticks for relative stock value comparisons of different companies with varying characteristics.

The P/E ratio is the relative value approach that you see and hear quoted most frequently by the media because it's simple to compute and understand. The P/E ratio is compared with the company's peers in conjunction with other fundamental factors—most notably earnings per share growth, net operating profit margin, and risk—to ascertain if a stock is overvalued or undervalued. The PEG ratio for the valuation of growth stocks has been popular of late because it is favored by the Motley Fool in its various publications and on its Web site.

A relative value analysis may read as follows: "McDonald's current P/E of 20 is below the P/Es of other fast-food restaurant chains. Given that the company's growth (10% for sales and earnings) is in line with industry peers, and its risk profile (as measured by earnings volatility and debt levels) is below that of its competitors, we conclude that McDonald's is undervalued."

Discounted Cash Flow Analysis. We use DCF analysis in this book. While DCF analysis is used in the valuation of all types of fixed income investments (bonds, mortgages, etc.), it gets much less attention from the media as a method to value common stocks. One apparent reason for this lack of attention may be the difficulty in explaining the DCF technique in simple terms to stock investors. This book overcomes that difficulty.

Under *discounted cash flow approaches,* a stock's value depends upon the analyst's estimate of expected cash flows of the company, discounted at an appropriate discount rate. The most basic DCF approach is the *dividend discount model (DDM),* under which the value of a stock is the present value of the dividends that an investor expects to receive. Using the DDM approach, the analyst estimates future dividend growth and the required rate of return on the stock and discounts those expected dividends to arrive at a stock's value.

Another DCF approach is the *free cash flow to equity (FCFE) model,* which measures the cash flow left over after payments for working capital, capital expenditures, the interest and principal on debt, and dividends on preferred stock. These cash flows are then discounted at the company's cost of equity to arrive at the stock's value. The final DCF approach involves *free cash flow to the firm (FCFF).* We use the FCFF approach and describe it herein.

Analysts who use DCF analysis tend to provide a simple value statement such as: "On a cash flow basis, we estimate McDonald's fair value to be $80 per share. Given the current price of $65, we recommend buying the stock."

In evaluating the fundamental approaches to stock valuation, it is important to note that both the *target stock price* and *relative value* methods employ a measure of value—primarily the P/E ratio—to establish intrinsic value. This is somewhat circular reasoning. P/E ratios represent the price that investors are willing to pay for a stock, given a company's earnings per share. P/Es for stocks are most closely related to expected earnings growth rates. Stocks with lower P/Es— such as banks and insurance companies, have projected earnings growth rates below 10%. On the other hand, stocks that sell at higher P/E multiples, such as Microsoft and Coca Cola, have projected earnings growth rates in excess of 20%.

When valuing a stock, it is important to note that P/E ratios are an outcome of the valuation process—not the process itself. Stocks are valued just like any other asset—by discounting expected future cash flows back to the present at a required rate of return. P/E ratios simply take the result of this valuation process, the stock price, and divide it by a company's current or projected earnings per share. In contrast to the target stock price and relative value approaches, DCF analysis involves a direct application of the valuation process.

Many market participants use fundamental analytic techniques as the basis for **long-term buy/sell decisions**. The basic investment rule of fundamental analysis is: If a stock price is well below its intrinsic value, buy the stock; if the stock price is well above its value, sell the stock.

Technical Analysis[2]

In contrast to fundamental analysts, *technical analysts* chart historic stock price movements, volume of trading activity, and the price/volume aspects of related equity and debt markets to predict or anticipate the *stock-buying behavior of other market participants.* The *animal spirits* of other market players are more important to technical analysts than to fundamental analysts. Technical analysts believe that stock prices are influenced more by investor psychology and the emotions of the "crowd" than by changes in the underlying fundamentals of the company. And the actions of the crowd of investors in the stock markets are driven by **fear** on the downside and **greed** on the upside.

The more famous advocates of technical analysis are Ralph Acampora of Prudential Securities, William O'Neil of *Investor's Business Daily*, and Richard McCabe of Merrill Lynch. The virtues of technical analysis are featured on the Internet at Wall Street City (http://www.wallstreetcity.com/), the Elliott Wave Chart Page (http://www.wavechart.com/), and the Short Term Stock Selector (http://www.flash.net/~hesler/).

Technical analysts focus on how market participants will behave in the near term and how stock market pessimism or optimism will affect their behavior. To a technical analyst, a stock's price would tend to go up, not necessarily because of better operating aspects of the company, but because of an upward trend and momentum in the company's stock price. Investors who exclusively use technical analysis generally have a shorter-term stock holding orientation and have more frequent trading activity than investors who employ only fundamental analytic techniques.

Many market participants use technical analytical techniques as the basis for **short-term buy/sell decisions**. The basic investment rule of technical analysis is: If your indicators signal that a stock's price will rise, buy the stock. If your indicators signal that a stock's price will fall, sell the stock.

Modern Portfolio Theory[3]

Advocates of modern portfolio theory (MPT) will tell you that stock prices **always** reflect intrinsic value. They believe that the value of any type of analysis is already reflected in the stock's price.

To support this claim, MPT advocates cite academic studies showing, among other things, that daily stock price changes are random (the *random walk hypothesis*); stock prices react very quickly to new company disclosures about earnings, dividend changes, and other corporate news (the *efficient market hypothesis*); and investment funds run by professional money managers (i.e., mutual and pension funds), on average, underperform the overall stock market as measured by the S&P 500. For a description of various tests of stock market efficiency, see Appendix B.

Overall, these findings suggest that investors cannot use past stock price information or public news releases of firm-specific information to find undervalued stocks; and that even investment fund managers, on average, cannot sleuth the market to detect undervalued stocks. MPT practitioners sometimes express disdain for technical and fundamental analysis. As such, MPT devotees tell investors not to bother searching for undervalued stocks; instead, pick a comfortable risk level and diversify holdings within a portfolio of stocks.

Our Valuation Philosophy

Most investors that we know (except for some staunch academician friends who actually believe in MPT) use either a combination of *fundamental and technical analysis* in coming up with investment picks and market timing or use *no analysis at all* and rely solely on hot tips from their golfing partners.

Where do we lie on the fundamental versus technical versus MPT debate? We'd **always prefer** to buy a stock that is priced below its intrinsic value. However, when a stock's price trend is upward, the trend can carry an overvalued stock even higher. Many investors who rely primarily on technical analysis have benefited from using a *momentum trading strategy.*

Conversely, if the market is bearish and stock prices are falling, a poor investment is a stock that is selling at a significant premium to its intrinsic value. An overvalued stock is a great short-selling opportunity in a bear market. We believe that technical price trends as well as fundamental value and diversification are all important. If an investment philosophy works for you, use it to your benefit. However, don't turn your back on other investment and valuation techniques, especially the DCF approach.

The MPT side of the story presumes that fundamental and technical analysis will get you nowhere in the investment world, since all this information is already reflected in today's stock price. While academics tend to believe this notion, investment professionals do not. The empirical evidence is beginning to turn against the idea that stock prices always reflect intrinsic stock values.

Since 1990, *The Wall Street Journal* has "tested" the notion of stock market efficiency in its "Investment Dartboard" column. The *Journal* compares the 6-month total return performance of four stocks, one selected by each of four different investment professionals, versus four stocks picked through the random method of tossing darts at the stock listings pages of the *Journal.* As of October 1998, the performance strongly supports the "fundamentalist" pros over the "random" darts. There have been 100 "contests" over the period *and the pros have beaten the darts in 60.* On a relative return basis, the pros have earned an average 6-month return of 10.8% over the period, compared with 6.8% for the DJIA and 4.5% for the dart stocks.[4]

We believe strongly that there is value to careful stock selection and that an investor should own a diversified portfolio of common stocks. Within that portfolio, the investor should value each stock individually, using the DCF technique that we describe. When a stock's price is *overvalued* and exceeds its intrinsic value by more than X% (the investor should pick that percentage, e.g., 15%), an investor should sell that stock and replace it with another stock that is *undervalued* by more than X% (e.g., 15%).

This approach allows an investor to benefit from the diversification that is advocated by modern portfolio theory, while also making the value play that we recommend. We also believe that in any analysis leading to a buy/sell stock decision, the investor should heed the *fear* and avoid the *greed* factors that regularly bubble through the stock market.

Tax considerations often complicate the timing of purchase and sale of stock, and we do not address this complex issue in the book.

Where Do We Go from Here?

Valuing common stocks is a mystery to most investors. The recent gyrations in the stock market have no doubt added to this mystery. Indeed, many market observers insist that these gyrations support the notion that stock valuation is less art and science and more hocus-pocus. This book's focus is on the art and science of stock valuation and how you can profitably use it in your investment decisions. In the pages that follow, we explain how **you** can apply the stock valuation principles used by professional money managers and Wall Street investment bankers to value your favorite stocks.

The crucial concept we will attempt to hammer home throughout this book is that the value of a stock—like the value of any other financial instrument—is equal to the discounted value of its expected cash flows, adjusted for risk and timing. For many investors, there are two general sources of confusion in the stock valuation process. First, what are the expected cash flows? We clear up this question in Chapter 4. Second, what is the appropriate rate to discount uncertain cash flows? We discuss this concern in Chapter 5. This book teaches you how to address these questions and use your answers to generate investment profits.

Since we believe it is helpful to know about a company in which you're considering an investment, Chapter 6 shows the what, where, and how of getting information instantaneously. Chapter 7 shows how to use the DCF approach and how to vary valuation assumptions to value stocks such as AT&T, Consolidated Edison, Microsoft, McDonald's, and Intel. In Chapter 8 we show you how to design a simple spreadsheet valuation program.

So let's go! If you get stuck on a term that is unfamiliar or a concept that is difficult to grasp, either reread the section or refer to the Glossary or Appendices. It's now time to learn how to value a stock.

Notes

1. For a description of the fundamental valuation techniques discussed in this section, see Aswath Damodaran, *Investment Valuation*, John Wiley & Sons, New York, 1996; and Tom Copeland, Tim Koller, and Jack Murrin, *Valuation—Measuring and Managing the Value of Companies*, John Wiley & Sons, New York, 1996.

2. For a good description of technical analytic techniques, along with linking them to stock selection criteria using the Internet, see David Brown and Kassandra Bentley, *Cyber Investing: Cracking Wall Street with Your Personal Computer*, John Wiley & Sons, New York, 1997.

3. Burton G. Malkiel explains the random walk hypothesis and modern portfolio theory in his classic, witty book, *A Random Walk Down Wall Street*, W.W. Norton & Co., New York, 1990.

CHAPTER 2

How to Value a Stock

Valuation Insights or Stock "Tips"

Are you worried that your shares of Dell Computer (NASDAQ—**DELL:** http://www.dell.com/) have run too far and may be overvalued? Has your cousin told you that her stock broker claims that WalMart (NYSE—**WMT:** http://www.wal-mart.com/) will hit $125 per share by year end? What type of return can you expect to earn on a stock? How can you test your stock valuation insights or the stock "tips" of others?

You can pick up investment reports from stock brokerage firms to see what others are saying about these stocks. Or you can test these notions yourself using the same valuation procedures employed by Wall Street investment bankers and stock analysts—with the techniques described in this book. This chapter provides a description of expected stock returns and an overview of the DCF approach to show how easily this procedure can be applied to stocks you own or are considering for purchase. To demonstrate the basic principles of the DCF approach, we show a simplified valuation of Microsoft (NASDAQ—**MSFT:** http://www.microsoft.com/) as an example.

What Do We Mean by Returns to Stockholders?

As a stockholder, you should be primarily concerned with your investment return, or *cash flows* from your stock. Have you received dividends? Has the stock price gone up? What has been your total rate of return? In other words, you're primarily concerned with stock performance measures that relate to your pocketbook.

Calculation of Return to Stockholders

Return to stockholders includes the dividend payments plus the increase (minus the decrease) in stock price that investors experience during an investment holding period. The market's focus is on *yearly return* to stockholders, as measured by percentage gains or losses, and usually uses the calendar year as the benchmark period over which to calculate the return. Return to stockholder refers to the annual return, which is equal to the sum of the dividends paid plus the net change in a stock's price, divided by the beginning price of the stock:

$$\%\text{Return to Stockholders} = \frac{(\text{Dividends} + \text{Change in Stock Price})}{\text{Beginning Stock Price}}$$

For example, if a stock's price started the year at $100, the stock paid $1 in dividends during the year, and it ended the year at $109, its percentage return to stockholders would equal ($1 + $9)/$100 = 10%. This is not a complex calculation.

The stock market sometimes acts in funny ways. The return to a stockholder may be negative even if the company had a successful year from an operations or earnings perspective. The stock market may have gone down as a result of macroeconomic concerns, such as higher interest rates, lowered earnings forecasts, or inflation or deflation fears, or geopolitical concerns, such as a deterioration in Middle East relations, a Russian currency crisis, or an improvement in Fidel Castro's health. This market downdraft may have pulled your stock with it, and there is nothing the company's management could have done to change the adverse stock price movement.

Conversely, the return to stockholders may be very positive, even though the company had a mediocre or poor operating performance. The stock market may have skyrocketed because of a positive economic event, such as the settlement of a major labor strike or reduced inflation fears. Poor performance may put the company into the *takeover candidate* category, and the increase in price may be the result of a tender offer for the company's stock. For example, large trading losses at Salomon Brothers triggered the 1997 takeover of Salomon, at a substantial premium to the then-market price, by the Smith Barney unit of Travelers Corporation.

Investor Expectations Regarding Stock Market Returns

What should an investor expect in the way of returns from a *diversified portfolio of common stocks?* During the 70-year period from 1928 to 1997, the S&P 500 had a compound average return of 10.6%. The S&P 500 is a value-weighted index. In more recent years stock returns have been spectacular. In calendar years 1995, 1996, and 1997, total returns on the S&P 500, according to Ibbotson Associates,[1] were 37.4%, 23.1%, and 33.4%, respectively. In 1998, while the S&P 500 was up 26.7%, the *average* stock in the S&P 500 gained just 10.8%.[2] General stock market performance that good can't last forever.

What are *reasonable* returns to be earned in the stock market over a long period of time? Jeremy Siegel, in *Stocks for the Long Run,* found that **7.13%** was the **average real yearly return,** dividends plus appreciation after adjusting for inflation, from owning stock over the 50-year period from 1946 to 1996. This return is very close to the **6.96% median earnings yield,** which he defines as corporate earnings per share divided by stock price, for the same time period.[3] As a company's earnings have increased, its stock price also has increased proportionately to maintain this earnings yield. Siegel finds *that real returns (after inflation) for common stock closely track real* growth in *corporate earnings,* and *stock prices in the long-run are a very strong function of real growth in corporate earnings.* For a first cut at expectations for stock returns from *a diversified portfolio of stocks,* **investors should expect a real return that is roughly in line with the growth of corporate earnings.**

Siegel also calculates that the companies that comprise the S&P 500 had an average earnings-per-share growth rate of 14.8% for the 5-year period from 1993 to 1997. That's a significantly lower percentage than the 21.4% average market performance of share prices of the S&P 500 for the same period. What is the reason for this recent large discrepancy between corporate performance and stock market performance?

Famed economist John Maynard Keynes said that in the long run we are all dead! Then what happens in the short run? In the *short run,* stock prices exhibit a very strong *inverse* relationship to movements in interest rates. In general, as interest rates (and a corporation's financing costs) go down—stock prices go up, and as interest rates go up—stock prices go down.

Siegel believes and we agree that **interest rates, in the short and intermediate time frame, are the single most important influence on stock prices.** He analyzed monetary policy, as implemented by the Federal Reserve, over a 42-year period from 1955 to 1996. His results were quite striking.

Siegel found that the 3-month average return for the stock market, after significant decreases in the Fed Funds rate (85 instances), was 5.6%. When the Fed increased the Fed Funds rate (92 instances), the 3-month average return for the stock market was only 0.85%. The *benchmark* 3-month average return during this period was 2.97%. The 3-month return of 5.6%, after Fed Funds rate decreases, versus the 3-month return of 0.85%, after Fed Funds rate increases, is a very healthy difference in stock market performance. Fed Funds rate movements have been a good predictor of short-term stock returns.[4]

During the time period described above, long-term interest rates, as measured by the 30-year U.S. Treasury yield, declined from 7.34% at the beginning of 1993 to under 5% in September 1998. This decline in interest rates has greatly increased intrinsic stock values and we explain why in Chapter 5.

The DCF approach uses **both cash flow and interest rate measures as the two primary influences on intrinsic stock value.** The direct relationship of a stock's value to corporate cash flow is examined in Chapter 4, and the inverse relationship of a stock's value to a change in a corporation's weighted average cost of capital (WACC), especially through changes in interest rates, is described in Chapter 5.

Investor Expectations Regarding Returns of a Stock

What are *reasonable* market expectations in the way of return on a *particular stock?* It depends in large part on the risk of the stock and the expected growth of the company's earnings and its free cash flows. **With increasing risk, a rational investor should require increasing expected return.**

Let's assume that the *risk-free,* long-term Treasury Bond yields 7%, the equity risk premium is 3%, and the stock is of *average* risk (beta = 1.0) relative to the stock market as a whole. (Don't worry, we describe beta, risk, and risk premiums below.) According to finance theory, our expected return for this stock is 10% (we rigged this example to result in a nice round number). The equation below shows the relationship between expected return, the risk-free rate, beta, and the equity risk premium:

Expected Return from Stock = Risk-Free Rate
+ (Beta × Equity Risk Premium)
Expected Return from (Beta = 1) Stock = 7% + (1.0 × 3%) = 10%

Beta, which is more fully described in Chapter 5, is a measure of the *price volatility* (a.k.a. *risk*) of an asset. If the risk of the stock is greater than average (e.g., the stock has a beta of 2.0), a rational investor would require an expected return that is greater than that of a lower beta stock. For example, based on a Treasury Bond yield of 7% and an equity risk premium of 3%, the expected return of a beta = 2.0 stock is:

Expected Return from (Beta = 2) Stock = 7% + (2.0 × 3%) = 13%

If you invest on January 1 (which is difficult, because the U.S. stock market is closed) in a $100 (beta = 1) stock that *pays no dividend* and has the risk characteristics described above, your expectation is that the stock will increase in value by 10% to $110 on December 31. Your hope is that it will become the next Microsoft or Intel and it will make you a millionaire.

If you assume the same yield/risk profiles, you expect that the stock will increase in price by another 10% to $121 the next December 31: $100 × 1.10 = $110 × 1.10 = $121. If the $100 stock has a beta = 2, your expectation is a progression in price to $113 (year 1) to $127.69 (year 2): $100 × 1.13 = $113 × 1.13 = $127.69. To paraphrase the late, great Sonny Bono and Cher, ". . . and the beta goes on!"

As long as the stock performs in accordance with its perceived risk profile, your gain of 10% or 13% per year compounded annually would have fulfilled your expectations. If the stock price exceeds your target levels, you're happy! If the stock price increases to less than your target levels, or decreases, you might still be happy, but you have been underpaid for the risk associated with owning that stock.

Is a Stock Fairly Valued?

A major concern for you as an investor is whether a stock's price is equal to, above, or below, its value, at the time you buy it. According to all measures of corporate performance, the company may be a great company and may have performed well operationally during the year. Nevertheless, if the stock's price is much greater than the stock's value when you purchase it, then the return on your investment may be dismal. This book and the ValuePro 2000 software will allow you to estimate a stock's value and help you avoid purchasing overpriced stock.

How are market expectations factored into stock prices? If stock market analysts and participants are expecting earnings or revenue growth for stocks like Microsoft or Dell Computer of 30% per year, **that expectation is factored into today's stock market price—especially for growth stocks.**

Growth stocks are companies whose rate of revenue or earnings growth (e.g., 15% and up) greatly exceeds the growth rate of the economy as a whole (e.g., 2% to 5%). If earnings growth for the stock meets market expectations, all other things equal, the stock return should be commensurate with a stock with a similar beta (e.g., according to our grossly hypothetical examples above—returns of 10% for a beta = 1.0 stock, and returns of 13% for a beta = 2.0 stock), not the 30% associated with the earnings or revenue growth rate associated with the company!

For example, after the markets closed on July 16, 1998, Microsoft reported a healthy 28% gain in its fiscal fourth-quarter earnings (Microsoft's fiscal year ends on June 30), a figure that was *in line with analysts' earnings estimates.* In NASDAQ trading for the day, Microsoft shares closed at $117⅞, unchanged for the day. In after-hours trading that day, shares of Microsoft fell slightly to $116⅞—an insignificant reaction to a 28% growth in earnings.

If growth exceeds expectations, the expected stock return should exceed the above-stated hypothetical 10% to 13% returns—perhaps by a very large margin. For example on July 20, 1998, Warner-Lambert (NYSE—**WLA:** http://www.warner-lambert.com/), a large pharmaceuticals company, reported a 46% gain in second-quarter earnings. The results surprised analysts, who *expected a 35% gain.* That day the shares of Warner-Lambert rose $3.56 to close at $83⅛ (a 4.5% gain) while the general stock market, as measured by the S&P 500, declined by approximately ¼%.

On July 28, 1998, American Express (NYSE—**AXP:** http://www.americanexpress.com/), the large travel and credit card company, reported second-quarter earnings of $1.24 per share—versus analysts' consensus expectations, according to First Call Corporation, of $1.22 per share—only 2 cents more than expectations. The shares of American Express rose $5.75 (5.4%) to close at $112.81, while the DJIA rose only 1% that day.

If revenue or earnings growth turns out to be or is projected to be less than expected, Katie bar the door! The return on that stock will probably be negative and could be disastrous. For example, on July 22, 1998, the stock of Computer Associates Int'l (NYSE—**CA:** http://www.cai.com/), a large computer software firm, dropped from $57 to $39.50, a decline of $17.50 (–30%). Management announced second-quarter basic income of 34 cents per share, in line with analysts' expectations of 33 cents per share. But management also issued a warning that slower growth in revenues was expected in the future. According to *The New York Times* (http://www.nytimes.com/), market analysts immediately reduced their expectations of 1998 earnings by 7%.

The intelligent investment decision rule in today's market (especially for growth stocks) is: If you believe that a company's performance will exceed expectations, buy the stock; if you believe the company will perform below expectations, sell the stock. Growth rates, net operating profit margins, net investment levels, and interest rates are all incorporated into today's stock price, and it's essential to know how they affect a stock's price if you want to be able to make intelligent investment decisions.

Stock Value versus Stock Price

Many professional investors will tell you that a stock's *value* is whatever *price* you can get for it on the open market—nothing more, nothing less. The law of supply and demand alone determines the fair price of a stock! It's hard to argue with that declaration, but we'll give it a try. Whether that fair price is determined by fundamental analysis resulting in a supportable intrinsic value, or whether that price is due to the *greater fool theory*[5] of valuation, in which there is always an ample supply of truly foolish buyers for overpriced stock, is another question.

Market players constantly are bombarded with information that may influence a stock's price, either positively or negatively. Some info is very stock-specific—an announcement of better or worse than expected earnings, the release of a dynamite new product, the death of the corporation's founder (which, in a morbid way, usually has a positive effect on the stock's price), the settling of a labor strike, or an exciting technological or medical breakthrough.

For example, on Monday May 4, 1998, EntreMed (NASDAQ—**ENMD:** http:/www.entremed.com/) jumped over $72 to an intraday high of $84⅞ from the previous trading day's closing price of $12¹/₁₆, before closing at $51¹³/₁₆. EntreMed is a start-up research and pharmaceuticals company that, to date, has never had a profitable year. This stock price movement was caused by a very bullish article in *The New York Times* that described a potential breakthrough relating to EntreMed's cancer research and drug development.

Do the stock market and stock prices ever overreact or underreact to new information? Absolutely! Did the market initially overreact to this information for EntreMed? We can't tell at the present. We would venture to guess, however, that the investor who paid $84⅞ for EntreMed on May 4 was feeling sheepish five months later. Its closing market price was $21.94 on March 17, 1999.

Emotions often play a large role in the stock market! Some market players may translate the information that they receive into overly optimistic or pessimistic influences on a company's future cash flow. A stock's price may be bid up for a time to an unrealistically high amount, or it may be driven down to an unbelievably low bargain level. Some info may affect an industry as a whole. For example, the discovery of a vast new supply of oil in the Caspian Sea may adversely affect the natural gas industry and favorably affect the Russian vodka industry.

Some information may affect the stock market as a whole. For example, political and labor stability, decreasing income taxes, low inflation, and low equity risk premiums (associated with lower interest rates and cost of capital) are major bonuses for the vast majority of stocks. On the other hand, labor and political unrest, higher inflation, increased income taxes, and greater perceived equity risk premiums (associated with higher interest rates and cost of capital) are huge downers for stocks in general.

With all this info bombarding investors and causing constant reevaluations, market prices see and saw quite a bit. As shown in Exhibit 2-1 the shares of Microsoft have gyrated considerably over the past five years. Despite these ups and downs, Microsoft has outperformed the S&P 500 by a considerable margin.

Does a stock's intrinsic value change as frequently as, and in unison with, its price? The evidence is to the contrary. A lot of academic research has been conducted regarding the movement of stock prices and the noise associated with that movement.[6] Because of overly optimistic or pessimistic views in the market, a stock's price may diverge significantly and for a long period of time from a stock's intrinsic value. Over time, however, the price and value of most stocks should converge on a regular basis.

Intrinsic value, like beauty, is somewhat in the eye of the beholder and is influenced by the valuation model used and the assumptions made in the analysis. Wall Street (and non-Wall Street) analysts incorporate their own spin to the models that they use to calculate a stock's value. An analyst's value may be based upon the current fundamentals (historic revenue growth, profit margins, etc.) associated with the stock or upon how the analyst believes those fundamentals will develop in the future.

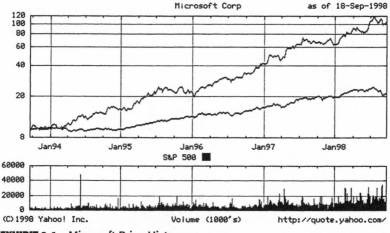

EXHIBIT 2-1   Microsoft Price History

An analyst who believes a stock's price is below its intrinsic value would recommend a purchase of the stock. On the flip side—an analyst, fearing retribution from an unhappy corporate client, may be more reticent to recommend a sale of a stock that is priced above its intrinsic value. An analyst who gives a stock a "sell" recommendation has a much more difficult time in getting information from that company in the future. Also, sell recommendations tend to strain relationships between the client and the firm's investment banking department, which may be trying to get a lucrative piece of business from the company, making that analyst persona non grata in the investment bank's corporate dining room. Instead of a sell recommendation, an analyst calls an overpriced stock a *fully valued* stock or a *long-term hold* situation. Be cautious when hearing those terms.

Given the stock inputs that you develop and our view of the stock valuation world, the DCF approach and the ValuePro 2000 software will help you determine a stock's intrinsic value—just like the approach used by Wall Street analysts. You control the inputs—the fundamentals—and you can see how those input changes are transformed into changes in a stock's value.

You determine what constitutes a reasonable revenue growth rate or net operating profit margin that you think that the company can achieve, or the cost of capital that you think the financial markets will demand. We'll describe in great detail how you can reasonably estimate these inputs and show you that you don't have to be a clairvoyant to do so. With the valuation approach and the spreadsheet software, you are now in charge of your stock-picking destiny. **You** are now able to empower yourself with information!

The DCF Approach: Microsoft— A Simplified Valuation Example

How complex is it to value stocks like a pro? To illustrate the valuation process, we will now take you through a simplified four-step valuation of Microsoft. These calculations can easily be performed using a spreadsheet program written in Excel or Lotus. Chapter 8 describes how you can write a program that does this type of valuation or how you can purchase the ValuePro 2000 software over the Internet.

Recall the four steps: Forecast expected cash flow; estimate the discount rate (the WACC); calculate the value of the corporation; and calculate per share intrinsic stock value.

Step 1: Forecast Expected Cash Flow

Expected cash flow to stockholders includes cash dividends, if any, and the expected increase (or decrease) in the stock's price during the investor's holding period. As we've shown in Chapter 1, it's easy to estimate the expected cash flow for your mortgage because you agree to pay the bank $734 per month. Accurate estimations of cash flow for common stock are considerably more challenging. Here we describe ways to help you to overcome the complications associated with this cash flow estimation.

The DCF valuation analysis that we use estimates *expected free cash flow to the firm.* Free cash flows are cash amounts that are available to be paid to debt holders and stockholders. *Earnings per share* is an accounting measure and an accountant's way of measuring corporate performance. *Discounted free cash flows* are an investor's way of measuring potential return to stockholders. DCF is more pocketbook-oriented, hence more meaningful to you—unless you happen to be an accountant.

The discounted free cash flow approach uses corporate performance measures that focus solely on real cash dollars flowing both into and out of the company.[7] Corporate activities that produce additional net *cash inflows* to the company, such as increased revenue growth or increased net operating profit margins have a **positive effect on stock value.** These are good activities.

Corporate activities that produce net *cash outflows* from the company—such as higher income tax rates, higher capital investment or working capital requirements, and lower net operating profit margins because of increased labor costs or other costs of production—have a **negative effect on stock value.** These payments may be necessary from the corporation's perspective but they are not particularly good activities for the stock's value.

Microsoft has been a darling of Wall Street for many years. Since it's initial public offering in March 1986, Microsoft's stock has produced an average annual return of almost 50% per year for investors, see Microsoft Price History-Exhibit 2-1.

We describe and examine how to estimate corporate cash flows in Chapter 4, where we focus on five key cash flow measures. We refer to these cash flow measures as *The Five Chinese Brothers* (taken from the Chinese folk tale of the same name): the revenue growth rate (e.g., 25%), the net operating profit margin (e.g., 50%), the net fixed capital investment rate (e.g., 4.84%), the incremental working capital investment rate (e.g., 5.7%), and the company's income tax rate (e.g., 35%). Briefly, these may be described as:

The Five Chinese Brothers

Revenue growth rate: Annual growth in revenue

Net operating profit margin: Operating income/revenue

Fixed capital investment: Net capital investment/revenue

Working capital investment: Working capital/% change in revenue

Tax rate: Taxes/pretax income

To compute net capital investment, we also provide the depreciation rate (e.g., 5%)—depreciation divided by revenue.

We did some analysis of the historic ratios for these cash flow measures for Microsoft, and we found on free Internet Web sites growth

			Valuation Date	10/14/98
	General Input Screen			
	Intrinsic Stock Value $107.72			
		General Inputs		
Company Name	Microsoft			
Fiscal Year	06/30/98	Depreciation Rate (% of Rev.)	5.00%	
Excess Return Period (years)	10	Investment Rate (% of Rev)	5.70%	
Revenues ($mil)	$14,484	Working Capital (% of change in Rev.)	4.84%	
Revenue Growth Rate (%)	25.00%	Excess Marketable Securities ($mil)	0	
Net Operating Profit Margin (%)	50.00%	Other Senior Claims	0	
Tax Rate (%)	35.00%			
		Cost of Capital Inputs		
Current Stock Price	$109.25			
Annual Dividend Per Share (e.g. $1.00)	$0.00			
Shares Outstanding (mil)	2464			
30-year Treasury Bond Yield (e.g 6.50%)	7.00%			
Bond Yield Spread to Treasury (e.g. 1.00%)	0.00%			
Preferred Stock Yield (e.g. 8.00%)	0.00%			
Equity Risk Premium (e.g. 3.00%)	3.00%			
Company Specific Beta (e.g. 1.00)	1.00			
Value of Debt Outstanding ($mil)	$0.0			
Value of Preferred Stock ($mil)	$0.0			
Weighted Average Cost of Capital	10.00%			

EXHIBIT 2-2   General Inputs Screen, Microsoft

projections of Wall Street analysts to come up with our estimates of Microsoft's cash flow measures. We show those estimates in Exhibit 2-2, the general input screen of the ValuePro 2000 spreadsheet. Our valuation spreadsheets will become more clear as we progress through the next six chapters.

Net operating profit (NDP) for Microsoft is projected to grow more than sevenfold—from $9,052 million in 1999 to $67,446 million in 2008. To convert from net operating profit to free cash flow to the firm (FCFF), we must (1) add depreciation (a noncash expense), and (2) subtract income taxes, incremental working capital and fixed capital investment. FCFF projections for Microsoft (in millions of dollars) are:

Year	1999		2000		2001		2002		.....		2008
FCFF	$5,582	+	$6,978	+	$8,722	+	$10,903	+	.....	+	$41,590

All of these numbers are shown in Exhibit 2-3: the General Pro Forma Screen.

Step 2: Estimate the Discount Rate—The WACC

Given the expected cash flow associated with the company, what is the appropriate rate to use to discount that uncertain (but expected) cash flow? There are several discounted cash flow methods used in the capital market. The method used in this book calculates *the after-tax weighted average cost of capital* (*WACC*) of the company and uses that WACC to discount the company's after-tax free cash flow. Again, we show you how to estimate a company's WACC longhand, and if you use the ValuePro 2000 software it automatically does all the work based on the inputs that you feed it.

How do you calculate a WACC? Finance theory tells us that a company's WACC is a function of three general categories of risk/return adjustments required by the market:

- As a *base rate of return* for any investment, the market's current long-term (which incorporates expectations of inflation), risk-free rate of interest. We use the current 30-year Treasury Bond yield.

- For the expected return associated with the *company's debt and preferred stock,* a *spread,* that reflects the company's *risk of default,* above the risk-free rate.

Microsoft
General Pro Forma Screen
10-year Excess Return Period

			Discounted Excess Return Period FCFF	$96,409	Total Corporate Value	$265,432
			Discounted Corporate Residual Value	$169,023	Less Debt	$0
			Excess Marketable Securities	$0.0	Less Preferred Stock	$0
			Total Corporate Value	$265,432	Less Other Senior Claims	0
					Total Value to Common Equity	$265,432
					Intrinsic Stock Value	$107.72

(1)	(2)	(3)	(4)	(5)	(6)	(7)	(8)	(9)	(10)	(11)	(12)	(13)
Period	Fiscal Year	Revenues	NOP	Adj. Taxes	NOPAT	Invest.	Deprec.	Net Invest.	Change in Working Capital	FCFF	Discount Factor	Discounted FCFF
0	06/30/98	14,484										
1	06/30/99	18,105	9,052	3,168	5,884	1,032	905	127	175	5,582	0.9091	5,075
2	06/30/2000	22,631	11,316	3,960	7,355	1,290	1,132	158	219	6,978	0.8264	5,767
3	06/30/2001	28,289	14,145	4,951	9,194	1,612	1,414	198	274	8,722	0.7513	6,553
4	06/30/2002	35,361	17,681	6,188	11,492	2,016	1,768	248	342	10,903	0.6830	7,447
5	06/30/2003	44,202	22,101	7,735	14,366	2,519	2,210	309	428	13,628	0.6209	8,462
6	06/30/2004	55,252	27,626	9,669	17,957	3,149	2,763	387	535	17,035	0.5645	9,616
7	06/30/2005	69,065	34,533	12,086	22,446	3,937	3,453	483	669	21,294	0.5132	10,927
8	06/30/2006	86,331	43,166	15,108	28,058	4,921	4,317	604	836	26,618	0.4665	12,417
9	06/30/2007	107,914	53,957	18,885	35,072	6,151	5,396	755	1,045	33,272	0.4241	14,111
10	06/30/2008	134,893	67,446	23,606	43,840	7,689	6,745	944	1,306	41,590	0.3855	16,035
Residual		134,893	67,446	23,606	43,840	6,745	6,745	0	0	438,401	0.3855	169,023

EXHIBIT 2-3 General Pro Forma Screen, Microsoft

- For the expected return associated with the *company's common stock,* the market's assessment of the current *equity risk premium,* in general, and the *specific risk premium (beta)* associated with the company's stock.

To arrive at the company's WACC, the capital cost inputs described above must be adjusted by two factors: the tax advantages of interest payments, and the percentage of debt, preferred stock, and common stock employed by the company in financing its operations. While this calculation may seem complex, it is actually quite simple with a calculator or software like ValuePro 2000.

The discount rate or WACC that is used in the valuation process, **and the movement of interest rates in general, can have an enormous effect on the market value of the stock.**[8] The discount rate that is used to value a stock reflects the three risk/return factors described above. Investments with similar risks should have similar discount rates.

Factors that reduce the discount rate, such as a decrease in interest rates due to expectations of lower inflation, or a decrease in the equity risk premium due to the fall of communism and an increase in free trade among nations, have greatly increased stock market valuations in the 1990s. Many market participants believe that the principal reason for the recent (1995–1998) large percentage increases in stock market valuation, in excess of the growth rate of corporate earnings, is due to the general reduction of interest rates and their subsequent lowering of corporate WACCs. **A lower WACC increases a stock's value.**

Conversely, factors that increase the discount rate, such as expectations of higher inflation, government policies that restrict free trade, or an increasing equity risk premium due to labor unrest, currency/trade crises, production bottlenecks or other reasons, will have a significant negative effect on stock market prices. **A higher WACC reduces a stock's value.** (We discuss all the WACCy stuff in detail in Chapter 5.)

The WACC for Microsoft is easier to compute than most, since the company is principally financed by common stock. Microsoft has no debt outstanding. There is a small issue of preferred stock outstanding but, for simplicity, we'll ignore it in our example. We include the preferred stock in our valuation of Microsoft in Chapter 7.

In this simple example, the WACC for Microsoft is entirely a function of its cost of common stock. The capitalization and the WACC for Microsoft look like this:

Capital Source	Capital Amount	Capital Cost Rate
Debt	0	0
Preferred stock	0	0
Common stock	$265,422 million	10%
WACC		**10%**

In 1998, Microsoft bypassed General Electric to become the most valuable company in the world as measured by market capitalization. Market capitalization is defined as the number of common shares outstanding times the stock price per share plus the value of debt and preferred stock outstanding. For Microsoft, this is computed as follows:

Common Shares Outstanding $\times$ Stock Price = Market Capitalization
2,464 million $\times$ $107.72 = $265,422 million

The cost of common stock for Microsoft is a function of the level of interest rates (the 30-year U.S. Treasury), the risk of Microsoft relative to the overall stock market (its beta), and the equity risk premium. While we do not go into particulars for Microsoft at this point (they are provided in Chapter 7), here we will use a 10% capital cost rate.

Step 3: Calculate the Value of the Corporation

Step 3 involves the arithmetic exercise of discounting the expected cash flow by the required rate of return. In the DCF approach, the required rate of return is the firm's WACC. Recall the mortgage example from Chapter 1. This concept is the same.

Step 3 involves two stages: (1) calculating the discounted value of the expected cash flows over the 10-year forecast horizon (called the excess return period, as described in Chapter 3), and (2) calculating the value of Microsoft beyond this 10-year period (called the residual value, as described in Chapter 3). Exhibit 2-4 gives the discounted expected cash flows for 1999–2008 for Microsoft. The sum of the discounted cash flows over the 10-year period is $96,409 million.

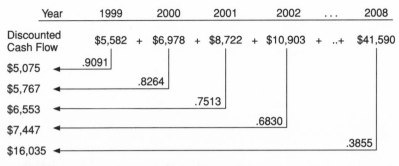

EXHIBIT 2-4 Discounted Cash Flow, Microsoft

Exhibit 2-3 shows the *total corporate value* calculation. We start with the sum of the discounted free cash flows from above ($96,409 million) and add the present value of the expected cash flows beyond the end of the excess return period (year 2008). Residual value can be expressed as net operating profit after tax (NOPAT) divided by the WACC. The residual value for Microsoft is $438,401 million ($43,840 million/.10). Since this is the value 10 years from now, we must discount it at the 10-year discount factor of 0.3855 to get the present value of $169,023 million.

The sum of the discounted free cash flow over the 10-year excess return period ($96,409 million) and the present value of the residual value ($169,023 million) is $265,432 million. This represents the total corporate value of Microsoft.

Step 4: Calculate Intrinsic Stock Value

The final step involves computing the *total value to common equity* by subtracting the market value of senior claims on the firm's cash flows and dividing that amount by shares outstanding. Exhibit 2-3 shows the total value to common equity calculation. The estimated market value of Microsoft's common stock is $265,432 million. Dividing this figure by the number of shares outstanding (2,464 million) gives an estimated stock value per share of $107.72.

The Next Step

In this chapter, we talked about stock returns and investor expectations. We've seen that market expectations are already factored into stock prices, and it is essential to know how those expectations affect a stock's value. We use the discounted cash flow approach in a simple valuation of Microsoft. In the valuation example we: forecast expected cash flow, estimate a simplified WACC for Microsoft, calculate the corporate value of Microsoft, and calculate Microsoft's per share intrinsic stock value of $107.72.

The valuation approach that we develop over the next three chapters is not much more complex than the approach used in our valuation of Microsoft. In Chapter 3 we look at the DCF approach in greater detail. In Chapter 4 we show how to estimate The Five Chinese Brothers—our five cash flow measures. And in Chapter 5 we examine how to estimate a company's WACC.

After that it gets easy. In Chapter 6 we show where to get the information that you need to estimate cash flow measures and cost of capital components. In Chapter 7 we perform some customized valuations on AT&T, Intel, Microsoft, McDonald's, and Consolidated Edison. And Chapter 8 describes how you can write a simple stock valuation program to make valuation easy.

Now let's plunge deeper into the DCF approach as we graduate to Chapter 3.

Notes

1. See Ibbotson Associates, *The Stocks, Bonds, Bills, and Inflation 1998 Yearbook*, Chicago, 1998.

2. Greg Ip, "Top-Heavy Stock Market May Become a Drag," *The Wall Street Journal*, January 18, 1999, p. C1.

3. Jeremy J. Siegel, *Stocks for the Long Run*, McGraw-Hill, New York, 1998, pp. 13, 79–80.

4. Siegel, pp. 153–154.

5. Malkiel labels it "The Castle-in-the-Air Theory." See Burton G. Malkiel, *A Random Walk Down Wall Street*, W.W. Norton & Co., New York, 1990.

6. Siegel describes tests of the efficient market theory and the movement of stock prices in great detail.

7. For an excellent description of the discounted free cash flow technique and its importance to shareholder wealth creation, see Alfred Rappaport, *Creating Shareholder Value*, The Free Press, New York, 1986. The consulting firm of Stern Stewart & Co also has been a major and vocal proponent of creating shareholder value and uses a DCF approach to measure Economic Value Added (EVA).

8. Malkiel explains how the stock market drop of 508 points (22.6%) on October 19, 1987, could have been caused solely by an increase in both interest rates and the equity risk premium (pp. 203–206).

CHAPTER 3

The Importance of Cash Flow

The Spirit of Cash Flow Yet to Come

There are those in the world of finance (including the authors of this book) who believe that Ebenezer Scrooge had it right the first time—before the spirits enlightened him—that the number one goal of a business is to make money. The aim of corporate management should be to make stockholders very happy, with more profits being preferred to less. If it succeeds at its task, the corporation's stock price should rise and management should cash in on exorbitant bonuses by way of exercising scads of stock options. If managers perform poorly, they will become *consultant*s and will exit—stage left.

Corporate Revenue, Expense, and Net Operating Profit Margin

How does a corporation make money? It makes money by developing and operating business lines and divisions where it manufactures products or provides services. A company generates *revenue* by selling its products and services to another party. In generating revenue, a company incurs *expenses* such as employee salaries, costs of goods sold, research and development costs, charges for depreciation of plant and equipment, and marketing expenses. Stockholders sincerely hope that corporate revenues are greater than the expenses associated with producing them. The difference between operating revenue and operating expense of a firm is called *operating income* or *net operating profit* (*NOP*).

Exactly what is net operating profit? NOP is the income that a company earns without taking into account the payment of income taxes on corporate earnings, or the interest payments on the company's debt. NOP is based upon income generated from continuing operations and excludes interest income, extraordinary gains or losses, and income from discontinued operations. **NOP should reflect the future revenue-generating ability and expense requirements of the operating businesses that comprise the ongoing operations of the company.**

In valuing a stock, investors are very concerned with corporate revenue, expense, and net operating profits. The corporation's *net operating profit margin* (*NOPM*) is an important cash flow measure that helps quantify a corporation's ongoing operating profitability. How do we calculate NOPM?

As an example, let's look at the revenue, expense, and operating income for the Intel Corporation (NASDAQ—**INTC:** http://www.intel .com/). Intel makes integrated circuits and microprocessors for computers. It is by far the dominant player in this market sector. Exhibit 3-1 shows the 1997 consolidated statement of income, from Intel's corporate Web site. We have circled its net revenues, operating costs and expenses, and operating income entries.

Using these entries, if we divide Intel's yearly operating income by its net revenues (operating income/net revenues), we see that Intel's NOPM equaled 39.4%, 36.2%, and 32.4% in years 1997, 1996, and 1995, respectively. NOPM increased each year and averaged 36% during this period. We also see that Intel's net revenues increased from $16,202 million to $20,847 million to $25,070 million, which represents revenue growth of 28.7% in 1996 and 20.3% in 1997. These are very impressive NOPMs and revenue growth rates for such a large company. We show how to use these ratios for valuation purposes, along with other cash flow measures that are taken from the company's balance sheet and cash flow statements, in Chapter 4.

Consolidated statements of income

int⊌l.

Three years ended December 27, 1997

(In millions—except per share amounts)

	1997	1996	1995
Net revenues	$ 25,070	$ 20,847	$ 16,202
Cost of sales	9,945	9,164	7,811
Research and development	2,347	1,808	1,296
Marketing, general and administrative	2,891	2,322	1,843
Operating costs and expenses	15,183	13,294	10,950
Operating income	9,887	7,553	5,252
Interest expense	(27)	(25)	(29)
Interest income and other, net	799	406	415
Income before taxes	10,659	7,934	5,638
Provision for taxes	3,714	2,777	2,072
Net income	$ 6,945	$ 5,157	$ 3,566
Basic earnings per common share	$ 4.25	$ 3.13	$ 2.16
Diluted earnings per common share	$ 3.87	$ 2.90	$ 2.02
Weighted average common shares outstanding	1,635	1,645	1,650
Dilutive effect of:			
Employee stock options	102	94	96
1998 Step-Up Warrants	58	37	22
Weighted average common shares outstanding, assuming dilution	1,795	1,776	1,768

See accompanying notes.

EXHIBIT 3-1   Intel Consolidated Statement of Income

Corporate Free Cash Flow

To produce these revenues, not only must a corporation incur operating expenses; it also must invest money in real estate, buildings
and equipment, and working capital to support its business activities. Working capital is a company's net investment in its accounts
receivable and its inventories (cash outflows), minus its accounts
payable (a cash inflow). Also, the corporation must pay income taxes
(big-time cash outflows) on its earnings. From Exhibit 3-1, we see
that Intel paid $3,714 million in taxes in 1997, which when divided
by its income before taxes of $10,659 million is equal to a tax rate of
34.8%.

These investments in real assets and working capital, along with tax
payments, represent real cash outflows from the corporation—hard
dollars flowing out to others and dollars that are not available to pay
the good guys, the stockholders.

How do we blend these cash flow measures to come up with a
stock's value? We use a *discounted free cash flow to the firm approach*
to calculate the **intrinsic value** of a company's stock. The number that
results from adjusting the *earnings measure* associated with NOP for
the actual cash flows of taxes, net investment in long-term assets
(which is equal to new investment minus depreciation expenses), and

net change in working capital is known as the *free cash flow to the firm* (*FCFF*).

FCFF is an important measure to stockholders. This is the cash that is left over after the payment of all hard cash expenses and all operating investment required by the firm. FCFF is the actual cash that is available to pay the company's various claimholders, especially the stockholders. The simple equation that we use to calculate FCFF is:

FCFF = NOP – Taxes – Net Investment – Net Change in Working Capital

The accounting definitions of *earnings and profits* are fine for accounting purposes, but from a stock valuation standpoint, stockholders should be more concerned about the amount of free cash flow to the firm.

The Investment Rule for Corporate Management

How are all these cash flows and acronyms related to a stock's value? It all boils down to this: On any corporate investment, a corporation creates additional value for stockholders if and only if it earns a rate of return, after all net cash flow adjustments, that is greater than the corporation's weighted average cost of capital. This occurs only when the investment generates *additional free cash flow to the firm.*

The investment decision rule for a corporation should be: Invest only in projects that earn a rate of return greater than its WACC; otherwise, pay out free cash flow to stockholders. A corporation should not invest in any project that earns a rate of return less than its WACC. This destroys stockholder value.

We have stated that the value (not necessarily the price) of an investment is equal to the present value of its expected cash flow, appropriately discounted for risk and timing. The value of a firm is not determined by historic performance or current performance. The firm's value is determined by expected **future** performance. Future performance is not easy to predict—particularly when you're putting your hard-earned money behind your prediction in the way of a stock purchase. However, there are some tried-and-true ways to estimate growth and other valuation inputs that are used by Wall Street analysts and savvy investors for valuation purposes. We talk about those later and we provide some tips on how to make well-informed assumptions.

The Free Cash Flow to the Firm Philosophy

This book uses a free cash flow to the firm approach to value the corporation. This approach has two underlying assumptions: (1) the company will maintain a relatively constant capital structure; and (2) company management will act in the best interests of its owners (a sometimes erroneous assumption) to maximize stockholder value.

The first assumption implies that the market capitalization of the company will have stable percentages of debt, preferred stock and common stock in its market capitalization ratio (this assumption affects the calculation of the company's WACC over time). As the market capitalization of the company increases, the amount of debt, preferred stock, and common stock will increase proportionately. For example, the company expects to have a relatively constant percentage market capitalization of 60% common stock, 10% preferred stock, and 30% debt.

The second assumption implies that the excess cash inflow that the firm receives (*earns*) will be reinvested only in *profitable* business projects, or else the free cash flow will be paid out to the stockholders. The term *reinvested in profitable business projects* means that those projects will create *additional* free cash flow for the firm and, therefore, will earn a rate of return that is higher than the company's WACC and will add to stockholder value.

What does this assumption mean for a corporation? As an example, let's look at Microsoft and again assume that its weighted average cost of capital is 10%. Bill Gates and the management of Microsoft should invest the billions of dollars they receive in excess of company costs of operation in investments that have a rate of return greater than 10%, or they should pay out the free cash flow to stockholders.

It's easier to find projects and investments with higher rates of return in growth sectors like computers, pharmaceuticals, and information technology rather than in the more mundane economic sectors. That's why most high-growth, high-tech companies like Microsoft and Intel invest their free cash flow in projects or acquisitions. It's more difficult to find investments with high rates of return in mature, low-growth industries like banking, manufacturing, and utilities.

Free Cash Flow—Share Repurchase Programs versus Dividends

Free cash flow can be paid out to stockholders as dividends, which are taxable payments, or through the corporation's repurchase of shares in the open market. Presently, share repurchase is the channel that many corporations prefer to use to pay out free cash flow. For instance, Microsoft used its excess free cash flow to repurchase $3 billion of stock in its fiscal year ending June 30, 1998. That's a huge chunk of change and is more money than most corporations have in the way of annual revenues.

Share repurchase programs reduce the number of shares outstanding that have claims on corporate cash flow. Share repurchases usually benefit the remaining stockholders by reducing the supply of the outstanding stock—thereby increasing the stock's price. Investors in the higher tax brackets of up to 39.6% find it very painful to pay taxes on dividends that they receive. Also, if investors don't currently need the dividends for spending purposes, they have to decide where they want to reinvest those dividends and may incur additional transaction costs in doing so.

Many investors prefer to see stock prices rise steadily over time rather than to receive quarterly dividend payments. They can decide when to sell their shares and cash out, and then pay taxes at lower (e.g., 20%) capital gains tax rates. Share repurchase programs allow investors to *minimize* their tax payments while still enabling the corporation to maintain the philosophy of paying out excess free cash flow.

Other investors buy stock in a company—a utility like Consolidated Edison, for example—for the dividend stream that it pays, along with the possibility of dividend growth. The differing dividend payout/stock repurchase philosophies associated with a company's payment of free cash flow create what is termed a *clientele effect*. Retirees and other investors who are interested in predictable current returns tend to purchase stock in companies that pay out their free cash flow through dividends. By contrast, investors who are interested more in capital gains and the growth of a stock's price, gravitate to low or no dividend paying companies that pay out their free cash flow through stock repurchase programs.

Free Cash Flow—The Corporation's Investment Decision

The investment rule underlying the free cash flow approach to corporate management is simple: Invest in a project or business strategy if and only if the project provides additional free cash flow to the firm. The result of this investment will be an increase in stockholder value. This approach is worthwhile, and those projects that increase FCFF should be undertaken. If the project decreases the discounted free cash flow to the firm, the result is a decrease in stockholder value. Rather than investing in a project that reduces stockholder value, the company should pay out the money to investors, through share repurchases or through dividend payments.

The FCFF Approach—Where Does It Work Well?

The stocks that the FCFF valuation approach handles well represent 95% of all common stocks traded on U.S. and international stock markets. However, in valuing highly-levered companies (such as real estate investment trusts (REITs) and financial institutions) or companies with no current free cash flow (such as EntreMed), the FCFF approach needs fine tuning.

Typically, the balance sheets of commercial banks and investment banks reflect a book value, not necessarily a market value, of approximately 90% debt and 10% equity. We discuss market versus book values in Chapter 5. Also, depreciation expense is minor, and there is very little investment in property, plant, and equipment for financial institutions. The bulk of their investments are in financial obligations that have characteristics that more closely resemble working capital investments.

Adjustments must be made for companies with little or no free cash flow or companies that are suffering net operating losses. These adjustments may involve reversals in and changing of NOPMs over time, and estimating the probability of and potential revenues from high-risk products, whose cash flows depend upon regulatory approval or future scientific breakthroughs.

All of this fine-tuning can be addressed in the FCFF approach, but it's beyond the scope of this simple, first book. We hope that a more detailed FCFF approach will be the subject of a sequel.

The Discounted FCFF Valuation Approach

The Four-Step Process

The discounted FCFF valuation approach, and the spreadsheet software that we describe later in Chapter 8, uses a four-step process to value the stock of a company. In this section, we add more detail to our Microsoft example from Chapter 2. As you work through a valuation by doing it longhand, by writing and using a spreadsheet, or by using the ValuePro 2000 software, the concepts and their implementation should quickly fall into place.

Step 1: Forecast Expected Cash Flow.   The first order of business is to forecast the expected cash flow for the company on the basis of most likely assumptions about the company's revenue growth rate, net operating profit margin, income tax rate, fixed investment requirement, and incremental working capital requirement. It's easier than it sounds. We describe these cash flows and how to reasonably estimate them in Chapter 4. The *expected cash flows* are separated into two time periods—the *excess return period,* in which the corporation generates *cash flows from operation;* and the *residual value period,* the time period after the excess return period, in which the corporation is not able to create additional free cash flow.

Step 2: Estimate the Discount Rate.   The next order of business is to estimate the company's WACC, which is the discount rate that's used in the valuation process. We show how to estimate the company's WACC using mostly easily observable inputs in Chapter 5.

Step 3: Calculate the Value of the Corporation.   We then use the company's WACC to discount the expected cash flow during the excess return period to get the aggregate of the corporation's *cash flow from operations.* To get the company's *residual value, which usually represents 60% to 90% of the corporation's total value,* we divide the company's net operating profit after taxes (NOPAT) at the end of the excess return period by its WACC. We then discount that future value back to today, also at a discount rate equal to the company's WACC. Finally, we add the cash flow from operations, the residual value, and the excess marketable securities on hand to get today's value of the corporation as a whole—the corporate value. We describe this procedure, which is represented by Equation 1, in greater depth later in this section.

Corporate Value = Cash Flow Operations
**   + Residual Value + Excess Securities   (Eq. 1)**

Our spreadsheet examples, which we discuss in Chapter 7, show this calculation at the top of the general pro forma page. Again, a simple spreadsheet program does all the work automatically. All you have to worry about is who is paying for the first round of drinks at the clubhouse.

Step 4: Calculate Intrinsic Stock Value. We subtract the value of the company's liabilities—debt, preferred stock, and other senior claims such as underfunded pension plans (all senior obligations collectively are defined as *senior claims*)—from corporate value to get value to common equity, as shown in Equation 2 below:

Value to Common Equity = Corporate Value – Senior Claims   (Eq. 2)

We divide that value by shares outstanding to get the **per share intrinsic value of common stock.**

Where do we get our information? The information necessary to accomplish Step 1, forecast expected cash flow, is the focus of Chapter 4. The inputs and information needed to accomplish Step 2, estimate the WACC, are the subjects of Chapter 5. Before we jump ahead, let's now spend a little time discussing **the theory of competitive advantage** that underlies the calculation of cash flow from operations described in Step 3 above.

The Excess Return Period and Competitive Advantage

The FCFF approach provides for several distinct time periods for estimating cash flow to allow differing value-creating periods for a corporation's business strategy. In the *excess return period*, because of a competitive advantage enjoyed by the firm, *the corporation is able to earn returns on new investments that are greater than its cost of capital.* Examples of companies that experienced a significant period of big-time competitive advantage are IBM in the 1950s and 1960s, Apple Computer in the 1980s, and Microsoft and Intel in the 1990s.

Success invariably attracts competitors whose aggressive practices cut into market share and revenue growth rates, and whose pricing and marketing activities drive down net operating profit margins. A reduction in NOPM drives return on new investment to levels that approach the corporation's WACC. When a company loses its competitive advantage and the return from its new investments just equals its WACC, the corporation is investing in business strategies in which the aggregate net present value is zero (or worse yet, negative—such as IBM in the 1980s and Apple in the 1990s).

The length of the excess return period for the corporation will depend on the particular products being produced, the industry in which the company operates, and the barriers for competitors to enter the business. Products that have a very high barrier to entry, extremely high growth potential, patent protection, strong brand names, or unique marketing channels might have an excess return period of competitive advantage that is quite long—10 to 15 years or longer. More typically, the excess return period for most companies is 5 to 7 years or shorter. All else equal, a shorter excess return period results in a lower stock value.

What do we use for the excess return period for our free cash flow estimation and in the spreadsheet software? This is a judgment call. We use the **1-5-7-10 Rule**—and we suggest that you do likewise.

We group companies into one of **four general categories** and excess return periods:

1. The *boring companies* that operate in a competitive, low-margin industry in which they have nothing particular going for them—a 1-year excess return period

2. The *decent companies* that have a recognizable name and decent reputation and perhaps a regulatory benefit (e.g., Consolidated Edison)—a 5-year excess return period

3. The large, economies of scale *good companies* with good growth potential, good brand names, marketing channels, and consumer identification (e.g., McDonald's and AT&T)—a 7-year excess return period

4. The *great companies* with great growth potential, tremendous marketing power, brand names, and in-place benefits (e.g., Intel, Microsoft, Coca Cola, and Disney)—a 10-year excess return period

We do not believe in going out more than *10 years* with an excess return period. Some fundamental stock valuation models, like the dividend discount model, incorporate earnings and dividend growth in excess of the company's WACC, over an infinite time period. Cash flow in these models is discounted until the *hereafter!* We think that 10 years is an ample amount of time to incorporate the product cycles of today's markets.

What happens after the excess return period? Does the company dry up, die, or go bankrupt? No. For valuation purposes, the company loses its competitive advantage. Because of this loss, the stock's value will grow only at the market's required rate of return for the stock. For example, if the common stock price of XYZ Boring Company (which does not pay dividends) is $20, and its required rate of return is 12%, its stockholders expect it to grow to $20 × 1.12 = $22.40 after year 1; $22.40 × 1.12 = $25.08 after year 2; $25.08 × 1.12 = $28.06 after year 3; ad infinitum. Once the excess return period ceases, the company should pay all its free cash flow to stock owners through dividends or share repurchases.

When return on investment equals a company's WACC, investors are just compensated for the risk that they are taking in owning the company's stock and no additional value is created from new business investments. **The stock price is still growing in value,** but its growth **does not exceed** its risk-adjusted market expectation (or match investors' hopes). At that point in time, the after-tax earnings of the company can be treated and valued as a *cash flow perpetuity*—which is equal to the company's NOPAT divided by its WACC (NOPAT/WACC—see note 1 at the end of the chapter). This number is discounted to the present also at the company's WACC.

This discounted value is called the company's *residual value*—a very important number which generally represents 60% to 90% of the total value of the company. The residual value is very sensitive to projections of the company's NOPAT and its WACC, as described below.

Does a corporation really lose its competitive advantage and the benefit of its excess return period? For well-managed corporations, the answer is probably not. Most well-run companies will continue to innovate, to reduce operating costs and increase efficiency, to create new business strategies, and to maintain their competitive advantage for a very long time. Some will go bankrupt. Some will be acquired or merge. But the concept of an excess return period or forecast period is one that should result in a more conservative, less aggressive stock valuation. When we invest, we would rather err on the side of conservatism than overpay for a stock.

The Three Valuation Categories

In calculating corporate value, the FCFF approach and the spreadsheet software segments and discounts corporate assets and cash flows into three categories and time periods:

Cash Flow from Operations. First, during the excess return period, we calculate free cash flow to the firm. This is the difference between operating cash inflows and cash outflows. These free cash flows are discounted at the discount factors associated with the firm's WACC and should create additional value for stockholders.

Corporate Residual Value. Second, we find the corporation's residual value. This is the value calculated by taking the company's NOPAT at the end of the excess return period and dividing it by the company's WACC and discounting it to today (also at the WACC). At this point in time it is assumed that the corporation is earning a return on investment equal to its WACC. The net present value (NPV) of additional investment by the corporation is assumed to be zero and no additional value is created for stockholders.[1]

Excess Marketable Securities. We then add the current value of marketable securities and other corporate financial investments that are not essential to operate the business. For example, according to its balance sheet on December 27, 1997, Intel had about $9.7 billion in cash and excess marketable securities on its books. These assets have no business operating risk (e.g., they could be paid out to stockholders without adversely affecting the ongoing business lines of the corporation) and should not be discounted in the valuation procedure.

As shown before in Equation 1, corporate value is the sum of the discounted free cash flow from operations, plus discounted corporate residual value, plus excess marketable securities:

Corporate Value = Cash Flow Operations
+ Residual Value + Excess Securities

Once total corporate value is calculated, the FCFF approach and the spreadsheet software subtract out the market value of senior claims and divide by shares of stock outstanding to get the per share intrinsic value. Again, Equation 2 states:

Value to Common Equity = Corporate Value – Senior Claims

Mathematically, this is as difficult as the discounted free cash flow approach gets—no calculus, no differential equations—just addition, subtraction, multiplication, and division. Through the magic of a Pentium II processor, the computations all occur rather quickly and without boredom.

Why DCF and Not EPS?

Often on Wall Street there is an intense focus on earnings per share (EPS). Several investment services, like First Call (http://www.firstcall.com/), IBES (http://www.ibes.com/), and Zacks (http://www.zacks.com/), and many analysts from stock brokerage firms give detailed estimates of quarterly earnings. The wise investor has sold the stock of a company that does not achieve or exceed those estimates.

There is no doubt that, all other things being equal, we prefer that the company in which we own stock has more earnings than less. But all other things often are not equal. If we're more concerned about real cash returns as evidenced by dividends and increases in share price than about earnings, then EPS calculations come up short in measuring returns. This is because EPS calculations do not include dividends paid by the corporation or the time value of money and the risk associated with a stock. There also is no consideration given to the timing of cash flows. In fact, there is no discounting process at all associated with the EPS measure. EPS implicitly and explicitly ignores the risks and timing of return issues that are included in a discounted cash flow analysis. EPS also fails to reflect *future expectations* of corporate performance.

There are two additional reasons that analysts prefer to work with discounted cash flow figures rather than earnings-related ratios. First, there are a number of ways to compute earnings, ranging from various types of inventory control accounting to various accounting methods for depreciation and cost of goods sold. These methods sometimes are manipulated by management in ways that affect the computation of earnings.

Second, there are no provisions for the additional investments in fixed assets and working capital that are necessary to support the increased growth of the firm. If EPS growth requires too much additional investment in fixed assets and working capital, then this earnings *growth* actually may result in a decrease in free cash flow and a decrease in the stock value.

Many corporations appear to be overly concerned with "managing" their EPS growth through accounting *gimmicks* to achieve or exceed the expectations of Wall Street. The two *gimmicks du jour,* according to *Business Week,*[2] are excessive "extraordinary restructuring charges" and write-offs for "in-process R&D."

These *one-time* accounting entries, though legal and in many cases justified, create opportunities to write off as extraordinary, expenses that otherwise may have adversely affected corporate operating earnings in the future and may well have been ordinary operating expenses. Charges for in-process R&D would otherwise have been amortized over time as *goodwill* associated with a corporate merger or acquisition. Presently, extraordinary charges seem to be incurred all too frequently by companies.

Valuation—Growth versus Value, Large Cap versus Small Cap

Often we read about mutual funds and investment managers specializing in *value stocks* or *growth stocks* or *large cap stocks* or *small cap stocks.* How should the classification of a stock into one of these categories affect the valuation of a stock?

Growth stocks are stocks that are expected to have high revenue or earnings growth rates, usually 15% and above, over the foreseeable future. Growth stocks are characterized by high P/E and P/BV (price/book value of equity) ratios and are in high-tech industries like telecommunications, pharmaceuticals, the Internet, and information technology.

Value stocks are stocks that are expected to have low revenue and/or earnings growth rates. Value stocks are stocks in mature industries like utilities, banks and brokerages, manufacturing, and automobiles. They are characterized by low P/E and P/BV ratios. Large cap stocks are stocks that have a market capitalization of equity in excess of $3 billion. Midcap and small cap stocks have a market capitalization that is less than $3 billion.

Depending upon the cycle of the moon and recent past successes or failures in fund management, different investing approaches targeting these stock categories come into or go out of favor. Investors concentrating in large caps performed well during the 1995–1998 stock market climb—with gains in the S&P 500 of 37.4%, 23.1%, 33.4%, and 26.7% during those four years.

According to Siegel, small cap stock returns exploded during the period between 1975 and 1983, when the compound annual return of small cap stocks averaged 35.3%.[3] Recently, small caps have not done nearly as well. Value and growth stock investment approaches also come into and go out of vogue on a fairly regular basis. The current darlings of the stock market are the stocks of companies with a large Internet presence.

Whether a stock is *large* or *small, growth* or *value, Internet* or *non-Internet,* the valuation procedure for each category is exactly the same. Investors should care **only** about expected future cash flows and the risks associated with those expected cash flows. The market price of any growth or value stock, large cap or small cap stock, Internet or non-Internet stock can be greatly under or over its intrinsic value. The valuations of some Internet stocks are presently in the stratosphere. Eventually they will return to levels that can be supported by their expected future cash flows. For valuation purposes relative to value stocks, growth stocks will have higher growth rates input into the valuation equation. Relative to large cap stocks, small cap stocks may have higher betas and WACCs input into the valuation equation. But the valuation procedure for each category of stock should be identical.

Valuation—The Next Step

Now that we've numbed you with discussions of free cash flow philosophies, DCF versus EPS, and all those other pesky acronyms—NOP, FCFF, NOPAT, WACC—it's time to wake up. We're about to apply the theory and demonstrate how to do something really useful in the way of cash flow analysis. In the next chapter we show you how to calculate FCFF and explain which variables are most important to the calculation. We also give you a sneak preview of *valuation in action.*

Notes

1. In the calculation of residual value of the corporation, it is assumed that there is no net new investment (i.e., investment = depreciation) and that no additional working capital is required.

As an example, at the end of an excess return period of 10 years, if the company's NOPAT = $1 million and its WACC = 10%, the company's future residual value is $1 million/(.10) = $10 million, which amount would be discounted to the present at the discount factor equal to 1.0 divided by (1.0 plus the company's WACC). That sum taken to the tenth power is $1.0/(1.0 + .1)^{10} = (.3855)$. Residual value is therefore $10 million × .3855 = $3,855 million.

2. See N. Byrnes, R. Melcher, and D. Sparks, "Earnings Hocus-Pocus," *Business Week*, October 5, 1998, pp. 134–142.

3. Siegel, p. 95.

The Five Most Important Cash Flow Measures

Forecasting Expected Cash Flows

Remember the folktale about The Five Chinese Brothers? Although they were identical in appearance, each brother had a unique trait or ability. One couldn't be burned. One could hold his breath indefinitely. One had a neck made of iron. You get the idea. By using all five of their special talents, The Five Chinese Brothers managed to escape every form of torture that the jealous local villagers could dream up. And so The Five Chinese Brothers lived happily ever after.

Similarly, in our DCF approach The Five Cash Flow Measures will be important to happy endings in your stock portfolio. The Five Cash Flow Measures that we focus on are: revenue growth rate (and the excess return period), net operating profit margin, company income tax rate, net investment, and incremental working capital investment. These are the cash flows that are the most important numbers in determining the *free cash flow to the firm* and the *intrinsic stock value*. Free cash flow to the firm represents the difference between a corporation's cash inflow and cash outflow:

Free Cash Flow to the Firm = Cash Inflow − Cash Outflow

Naturally, many of the company's operating decisions affect these cash flow measures in one way or another. Decisions relating to salaries, hiring, executive bonuses, new suppliers, and so on, will affect net operating profit margins. Decisions regarding research and development, new product development, advertising campaigns, and the like, will affect revenue growth rates, periods of competitive advantage, net operating profit margins, and net investment. And management decisions affecting these variables are occurring every day within the company.

This chapter shows how these five cash flow measures affect the value of the corporation, and this is where the rubber really begins to meet the road. The cash flow estimation process is sometimes more tedious than toenail clipping—but it's the most important part of valuation. In the process of estimating cash flow you learn a great deal about the company that you are valuing.

Revenue Growth Rate and the Excess Return Period

The current revenue of the corporation and the expected growth (or shrinkage?) rate of revenue during the period of competitive advantage, or excess return period, are extremely important inputs in valuing a company. These variables act as the first step in forecasting the expected revenue, or cash inflow of the corporation. The term *revenue growth rate* is self-explanatory. How it is calculated—or, more importantly, how it is *estimated*—is more complicated.

Where do you get revenue growth rates? Do you need to be a swami or a fortuneteller to come up with a good prediction? That may be helpful but, thankfully, it is not necessary. Several Web sites such as Yahoo Finance, IBES, First Call, and Zacks have 5-year expected profit or revenue growth projections. Many Wall Street brokerage firms also forecast these numbers. Finally, the corporation's recent history of revenue growth can act as a good indicator of potential revenue growth.

Just as science tells us that the universe can't expand forever, so mathematics tells us that a corporation cannot continue to grow forever at a rate appreciably higher than the nominal growth rate of the economy in which it operates. If it did, the company eventually would grow to be larger than the economy—not a very stable condition.

Microsoft's Revenue Growth Rate

Let's look at the revenue growth rate associated with Microsoft, one of the bellwether high-tech stocks of the 1990s. We downloaded its 1997 annual report from its corporate Web site and have reproduced its 1997 income statement as Exhibit 4-1. To get a perspective on its phenomenal growth and performance over the years, we have used other information sources to include 10 years of revenue data (an annual report typically has only 3 years of revenue data) in Table 4-1. Consider

Microsoft Corporation Income Statements
(In millions, except earnings per share)

	Year Ended June 30		
	1995	1996	1997
Revenue	$5,937	$8,671	**$11,358**
Operating expenses:			
Cost of revenue	877	1,188	**1,085**
Research and development	860	1,432	**1,925**
Sales and marketing	1,895	2,657	**2,856**
General and administrative	267	316	**362**
Total operating expenses	3,899	5,593	**6,228**
Operating income	2,038	3,078	**5,130**
Interest income	191	320	**443**
Other expenses	(62)	(19)	**(259)**
Income before income taxes	2,167	3,379	**5,314**
Provision for income taxes	714	1,184	**1,860**
Net income	1,453	2,195	**3,454**
Preferred stock dividends			**15**
Net income available for common shareholders	$1,453	$2,195	**$ 3,439**
Earnings per share[1]	$ 1.16	$ 1.71	**$ 2.63**
Weighted average shares outstanding[1]	1,254	1,281	**1,312**

See accompanying notes.

[1] Share and per share amounts have been restated to reflect a two-for-one stock split in December 1996.

EXHIBIT 4-1   Microsoft Income Statement

TABLE 4-1 Microsoft Corporation 10-Year Revenue Record
(millions of dollars)

	Revenues	$ Increase	% Increase
1997	$11,358	$2,687	31.0%
1996	8,671	2,734	46.1
1995	5,937	1,288	27.7
1994	4,649	896	23.9
1993	3,753	994	36.0
1992	2,759	916	33.2
1991	1,843	660	55.8
1990	1,183	379	47.1
1989	804	213	36.0
1988	591	245	70.8
1987	346	—	—
10-year average growth rate = 40.7%			
10-year compound annual growth rate = 41.78%			

Microsoft's phenomenal revenue growth, from $346 million in 1987 to $11,358 million in 1997—a net 33-fold increase over the 10-year period.

It's a simple procedure to calculate the historic percentage yearly growth in revenue. You divide one year's revenue by the previous year's revenue and subtract 1.0. For example, we calculate Microsoft's 1-year growth rate by dividing its 1997 revenue of $11,358 million by its 1996 revenue of $8,671 million and subtracting 1.0. In math terms, we get ($11,358/$8,671) – 1.0 = 1.31 – 1.0 = .31, a 31% growth rate.

The 10-year *compound annual growth rate* (*CAGR*) of Microsoft's revenues has been 41.78%.[1] Annual revenue growth in fiscal year 1997 was 31%. In fiscal year 1996, revenue growth had a *pop* and at 46.1% exceeded historic averages because of the phenomenal success that Microsoft experienced with the introduction of Windows 95. Absent fiscal year 1996, Microsoft's rate of revenue growth has been declining. Clearly, as the size of Microsoft increases, it becomes more and more difficult to sustain its historic revenue growth rate—replicating it over the next several years would give Microsoft $374 billion in sales in 2006, a very difficult goal to achieve!

How did Microsoft's profits perform during this period? Microsoft increased its net operating profit margin from 35.5% in 1996 to 45.2% in 1997, and its net operating profit increased from $3,078 million in 1996 to $5,130 million in 1997—a gain of 67%. Microsoft has been on an impressive roll. But, at some point, its rates of revenue growth and earnings growth will decrease. As a firm increases in size, it becomes more and more difficult to keep growing at an extraordinarily high growth rate. The growth rate, mathematically and realistically, eventually has to converge to or go below the economy's growth rate. So even Microsoft, despite recent evidence to the contrary, will obey the laws of economics.

Presently, Microsoft is embroiled in an antitrust suit with the federal and certain state governments. Investors do not like the uncertainty that comes with legal proceedings. This lawsuit could adversely affect future revenues and profits. At the least, it is a distraction to a company whose industry dominance has been legendary.

It's a lot easier for a CEO to talk about revenue and earnings growth than it is to develop the products and strategies to actually accomplish that growth. As an investor, you need to look past the public relations spiel, inject realistic estimates, and be aware of how reasonable future growth prospects affect stock value.

What about Microsoft's future growth rates? Most market participants generally talk about and look at a company's growth in earnings or profits, as opposed to its revenue. *Growth in earnings* will come from either one of two sources: *growth in revenue*—known as *top-line growth* (because revenue is the initial entry on an income statement) *or growth in operating income* as a result of higher net operating profit margin—known as *bottom-line growth* (because operating income is the result of a lot of addition and subtraction on an income statement). Bottom-line growth may be caused by higher revenue or, more likely in today's downsizing environment, by a reduction in costs.

Exactly where the growth in earnings comes from, revenue growth versus increasing NOPM, although important to many people, does not significantly change the valuation outcome in the DCF analysis. When we discuss growth rates, we assume growth in revenue because it is subject to less manipulation and "gimmicks du jour."

What are Wall Street analysts saying about Microsoft's expected future growth rates? Zacks survey of 26 analysts that follow Microsoft finds a median estimate for a 5-year CAGR of 25% per year. IBES also estimates a 5-year CAGR of 25% and notes that Microsoft's actual CAGR for the last 5 years was 33.7%. We use both analyst's and historic growth estimates to value Microsoft in Chapter 7. But first we want to turn to a company whose products most of us understand and have digested—McDonald's Corporation.

McDonald's Revenue Growth Rate

Let's examine the revenue growth rate of one of the favorite corporations of Generations X, Y, and Z—the McDonald's Corporation (NYSE—**MCD:** http://www.mcdonalds.com/). McDonald's market capitalization, according to the July 13, 1998 issue of *Business Week,* made it the seventy-ninth largest corporation in the world. Morningstar, Inc. (http://www.morningstar.com/) gives this company description on the Internet:

McDonald's operates, franchises, and services a system of more than 21,000 fast-food restaurants in 103 countries. The company's restaurants prepare, assemble, package, and sell a limited menu of low-to-moderate-price foods. These restaurants are operated by the company with franchise agreements, by independent third parties, or joint venture agreements between the company and local businesspeople. The substantially uniform menu consists of hamburgers and cheeseburgers, salads, milkshakes, breakfast items, chicken sandwiches, french-fried potatoes, and soft drinks.

Let's look at McDonald's revenue growth rates over the past 3 years with the thought that the information about past performance may be helpful in our estimate of future performance. We downloaded the 1997 annual report of McDonald's from its corporate Web site. The source for our information about McDonald's revenue is its 1997 income statement, presented as Exhibit 4-2, and shows revenue for 1997, 1996, and 1995. Table 4-2 shows McDonald's revenue growth rates over the last 3 years.

The 3-year average growth rate for McDonald's is 11.2% and the compound annual growth rate is 11.1%. Most analysts agree that the compound annual growth rate, rather than an average growth rate, is more appropriate for a valuation.

TABLE 4-2   McDonald's Corporation 3-Year Revenue Record
(millions of dollars)

	Revenue	$ Increase	% Increase
1997	$11,409	$722	6.8%
1996	10,687	892	9.1
1995	9,795	1,473	17.7
1994	8,320	—	—
3-year average growth rate = 11.2%			
3-year compound annual growth Rate = 11.1%			

Next, let's see what the pros are saying about McDonald's expected growth rates. Their projections are a little more optimistic than the historic averages. Zacks has a median 5-year estimate of 12.5% from the 17 analysts that it polled, while IBES estimates a 13% growth rate over the 3- to 5-year period.

When valuing a stock, we use the most recent publicly available information about the company. This means that we would examine the company's most recent quarterly reports and earnings releases. Most companies post these reports on their corporate Web sites. The SEC site is also a great central repository of quarterly and annual corporate information.

The most recent quarterly report will give a good current indication of the revenue and earnings prospects of the company. Analysts cover quarterly report filings and earnings releases closely. Negative surprises almost always result in very significant adverse stock price movements, while positive surprises often result in large upticks in the stock's price performance.

Why are there such significant stock price reactions to relatively small surprises in earnings? Recall that a stock's value is based upon expected *future* cash flows. If growth rates are reduced or NOPMs decline, then when analysts and investors plug these lower numbers into a discounted cash flow pricing model, the resulting value change can be quite significant. We examine these value changes in our examples in Chapter 7.

To keep this example simple, we focus on McDonald's annual report and we'll save introducing quarterly data and earnings surprises until Chapter 7. What does our own personal experience tell us about the growth prospects for McDonald's?

Although not federally mandated, virtually every U.S. Interstate exit, suburban intersection, and Main Street, USA already sports a McDonald's. This *market saturation* reduces the likelihood of increasing revenue growth, especially with additional Mickey D restaurants being built in new, high-visibility areas in the United States. Internationally, however, there has been a tremendous increase in high-volume McDonald's restaurants. From Bangkok to Santiago to the Puerta del Sol in Madrid, the Golden Arches are illuminating foreign skylines. In fact, Hoover's Online (http://www.hoovers.com/) notes that overseas restaurants accounted for nearly 60% of McDonald's profits in fiscal 1997.

It seems like outside the United States, the rest of the world is waking up to Egg McMuffins, is snacking on Chicken McNuggets, and is wolfing down McDonald's burgers and french fries. Revenue and earnings growth for McDonald's now and for the future seems to be highly dependent upon its international success—which to date has been stellar. Let's also assume that we are not privy to any nonpublic information about McDonald's that would negatively affect its sales of Happy Meals (e.g., our children are going to launch a boycott to protest a shortage of Beanie Babies).

Suppose that we like McDonald's internationally oriented strategy and believe that greater revenue growth will follow as it peddles its Big Macs in Macao. For simplicity and to be consistent with historic averages, we estimate a constant revenue growth rate of 11.1%. This may be an aggressive assumption, because over the past 3 years revenue growth has declined—from 17.7% to 9.1% to 6.8%. This is not a good trend. But IBES and Zacks do have slightly more positive growth assumptions, which we'll incorporate when we take a more detailed look at McDonald's in Chapter 7.

McDonald's Excess Return Period

Recall the **1-5-7-10 Rule** from Chapter 3. We think McDonald's is a *good company*—worthy of a 7-year excess return period. Why? The length of the excess return period should correspond to the time period over which the investor expects the corporation's business strategy to be successful. This means that the strategy will generate free cash flow—that is, earn a rate of return in excess of the company's WACC. Business strategies based on patent protection, high growth rates, superior marketing channels, or valuable brand names should have a relatively longer-term excess return period.

McDonald's has terrific brand name recognition and marketing channels. However, after a certain point fast food is fast food and intense competition in the fast-food market has resulted in shrinking profit margins. It may be possible for consumers to grow tired even of Big Macs and milkshakes. Also, McDonald's recent history of declining revenue growth rates and diminishing net operating profit margins, which we examine in the next section, is a bit troubling to us.

We use an excess return period for McDonald's of 7 years as we go through the cash flow analysis. Because of McDonald's strong brand name, this may be a conservative assumption for the excess return period. Erring on the side of conservatism is better than overpaying for a stock.

Valuation Inputs Relating to Revenue Growth and Excess Return Period

As of June 1, 1998, our general inputs and our inputs relating to revenue, revenue growth rate, and excess return period on our general input screen, as generated by the ValuePro 2000 software (see Exhibit 4-5, at the end of this chapter), are:

Company name	McDonald's Corporation
Fiscal year ending	12/31/1997
Excess return period (years)	7
Revenues ($mil)	$11,409
Revenue growth rate (%)	11.10%

Given the above *inputs*, we come up with the 7-year excess return period revenue projections for McDonald's, shown in Table 4-3. We also show McDonald's general pro forma screen, as generated by the ValuePro 2000 software, at the end of this chapter (see Exhibit 4-6).

The FCFF approach allows for different individual yearly inputs of revenue growth rates over the excess return period. For example, valu-

TABLE 4-3 McDonald's Corporation Projected Revenue Schedule (millions of dollars)

	Year	Revenue	$ Increase	% Increase
1997	0	$11,409	—	—
1998	1	12,675	$1,266	11.1%
1999	2	14,082	1,407	11.1
2000	3	15,646	1,564	11.1
2001	4	17,382	1,736	11.1
2002	5	19,312	1,930	11.1
2003	6	21,455	2,143	11.1
2004	7	23,837	2,382	11.1
	Residual	23,837	0	0

ation analyses can be based on growth rates increasing or decreasing over time, and they can accommodate numerous multistage growth valuation assumptions. We examine multistage growth valuation approaches in Chapter 7.

Net Operating Profit Margin and NOP

In this section, the acronyms start to flow heavily. They're only letters, and they're all described in our List of Acronyms (pp. 225–226). The *net operating profit margin* (*NOPM*) is the percentage ratio of the corporation's pre-tax, and pre-interest net operating profit (NOP) to operating revenues. To arrive at this ratio, we subtract costs of goods sold (CGS), selling, general and administrative expenses (SGA), and research and development costs (R&D—McDonald's does not list R&D costs separately, but high-tech companies like Intel and Microsoft do) from operating revenue and divide the resulting number by operating revenue:

$$\text{NOPM} = \frac{\text{Revenue} - (\text{CGS} + \text{SGA} + \text{R\&D})}{\text{Operating Revenue}} = \frac{\text{Net Operating Profit}}{\text{Operating Revenue}}$$

SGA, CGS, and R&D data also come from the corporation's income statement. Look again at McDonald's 1997 income statement (Exhibit 4-2) to find its NOP and calculate its NOPM over the last 3 years (see Table 4-4). As an example, consider how McDonald's NOPM is calculated for 1997:

$$\text{NOPM} = \frac{\$11,409 - (\$6,650 + \$1,950)}{\$11,409} = \frac{\$2,808}{\$11,409} = .246 = 24.6\%$$

Warning: Different companies may use different names and labels for various revenue and expense figures in their annual reports. For instance on the cash inflow side, McDonald's uses total revenues, Microsoft uses revenue, and Intel uses net revenues. There are greater differences in labeling on the expense side. Be careful when you examine annual reports and be sure to group entries consistently!

Now that we know what McDonald's has done historically, we must estimate its performance over the 7-year excess return period. For now, assume that McDonald's continues to operate at its 3-year average 25.2% NOPM for the foreseeable future. Note, however, that such an assumption may be aggressive, because the trend in McDonald's NOPM has been declining, from 26.5% to 24.6% over the 3-year period—but we'll go with the 25.2% estimate anyway.

Valuation Input Relating to NOPM

The input relating to NOPM for the ValuePro 2000 software on the general input screen is:

Net operating profit margin (%)   25.2%

TABLE 4-4 McDonald's Corporation NOPM Schedule (millions of dollars)

Year	Revenue	CGS	SGA	NOP	% NOPM
1997	$11,409	$6,650	$1,950	$2,808	24.6%
1996	10,687	6,163	1,891	2,623	24.6
1995	9,795	5,548	1,645	2,601	26.5

3-year average net operating profit margin = 25.2%

What do we have so far in our analysis of McDonald's? Based on an estimated growth rate of 11.1% per year and an estimated NOPM of 25.2% per year, we get the projected NOPM and NOP shown in Table 4-5. NOP is also shown in the general pro forma screen (see Exhibit 4-5, later in this chapter).

The FCFF approach allows for differing individual yearly inputs of net operating profit margins over the excess return period and can accommodate numerous assumptions in the valuation process. This allows NOP (operating income) to vary as the product of revenues (with varying growth rate capabilities) times NOPMs (with varying percentage capabilities).

The FCFF approach allows an infinite number of NOPM/revenue growth rate input options to create more multistage growth valuation capabilities than we will ever want to think about. We examine a multi-NOPM valuation example in Chapter 7.

Income Tax Rate and Adjusted Taxes

We all are painfully aware that the geopolitical units where we reside have developed great resourcefulness in expropriating a large portion of our income in the form of taxation. Likewise, corporations have to pay the various jurisdictions where they do business—federal, state,

TABLE 4-5 McDonald's Corporation Projected NOPM and NOP Schedule

	Year	Revenue	% NOPM	NOP
1997	0	$11,409	—	—
1998	1	12,675	25.2%	$3,194
1999	2	14,082	25.2	3,549
2000	3	15,646	25.2	3,943
2001	4	17,382	25.2	4,380
2002	5	19,312	25.2	4,867
2003	6	21,455	25.2	5,407
2004	7	23,837	25.2	6,007
	Residual	23,837	25.2	6,007

local, and international governments—their respective pounds of flesh. So we must make appropriate adjustments for taxes in our calculation of corporate free cash flow to see what is left over for the good guys—the stockholders.

The FCFF approach takes net operating profit, estimates an *adjusted tax payment* on the basis of the corporation's income tax rate, and subtracts out *adjusted taxes* to calculate NOPAT. We call them *adjusted tax payments* because the actual tax payments to the various government taxing entities are arrived at through complex calculations following arcane tax laws, with the associated $500 per hour New York tax lawyer's fee tacked on. These calculations include deferred components and complicated tax code treatments.

Tax deductions for interest expense associated with debt and the tax shield that debt provides are not included here in the cash flow section of the FCFF approach. They are introduced into the FCFF valuation process by adjusting the weighted average cost of capital. These adjustments, which are described in Chapter 5, reduce the cost of the debt component of the WACC to convert it to an after-tax WACC.

The FCFF approach to tax payments is to take NOP and subtract out adjusted taxes by multiplying it by (1 − tax rate) to get NOPAT:

$$\text{NOPAT} = \text{NOP} - \text{Taxes} = \text{NOP} \times (1 - \text{Tax Rate})$$

We also derive McDonald's tax rate from its income statement by dividing its *income before provision for income taxes* by its *provision for income taxes*. The 1997 income statement for McDonald's (see Exhibit 4-2) shows income before provision of income taxes of $2,407.3 million and a provision for income taxes of $764.8 million, giving McDonald's a tax rate of approximately 31.8% ($764.8/$2,407.3). We'll use this number for our 7-year projection of NOPAT, shown in Table 4-6.

Valuation Input Relating to Tax Rate

The input relating to the tax rate for the ValuePro 2000 software on the general input screen is:

Tax rate (%)   31.80%

The FCFF approach allows for individual yearly inputs of tax rates over the excess return period of up to 30 years and can accommodate numerous tax rate assumptions in the valuation process.

FINANCIAL REVIEW
Consolidated Statement of Income

(In millions, except per common share data)	Years ended December 31, **1997**	1996	1995
Revenues			
Sales by Company-operated restaurants	$ 8,136.5	$ 7,570.7	$6,863.5
Revenues from franchised and affiliated restaurants	3,272.3	3,115.8	2,931.0
Total revenues	11,408.8	10,686.5	9,794.5
Operating costs and expenses			
Company-operated restaurants			
Food and packaging	2,772.6	2,546.6	2,319.4
Payroll and other employee benefits	2,025.1	1,909.8	1,730.9
Occupancy and other operating expenses	1,851.9	1,706.8	1,497.4
	6,649.6	6,163.2	5,547.7
Franchised restaurants–occupancy expenses	613.9	570.1	514.9
Selling, general and administrative expenses	1,450.5	1,366.4	1,236.3
Other operating (income) expense–net	(113.5)	(45.8)	(105.7)
Total operating costs and expenses	8,600.5	8,053.9	7,193.2
Operating income	2,808.3	2,632.6	2,601.3
Interest expense–net of capitalized interest of $22.7, $22.2 and $22.5	364.4	342.5	340.2
Nonoperating (income) expense–net	36.6	39.1	92.0
Income before provision for income taxes	2,407.3	2,251.0	2,169.1
Provision for income taxes	764.8	678.4	741.8
Net income	$ 1,642.5	$ 1,572.6	$1,427.3
Net income per common share	$ 2.35	$ 2.21	$ 1.97
Net income per common share–diluted	2.29	2.16	1.93
Dividends per common share	$ .32	$ .29	$ .26
Weighted average shares	689.3	698.2	701.5
Weighted average shares–diluted	705.1	716.6	717.7

The accompanying Financial Comments are an integral part of the consolidated financial statements.

EXHIBIT 4-2   McDonald's Consolidated Statement of Income

Net Investment

Net investment by the corporation is the dollar amount needed to support the growth of the firm, and it includes new investment in property, plant, and equipment in excess of the depreciation expense associated with previous investments. Net investment, in math terms is:

Net Investment = New Investment – Depreciation Expense

For example, the growth of McDonald's revenue is in large part due to its opening of new stores both nationally and internationally. The information for this calculation comes from McDonald's cash flow statement, which is part of its annual report. The 1997 cash flow statement (see Exhibit 4-3) shows that Mickey D increased its *property and equipment expenditures* by approximately $2 billion in fiscal years 1997, 1996, and 1995.

TABLE 4-6   McDonald's Corporation Estimated NOPAT Schedule (millions of dollars)

	Year	NOP	Tax	NOPAT
1997	0	—	—	—
1998	1	$3,194	$1,016	$2,178
1999	2	3,549	1,129	2,420
2000	3	3,943	1,254	2,689
2001	4	4,380	1,393	2,987
2002	5	4,867	1,548	3,319
2003	6	5,407	1,719	3,687
2004	7	6,007	1,910	4,097
	Residual	6,007	1,910	4,097

An expenditure of $2 billion is a lot of money for a company with $11 billion coming in. It represents 18% of revenues. This investment has been significantly greater than the depreciation expense shown on the cash flow statement for McDonald's during 1997, 1996, and 1995. To generate increased revenue and net operating income figures, McDonald's made a substantial net investment in property, plant, and equipment. The net investment decreases the amount of money available for stockholders.

Net investment depends to a great extent on management investment decisions that are specific to and frequently guarded by a company. Management does not want competitors to be aware of what the company is doing, and information about planned investment may be difficult to procure. Investment in property, plant, and equipment is necessary both to maintain service and sales and also to grow revenues and profits.

The easiest way to estimate net investment as a valuation input is to do the following:

1. *During the excess return period,* which assumes revenue growth, project as though new investment and depreciation expense continue at the company's historic average percentages of revenues.

Consolidated Statement of Cash Flows

(In millions)	Years ended December 31, **1997**	1996	1995
Operating activities			
Net income	$ 1,642.5	$ 1,572.6	$ 1,427.3
Adjustments to reconcile to cash provided by operations			
Depreciation and amortization	793.8	742.9	709.0
Deferred income taxes	(1.1)	32.9	(4.2)
Changes in operating working capital items			
Accounts receivable increase	(57.6)	(77.5)	(49.5)
Inventories, prepaid expenses and other current assets increase	(34.5)	(18.7)	(20.4)
Accounts payable increase	52.8	44.5	52.6
Taxes and other liabilities increase	221.9	121.4	171.3
Refund of U.S. franchisee security deposits	(109.6)		
Other	(65.9)	42.9	10.1
Cash provided by operations	2,442.3	2,461.0	2,296.2
Investing activities			
Property and equipment expenditures	(2,111.2)	(2,375.3)	(2,063.7)
Purchases of restaurant businesses	(113.6)	(137.7)	(110.1)
Sales of restaurant businesses	149.5	198.8	151.6
Property sales	26.9	35.5	66.2
Other	(168.8)	(291.6)	(153.0)
Cash used for investing activities	(2,217.2)	(2,570.3)	(2,109.0)
Financing activities			
Net short-term borrowings (repayments)	1,097.4	228.8	(272.9)
Long-term financing issuances	1,037.9	1,391.8	1,250.2
Long-term financing repayments	(1,133.8)	(841.3)	(532.2)
Treasury stock purchases	(755.1)	(599.9)	(314.5)
Common and preferred stock dividends	(247.7)	(232.0)	(226.5)
Series E preferred stock redemption	(358.0)		
Other	145.7	157.0	63.6
Cash provided by (used for) financing activities	(213.6)	104.4	(32.3)
Cash and equivalents increase (decrease)	11.5	(4.9)	154.9
Cash and equivalents at beginning of year	329.9	334.8	179.9
Cash and equivalents at end of year	$ 341.4	$ 329.9	$ 334.8
Supplemental cash flow disclosures			
Interest paid	$ 401.7	$ 369.0	$ 331.0
Income taxes paid	$ 650.8	$ 558.1	$ 667.6

The accompanying Financial Comments are an integral part of the consolidated financial statements.

EXHIBIT 4-3   McDonald's Consolidated Statement of Cash Flows

2. *After the excess return period,* which assumes that the return from new investment only equals the company's WACC, set new investment equal to depreciation so that the property, plant, and equipment can be adequately maintained by the company.

The estimation procedure described above assures that for a company to maintain its revenue growth, new investment will keep pace on a percentage basis with total revenue. When revenue growth stops, new investment just keeps pace with depreciation expense and net investment. That is:

New Investment – Depreciation Expense = 0

Some analysts believe that it's more accurate to project net invest-ment and new investment in terms of a percentage of incremental rev-enue growth. We find that adjustment confusing and, in most cases, we prefer to use the percentage of revenue approach. Let's look at McDonald's historic investment versus revenue, and depreciation ver-sus revenue, schedules to get comfortable with this calculation.

As shown in Table 4-7, over the last 3 years, McDonald's has in-vested approximately 20.6% of its revenues in new property, plant, and equipment and has expensed only 7% of its revenues for depreciation charges. Those new investments are expected to translate into a lot of Happy Meals and McNuggets sales over the next umpteen years. If we assume that, over the next 7 years, it continues to cost McDonald's similar investment and depreciation percentage of revenue amounts to increase sales, then the schedule of net investment for McDonald's would be as shown in Table 4-8:

Valuation Inputs Relating to Net Investment

The inputs relating to new investment and depreciation expense, used to calculate net investment on the general input screen for the Value-Pro 2000 software, are:

New investment rate (% of revenue)   20.6%

Depreciation rate (% of revenue)   7.0%

The FCFF approach allows for individual yearly inputs of new investment and depreciation expense ratios over the excess return

TABLE 4-7 McDonald's Corporation 3-Year Revenue Versus Investment and Depreciation Schedule (millions of dollars)

	Revenue	New Investment	% New Investment	Depreciation	% Depreciation	Net Investment
1997	$11,409	$2,111	18.5%	$794	7.0%	$1,317
1996	10,687	2,375	22.2	743	6.9	1,632
1995	9,795	2,064	21.1	709	7.2	1,288
3-year average depreciation/revenue percentage = 7.0%
3-year average investment/revenue percentage = 20.6%

TABLE 4-8 McDonald's Corporation Projected Net Investment Schedule (millions of dollars)

	Year	Revenue	Investment	Depreciation	Net Investment
1997	0	$11,409	—	—	—
1998	1	12,675	$2,611	$ 887	$1,724
1999	2	14,082	2,901	986	1,915
2000	3	15,646	3,223	1,095	2,128
2001	4	17,382	3,581	1,217	2,364
2002	5	19,312	3,978	1,352	2,626
2003	6	21,455	4,420	1,502	2,918
2004	7	23,837	4,910	1,669	3,242
	Residual	23,837	1,669	1,669	0

period, and it can accommodate numerous capital investment and depreciation assumptions in the valuation process.

Incremental Working Capital

Working capital is needed to support the corporate sales effort of any company. Money is needed to finance accounts receivable from a company's customers and to finance the purchase of inventory prior to its sale. Working capital is usually defined as accounts receivable plus inventory minus accounts payable:

Working Capital = (Accounts Receivable + Inventory)
– Accounts Payable

Companies like Intel—which has over $3.7 billion (14.8% of revenues) in net working capital—have a very large amount of cash tied up in working capital. Other companies like McDonald's have a cash inflow generated by a surplus associated with working capital. It's not wise to keep a large inventory of hamburgers in India, for example.

Often a company's incremental change in net working capital, either positive or negative, is approximately proportional to its *change* in revenues. As an example, let's take a look at McDonald's working capital (taken from McDonald's balance sheet in Exhibit 4-4) over the

F I N A N C I A L   R E V I E W

Consolidated Balance Sheet

(In millions, except per share data)	December 31, 1997	1996
Assets		
Current assets		
Cash and equivalents	$ 341.4	$ 329.9
Accounts and notes receivable	483.5	495.4
Inventories, at cost, not in excess of market	70.5	69.6
Prepaid expenses and other current assets	246.9	207.6
Total current assets	1,142.3	1,102.5
Other assets		
Notes receivable due after one year	67.0	85.3
Investments in and advances to affiliates	634.8	694.0
Intangible assets – net	827.5	747.0
Miscellaneous	608.5	405.1
Total other assets	2,137.8	1,931.4
Property and equipment		
Property and equipment, at cost	20,088.2	19,133.9
Accumulated depreciation and amortization	(5,126.8)	(4,781.8)
Net property and equipment	14,961.4	14,352.1
Total assets	$18,241.5	$17,386.0
Liabilities and shareholders' equity		
Current liabilities		
Notes payable	$ 1,293.8	$ 597.8
Accounts payable	650.6	638.0
Income taxes	52.5	22.5
Other taxes	148.5	136.7
Accrued interest	107.1	121.7
Other accrued liabilities	396.4	523.1
Current maturities of long-term debt	335.6	95.5
Total current liabilities	2,984.5	2,135.3
Long-term debt	4,834.1	4,830.1
Other long-term liabilities and minority interests	427.5	726.5
Deferred income taxes	1,063.5	975.9
Common equity put options	80.3	
Shareholders' equity		
Preferred stock, no par value; authorized – 165.0 million shares; issued, 1997 – none; 1996 – 7.2 thousand		358.0
Common stock – $.01 par value; authorized – 3.5 billion shares; issued – 830.3 million	8.3	8.3
Additional paid-in capital	699.2	574.2
Guarantee of ESOP Notes	(171.3)	(193.2)
Retained earnings	12,569.0	11,173.0
Accumulated other comprehensive income	(470.5)	(175.1)
Common stock in treasury, at cost; 144.6 and 135.7 million shares	(3,783.1)	(3,027.0)
Total shareholders' equity	8,851.6	8,718.2
Total liabilities and shareholders' equity	$18,241.5	$17,386.0

The accompanying Financial Comments are an integral part of the consolidated financial statements.

EXHIBIT 4-4   McDonald's Consolidated Balance Sheet

past 3 years for some insight as to what cash flow effect increased revenue will have on working capital.

Table 4-9 shows that McDonald's net working capital requirements actually decrease on a cash flow basis as revenue increases. For our estimate of incremental working capital, we make projections that show working capital cash flows *coming into* McDonald's at a rate of 1% times the yearly increase in sales, as shown in Table 4-10.

TABLE 4-9 McDonald's Corporation Working Capital Schedule (millions of dollars)

	Revenue	Accounts Receivable	Inventory	Accounts Payable	Working Capital	% Working Capital
1997	$11,409	$483	$71	$651	$−97	−0.9%
1996	10,687	495	69	639	−75	−0.7
1995	9,795	377	58	564	−129	−1.3

3-year average working capital as percentage of revenue = −1.0%

Valuation Input Relating to Incremental Working Capital

The input relating to incremental working capital for the ValuePro 2000 software on the general input screen is:

Working capital (% of change in revenue)   −1.0%

The FCFF approach allows for individual yearly inputs of incremental working capital ratios over the excess return period, and it can accommodate numerous working capital investment assumptions in the valuation process.

TABLE 4-10 McDonald's Corporation Projected Incremental Working Capital (millions of dollars)

	Year	Revenue	Increase in Revenue	Incremental Working Capital
1997	0	$11,409	—	—
1998	1	12,675	$1,266	−13
1999	2	14,082	1,407	−14
2000	3	15,646	1,564	−16
2001	4	17,382	1,736	−17
2002	5	19,312	1,930	−19
2003	6	21,455	2,143	−21
2004	7	23,837	2,382	−24
	Residual	23,837	0	0

Free Cash Flow to the Firm— The Next Step

That was torture, but now we're home free! We have all the cash flow estimates that we need for the calculation of free cash flow to the firm. We have to take the net operating profit after tax and subtract out net investment and incremental working capital cash flow to get free cash flow to the firm. Remember our FCFF equation from Chapter 3:

FCFF = NOP − Taxes − Net Investment − Net Change in Working Capital

Earlier in this chapter we saw that NOPAT is equal to NOP minus taxes. Therefore:

FCFF = NOPAT − Net Investment − Net Change in Working Capital

Table 4-11 uses this equation to make the calculations for McDonald's FCFF.

Valuation Exercise: Estimating Free Cash Flow for McDonalds

Suffering through the pain and agony of creating all these schedules longhand is reminiscent of the third grade at St. Michael's Elemen-

TABLE 4-11 McDonald's Corporation Projection of Free Cash Flow to the Firm

	Year	Revenue	NOPAT	Net Investment	Net Change in Working Capital	FCFF
1997	0	$11,409	—	—	—	—
1998	1	12,675	$2,178	$1,724	−$13	$ 467
1999	2	14,082	2,420	1,915	−14	519
2000	3	15,646	2,689	2,128	−16	577
2001	4	17,382	2,987	2,364	−17	641
2002	5	19,312	3,319	2,626	−19	716
2003	6	21,455	3,687	2,918	−21	791
2004	7	23,837	4,097	3,242	−24	879
	Residual	23,837	4,097	0	0	49,248

tary School in Levittown, PA in 1958. Sister Mary Ignatius would be quite impressed by the ease with which a spreadsheet solves the divine mystery of stock valuation with a few strokes of the miraculous key pad! Exhibit 4-5 displays the inputs in **bold** relating to free cash flow estimation for our McDonald's example. Shown is the general input screen from the ValuePro 2000 integrated valuation software program.

Given those inputs, ValuePro 2000 produces the general pro forma cash screen for the excess return period that you specify—7 years in the example shown in Exhibit 4-6. Revenue, compounded at its estimated 11.1% growth rate, is shown in column 3. NOP, found by multiplying revenue by the NOPM of 25.2%, is shown in column 4. Adjusted taxes equals NOP times the tax rate of 31.8% and are shown in column 5. NOPAT, equal to NOP minus adjusted taxes (column 4 – column 5), is shown in column 6.

New investment, equal to revenue times the 20.6% estimated investment rate, is shown in column 7. Depreciation, equal to revenue times the 7% estimated depreciation rate, is shown in column 8. And net investment, equal to new investment minus depreciation (column

		Valuation Date	10/14/98
	General Input Screen		
	Intrinsic Stock Value $38.42		

General Inputs

Company Name **McDonald's Corporation**

Fiscal Year	12/31/97	Depreciation Rate (% of Rev.)	**7.00%**
Excess Return Period (years)	7	Investment Rate (% of Rev)	**20.60%**
Revenues ($mil)	**$11,409**	Working Capital (% of change in Rev.)	**-1.00%**
Revenue Growth Rate (%)	**11.10%**	Excess Marketable Securities ($mil)	0
Net Operating Profit Margin (%)	**25.20%**	Other Senior Claims	0
Tax Rate (%)	**31.80%**		

Cost of Capital Inputs

Current Stock Price	$67.25
Annual Dividend Per Share (e.g. $1.00)	$0.36
Shares Outstanding (mil)	689.3
30-year Treasury Bond Yield (e.g 6.50%)	5.80%
Bond Yield Spread to Treasury (e.g. 1.00%)	1.00%
Preferred Stock Yield (e.g. 8.00%)	0.00%
Equity Risk Premium (e.g. 3.00%)	3.00%
Company Specific Beta (e.g. 1.00)	0.97
Value of Debt Outstanding ($mil)	$4,931.0
Value of Preferred Stock ($mil)	$0.0
Weighted Average Cost of Capital	8.32%

EXHIBIT 4-5   General Input Screen, McDonald's

7 – column 8), is shown in column 9. The change in working capital, equal to the change in yearly revenues times the incremental working capital rate of –1%, is shown in column 10.

Column 11 shows the free cash flow to the firm—which is equal to column 6 – (column 9 + Column 10). Columns 12 and 13 are used to discount and total those FCFF numbers. You'll note that FCFF is calculated for the 7-year excess return period. At the end of the 7-year period, ValuePro 2000 calculates the residual value by dividing McDonald's NOPAT, estimated to be equal to $4,097 million, by McDonald's WACC (which, as we'll see later, turns out to be 8.32%) to get a $49,248 million residual value in 2004. You'll see how and where we get the inputs to calculate McDonald's WACC in Chapters 5 and 6.

We then discount the company's yearly free cash flow and the residual value at the discount factors, shown in column 12, associated with the WACC. Column 13 shows the product of FCFF (column 11) times the discount factors (column 12). The sum of these discounted numbers, along with excess marketable securities, is the total corporate value of $31,412 million, shown above column 7 in Exhibit 4-6. From total corporate value, we subtract the value of debt and preferred stock to get total value to common equity—$26,481 million in Exhibit 4-6—and divide by the shares outstanding to calculate the per share intrinsic stock value.

Our cash flow estimates, *based on historic data,* show the **intrinsic value for McDonald's stock to be $38.42 versus an observed market price of $65.50 on June 1, 1998.** On the basis of these assumptions, a strong sell recommendation was in order on that date. Could it be that the market knows something that we do not, or that market players are using valuation assumptions that are more advantageous to McDonald's stock value? In fact, recent management decisions have very favorably affected McDonald's stock price. We talk about these decisions as we look at McDonald's in greater depth later in the book.

The cash flow estimation process may be tedious but it is not difficult. It's important to know that if you follow the FCFF approach properly, you'll gain the talent of at least one of The Five Chinese Brothers—**you won't get burned.**

McDonald's Corporation
General Pro Forma Screen
7-year Excess Return Period

Discounted Excess Return Period FCFF	$3,262	Total Corporate Value
Discounted Corporate Residual Value	$28,150	Less Debt
Excess Marketable Securities	$0.0	Less Preferred Stock
Total Corporate Value	$31,412	Less Other Senior Claims

Total Corporate Value	$31,412
Less Debt	($4,931)
Less Preferred Stock	$0
Less Other Senior Claims	0
Total Value to Common Equity	$26,481
Intrinsic Stock Value	$38.42

(1)	(2)	(3)	(4)	(5)	(6)	(7)	(8)	(9)	(10)	(11)	(12)	(13)
Period	Fiscal Year	Revenues	NOP	Adj. Taxes	NOPAT	Invest.	Deprec.	Net Invest.	Change in Working Capital	FCFF	Discount Factor	Discounted FCFF
0	12/31/97	11,409										
1	12/31/98	12,675	3,194	1,016	2,178	2,611	887	1,724	-13	467	0.9232	431
2	12/31/99	14,082	3,549	1,129	2,420	2,901	996	1,915	-14	519	0.8523	442
3	12/31/2000	15,646	3,943	1,254	2,689	3,223	1,095	2,128	-16	577	0.7869	454
4	12/31/2001	17,382	4,380	1,393	2,987	3,581	1,217	2,364	-17	641	0.7264	465
5	12/31/2002	19,312	4,867	1,548	3,319	3,978	1,352	2,626	-19	712	0.6706	477
6	12/31/2003	21,455	5,407	1,719	3,687	4,420	1,502	2,918	-21	791	0.6191	490
7	12/31/2004	23,837	6,007	1,910	4,097	4,910	1,669	3,242	-24	879	0.5716	502
Residual		23,837	6,007	1,910	4,097	1,669	1,669	0	0	49,248	0.5716	28,150

EXHIBIT 4-6 General Pro Forma, McDonald's

Notes

1. The CAGR for revenue growth is calculated by dividing the most recent revenue number (A) (e.g., $11,358 for 1997) by an earlier revenue number (B) (e.g., $4,659 for 1994); taking the resulting ratio to the $1/T$ power, where T is the number of years in the compounding period; and subtracting 1.0 to bring it into percentage terms. In math talk, the previous sentence looks like this: $[(A/B)^{1/T} - 1.0]$. The calculation of the CAGR for the 3-year period (1994–1997) for Microsoft is $[(11{,}358/4{,}659)^{1/3} - 1.0] = 1.3458 - 1.0 = 34.58\%$. Likewise, for Microsoft's 10-year CAGR, the calculation (see Table 4-1) would be $[(11{,}358/346)^{1/10} - 1.0] = 1.4178 - 1.0 = 41.78\%$.

"Don't Count Until You Discount!"

Estimating the Cost of Capital

"Don't count until you discount." Writing this chapter brings to mind that oft-repeated phrase of Professor Russ Ezzell, who teaches Finance 301 at The Pennsylvania State University. The discounting of cash flow is based upon two fundamental principles underlying the theory of finance. The first principle is that of *positive interest rates* and may be characterized by the saying "A dollar invested today is worth more than a dollar promised tomorrow." The second principle is that of *risk aversion* and may be characterized by the saying "A safe dollar is worth more than a risky one."

The FCFF approach and the ValuePro 2000 software follow Dr. Ezzell's rule and develop a set of expected cash flows for a corporation and then adjust or *discount* those cash flows to account for their timing and risks. In Chapter 4 we examined the expected free cash flow of the corporation. In this chapter we address the estimation of the company's discount rate.

In accordance with generally accepted finance theory, a company's *after-tax weighted average cost of capital* is the rate we use to discount the *company's after-tax free cash flow*. A company's WACC is the weighted average of the company's **current cost of debt and equity claims** calculated by using debt, preferred stock, and current market common stock values. Later in this chapter, we show you how to calculate a company's WACC longhand.

The WACC as a Portfolio Return

A company's WACC may be a strange concept for most people to understand. It may be helpful for you to think of a company's WACC in relation to the weighted average return on your own investment portfolio. You may own $10,000 in a money market fund that has an expected yearly return of 6%. You also may own $10,000 of a preferred stock with an expected return of 8%. And you may own $80,000 market value of a common stock with an expected return of 10%. The expected weighted average return of your $100,000 (in total) investment portfolio equals:

Expected Portfolio Return

$$= \frac{(\$10,000 \times .06) + (\$10,000 \times .08) + (\$80,000 \times .10)}{\$100,000}$$

$$= \frac{\$9,400}{\$100,000} = 9.4\%$$

A company's WACC is similar to your investment portfolio's weighted average return. It's simply the weighted average expected cost for the various types of obligations—debt, preferred stock, and common stock—that are issued by the corporation to finance its operations and investments.

The company's WACC is an important number, both to the stock market for stock valuation purposes and to the company's management for capital budgeting purposes. In the analysis of a potential investment by the company, projects that have an expected return that is greater than the company's WACC will generate additional free cash flow and will create an additional positive net present value for stock owners. These corporate investments should result in an increase in stock prices.

Conversely, projects that have an expected return that's lower than the company's WACC will reduce free cash flow and decrease the value of the company. Management should just say **no!** Negative NPV projects result in a decrease in stock value. In fact, investing in negative NPV corporate projects has caused the early exit of many a chief executive in recent years.

How to Measure the Cost of Capital

In WACC calculations, the capital claims of the company are classified into debt, preferred stock, and common equity. The company may have outstanding many different issues of debt and preferred stock with varying coupon or dividend and maturity structures. Other than the effect on the market value of outstanding debt and preferred stock, the *historic* interest rates on a corporation's debt and the dividend rates on its preferred stock issues are fairly unimportant numbers. The past capital structure of the corporation is not as important as the expected *future* capital structure of the corporation and *expected market yield levels.*

The percentage weights (discussed in the next section) used in the FCFF approach and the ValuePro 2000 software to calculate the WACC are the percentages that the company plans to use in its capital structure over the valuation period. Generally, we use the current capital structure of the company to estimate what its capital structure will look like in the future. The discount rates used in the valuation process should be current rates demanded *today* (as a proxy for expected rates) by the market for securities with similar risk and cash flow characteristics.

Because of the tax benefits associated with the deduction of interest payments by the corporation, debt is treated in a special manner in the FCFF approach. The *after-tax* cost of debt is used in the calculation of the corporation's WACC. The ValuePro 2000 software is designed such that, given the current market yield on a company's debt and the company's tax rate, the after-tax adjustment to the WACC is calculated automatically.

Interest Rates, the Company's WACC, and Stock Values

Let's take a closer look at the relationship among interest rates, a company's WACC, and its stock value. Assume that changes in interest rates and a company's WACC don't affect a firm's amount of future free cash flows or earnings. However, changes in interest rates and

WACC will greatly affect the *present value* of those same cash flows and earnings. Lower interest rates will result in a lower weighted average cost of capital. A lower cost of capital will raise the present value of a company's future earnings or cash flow and its stock value. Conversely, higher interest rates and WACCs will result in a lower present value of FCFF and a lower stock value.

How much does a change in interest rates affect a stock's value? To get a better handle on this question, it's helpful to understand the *mathematics underlying bond pricing.* Suppose that an investor owns a $10,000 U.S. Treasury Bond that pays all its interest at maturity in 30 years (called a *zero coupon* or *stripped bond*). Assume that the yield or discount rate associated with that bond is 8%. From our discussion of compounding and compound annual growth rates, we can calculate the *discount factor* for the bond, which would be equal to 1 divided by 1.08 raised to the thirtieth power or $1/(1.08)^{30} = .0994$. The present value of this U.S. Treasury Bond is $10,000 \times .0994 = \$994$.

If interest rates were to drop by 1 percentage point and the new discount rate associated with that bond is 7%, its *discount factor* would now be equal to $1/(1.07)^{30} = .1314$. The present value of the bond is now $10,000 \times .1314 = \$1,314$, an increase of $320, or 32%, over the value of the same bond discounted at 8%.

If interest rates were to drop by an additional 1 percentage point, so that the discount rate associated with that bond is 6%, its *discount factor* would equal $1/(1.06)^{30} = .1714$, and its present value would equal $1,714—an increase of $427, or 33% over the value of the same bond discounted at 7%.

The stock valuation is a parallel analysis to bond valuation. Stocks, particularly growth stocks, have most of their value associated with growth in future cash flow and earnings far into the future. Stocks, by definition have no "stated maturity" or "principal value," and growth stocks specifically are *way out there* in terms of average life or duration of cash flows.

Ignoring the 1-5-7-10 Rule, which effectively shortens the average life and duration of cash flows for valuation purposes, **stock values are extremely sensitive to changes in interest rates!** From our interest rate analysis discussed above, a 1% change in interest rates in today's U.S. Treasury market, all else equal, can result in a 33% change in stock values. This is a huge effect!

Stock price/interest rate sensitivity is a two-edged sword. Stock values, particularly those of growth stocks that pay little or no dividends, benefit greatly when interest rates are falling. We saw this clearly during the 1990s. Be aware that rising interest rates will act to drive down stock values as quickly as falling interest rates have recently propelled stock values skyward. This is the effect that the discounting rate has on stock values!

Calculating the WACC and Market Capitalization

Let's look at the weighting procedure and how to estimate a company's cost of debt, preferred stock, and common equity. As our test case, we take a freeze-frame look at the capital structure of McDonald's on June 1, 1998. Initially, we use the *book value* of McDonald's *debt and preferred stock outstanding,* as shown on its 1997 balance sheet and *the market value of its common stock* on June 1, 1998 (see Table 5-1).

Market Value versus Book Value

Financial theory states that the market capitalization of a company is equal to the total market value, not book value, of the outstanding debt, preferred stock, and common stock of the company. The FCFF approach uses the various market values to calculate a company's market capitalization and debt and equity weightings. To illustrate this point, consider the book versus market values of McDonald's common stock. As of June 1, 1998 there were 689.3 million shares of common

TABLE 5-1 McDonald's Market Capitalization, June 1, 1998 (millions of dollars)

	Book Value		Market Value	
	Total	%	Total	%
Debt	$4,931	35.8%	$4,931	9.6%
Preferred stock	0	0 %	0	0 %
Common equity	8,851	64.2%	46,355	90.4%
Total capitalization	$13,782	100.0%	$51,286	100.0%

stock outstanding with market value and book value of $67.25 and $12.84 per share, respectively.

The *book value of debt and preferred stock* is an accounting measure that relates to how much money was raised by the company when each security initially was issued. The *book value of common stock* is also an accounting measure that relates to the amount of money raised per share when the stock was issued, plus the amount of aggregate earnings per share that has been retained by the company.

The *market value of debt and preferred and common stock* is the price that the specific obligation would trade at in today's market. Because of the frequent trading of stocks and the fact that prices are readily observable, it is easy to determine the market value of common stock. Since debt and preferred stock trade less frequently, and often only in the dealer-to-dealer market, market prices of these securities are not easily observable and are harder to determine.

If we're expecting a 10% return on a share of common stock of McDonald's, and its market value is $67.25 per share, our expectation is that we will earn 10% per year on our $67.25 investment, or $6.72 between dividends and stock price appreciation. We'd be more than mildly disappointed if we received 10% on the much lower $12.84 book value of the share, or $1.28 per year. Hence, market professionals use market values when they look at market capitalization of common stock.

The current quotes of market value for debt and preferred stock are often difficult to obtain. Also, the market values of preferred stock and debt for the most part do not stray significantly from their respective book values. In an effort to conserve time and to simplify their valuation task, most market professionals use the company's reported book values for debt and preferred stock when they examine the market's capitalization of the corporation.

Market professionals **always use the market value of common stock** when they examine the market's capitalization of the corporation. As we see in the McDonald's example above, the market value of common stock sometimes bears little relationship to its book value. Stock prices are easy to observe and current market quotes are readily available. In keeping with this market practice, we use book values for debt and preferred stock and market values for common stock in all our valuation examples.

Estimating McDonald's WACC

Previously, we discussed the importance of using the company's *expected* capital structure for valuation purposes. Since most of us don't have a pipeline into the finance department of the corporation, unless the corporation has publicly announced a target capitalization structure, the best estimate to use to calculate a company's WACC is the capital structure as reported in the most recent annual or quarterly report.

Assume that the pre-tax cost of debt for McDonald's is 6.8%, which represents a 1% *spread to Treasuries,* its after-tax cost of debt is 4.64% (equal to $6.8\% \times (1 - .318)$), it has no preferred stock outstanding, and the cost of common equity is 8.71%. You will see in the sections below that we didn't just pull those values out of Ronald McDonald's hat. Under the above assumptions, McDonald's WACC on June 1, 1998, based on *a market value weighting of common stock and book value weightings of debt and preferred stock,* was:

McDonald's WACC = $.096 \times (4.64\%) + .904 \times (8.71\%) = 8.32\%$

Below we show our inputs into the ValuePro 2000 software relating to the cost of capital and market capitalization. We'll explain how and where we come up with these numbers in the pages that follow. By the way, Ronald McDonald doesn't wear a hat.

Valuation Inputs Relating to Cost of Capital and Market Capitalization

Our initial inputs relating to cost of capital and market capitalization for the ValuePro 2000 software on the general input screen (which appear in **bold** in Exhibit 5-1) on June 1, 1998 are:

Current stock price	$67.25
Shares outstanding (mil.)	689.3
30-year Treasury Bond yield (e.g., 6.5%)	5.80%
Bond yield spread to Treasury (e.g., 1%)	1.0%
Preferred stock yield (e.g., 8%)	0.00%
Risk premium to stock market (e.g., 3%)	3.00%

		Valuation Date	10/14/98
	General Input Screen		
	Intrinsic Stock Value $38.42		

General Inputs

Company Name	McDonald's Corporation		
Fiscal Year	12/31/97	Depreciation Rate (% of Rev.)	7.00%
Excess Return Period (years)	7	Investment Rate (% of Rev)	20.60%
Revenues ($mil)	$11,409	Working Capital (% of change in Rev.)	-1.00%
Revenue Growth Rate (%)	11.10%	Excess Marketable Securities ($mil)	0
Net Operating Profit Margin (%)	25.20%	Other Senior Claims	0
Tax Rate (%)	31.80%		

Cost of Capital Inputs

Current Stock Price	$67.25
Annual Dividend Per Share (e.g. $1.00)	$0.36
Shares Outstanding (mil)	689.3
30-year Treasury Bond Yield (e.g 6.50%)	5.80%
Bond Yield Spread to Treasury (e.g. 1.00%)	1.00%
Preferred Stock Yield (e.g. 8.00%)	0.00%
Equity Risk Premium (e.g. 3.00%)	3.00%
Company Specific Beta (e.g. 1.00)	0.97
Value of Debt Outstanding ($mil)	$4,931.0
Value of Preferred Stock ($mil)	$0.0
Weighted Average Cost of Capital	8.32%

EXHIBIT 5-1   General Input Screen, McDonald's

Company-specific beta (e.g., 1.0)	0.97
Value of debt outstanding ($ mil.)	$4,930.7
Value of preferred stock ($ mil.)	$0

The FCFF approach allows for individual yearly inputs of the WACC over the excess return period. This enables us to incorporate the effect of changing leverage, capital structure, and discount rates into the valuation process.

The Cost of Common Equity and Shares Outstanding

The annual rate of return that an investor expects to earn when investing in shares of a company is known as the *cost of common equity*. That return is composed of the dividends paid on the shares and any increase (or decrease) in the market value of the shares. For example, if an investor expects a 10% return from McDonald's stock and buys a share at $67.25, her expectation is to receive $6.72 during the year through a combination of dividends (currently $.34 per share during 1998) and the appreciation of the stock price (presumed to be $6.38 to give the 10% expected return totaling $6.72) during the year.

The Risk-Free Rate and Expected Returns

Let's take a look at what rate of return, in general, an investor should expect from a stock. The return expected for any *risky* common stock should be composed of at least three different components: (1) a return that is commensurate with a risk-free security (R_f) of a comparable-term or maturity and that incorporates expectations of inflation; (2) a return that incorporates the market risk associated with common stocks as a whole (R_m); and (3) a return that incorporates the business and financial risks specific to the stock of the company itself, known as the company's *beta*.

The first measure of return (R_f) relates to the market rate of return currently available on a risk-free security. A rational investor who values a security that has risk, such as common stock, would expect it to earn a return at least equal to and probably greater than that of a risk-free security, such as the yield associated with a long-term Treasury Bond. If the yield on a Treasury Bond is 6.5%, an investor should expect a return greater than 6.5% for a common stock.

The Return Relating to Common Stock in General

The second measure of return (R_m) relates to what market returns are currently available from and what risks are associated with stocks in general. There is a general risk premium (the *equity risk premium*) associated with the stock market as a whole. That risk premium should be priced into any equity investment. For example, if you expect to earn 9.5% on average from a diversified market portfolio and the risk-free rate is 6.5%, the *equity risk premium* (R_{erp}) would be 9.5% − 6.5% = 3%.

Equity Risk Premium(R_{erp}) = Expected Return on Market(R_m)
$$- \text{Risk-Free Rate}(R_f)$$

There is much debate about how to measure or estimate the equity risk premium. Rerp is an ***expectation*** *of the excess return associated with the investment in a diversified portfolio of common stocks versus the expected return of a risk-free security.* It is the additional return that an investor expects to receive in excess of a risk-free yield to compensate for the price volatility associated with the stock market.

Damodaran observes that the actual compound annual rate of return difference between the stock market and Treasury Bonds has *decreased significantly* in recent years.[1] He notes that the stock market/T-Bond risk premium, on a compound annual return basis, has decreased from 5.5% for the period 1926–1990, to 3.25% for the period 1962–1990, to 0.19% for the period 1981–1990. In the valuation examples in his text, despite the decrease in observed R_{erp}, he uses the longer-term 75-year average, 5.5% equity risk premium, in his cost of capital calculations and in his valuation examples.

Investors also have noticed this decrease in the historic equity risk premium, and it appears to us that their *expectations* of this risk premium have lessened. A reasonable equity risk premium for the stock market of mid-1998 is approximately 3%.[2] This 3% equity risk premium estimate is what we use in our valuations. Both equity and debt market volatility increased in August and September 1998, and there had been concerns that the "price of risk" has been increasing as well. However, with the lowering of interest rates by the Federal Reserve in October 1998, the stock market recovered and ended 1998 near record levels.

The Return Relating to an Individual Stock

The third measure of return versus risk (beta) should be related to the specific stock being purchased: How risky is the type of business the firm does? How risky is the financial structure or leverage of the firm? Beta measures the risk of the company relative to the risk of the stock market in general. Greater risk (business or operating risk), as measured by larger variability of returns, increases a company's beta. Likewise, with greater leverage (higher debt/value ratio) increasing financial risk, a company's stock will have a larger beta. **With a larger beta, an investor should expect a greater return.**

The beta of an *average-risk* firm in the stock market is 1.0. The beta of a below-average-risk firm in the stock market, such as a firm operating in a regulated industry, is less than 1.0. For example, the beta of Consolidated Edison (according to S&P Comstock) is 0.8. The beta of an above-average-risk firm—such as Microsoft, which operates in the quickly changing industry of software and computers—is greater than

1.0. Microsoft's beta (according to Yahoo through its Market Guide link) is 1.26. McDonald's beta (according to Yahoo) is 0.97. Clearly, megabytes are more volatile than McNuggets and are much more volatile than megawatts. Betas are even higher for Internet-dependent stocks. For example, Amazon.com (http://www.amazon.com/), according to Thomson Investors Network accessed through Netscape's portal, is 3.26, while the beta of Yahoo! (http://www.Yahoo.com) is 3.24.

Expected Return and the Capital Asset Pricing Model

The financial risk model that uses beta as its sole measure of risk (a *single-factor model*) is called the *capital asset pricing model* (*CAPM*) and is used by many market analysts in their valuation process. The relationship between risk and return that comes out of that model and the one that is incorporated into our FCFF analysis and ValuePro 2000 is:

$$\text{Expected Return (Rs)} = \text{(Rf)} + \text{beta(Rerp)}$$

which in English translates as follows: "The expected return on a stock (e.g., McDonald's) is equal to the risk-free rate (e.g., 5.8%) plus the specific stock's beta (e.g., 0.97) times the equity risk premium (e.g., 3%)." In numbers it looks like this:

$$\text{Expected Return on McDonald's Stock} = 5.8\% + 0.97(3\%) = 8.71\%$$

The above equation results in is a linear relationship between the expected return on a stock and its specific risk measure, beta. A graph of this risk/return relationship with a risk-free rate of 5.8%, a stock market risk premium of 3%, and a beta of .97, is shown in Exhibit 5-2.

There's a lot of academic theory behind the capital asset pricing model, the equity risk premium, and the calculation of beta. We describe that theory, along with a multirisk measure asset pricing model called the arbitrage pricing model (APT), in Appendix C.

The Amount of Stock Outstanding—The Problem with Options

The final input associated with the cost of common equity is the amount of stock outstanding. There currently is a lot of discussion in the accounting industry about what this number truly should be—the actual number of shares outstanding; a number that takes into account any *in-the-money options* that have been granted (in-the-

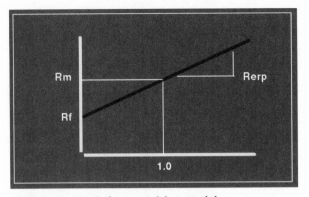

EXHIBIT 5-2   Capital Asset Pricing Model

money options are options that have an exercise price below the current market price of the stock); or an amount that takes into account all options that have been granted by the company.

It seems that many corporations, especially high-tech companies like Microsoft and Intel, are making stock options a large part of the compensation package for employees—and not just for top management. When and if those options become vested and are in the money, they are going to **represent a serious dilution problem for stockholders and will strongly and negatively affect stock values.** In our valuations for Microsoft and Intel in Chapter 7, we adjust the "amount of stock outstanding" input to take into account the dilution aspects of stock options.

What we use, for our *first cut* at valuation, is the most recent "amount outstanding" number that is reported on S&P Comstock. To our knowledge, S&P Comstock reports the actual number of shares outstanding. For more detailed valuations, we take into account the "fully diluted" amount of stock outstanding as reported in the annual and quarterly reports to get a better handle on the corporation's option dilution problem.

In summary, the inputs for valuation relating to the cost of common equity are the current rate of return on the risk-free Treasury Bond, the beta of the stock, which is 0.97 for McDonald's (estimates of beta are available from a number of sources, as discussed in Chapter 6), the current estimate of the equity risk premium, and the amount of common stock outstanding.

The After-Tax Cost of Debt and Debt Outstanding

The after-tax cost of debt securities represents the cost to the firm of *borrowing funds at today's interest rates and market yields in the debt markets* to finance investments in the operations of the company, after taking into account the tax deductibility of interest payments by the corporation.

It's important to use **today's interest rates** in calculating the company's WACC, because they represent today's best expectation of relative opportunity costs for providers of new capital to the company. By contrast, historic or *sunk* costs are associated with the coupon rates and original offering yields on outstanding debt and preferred stock issues of the company. These historic rates should not affect the corporation's investment decisions or the calculation of the corporation's WACC.

Because a company's debt securities are *risky* investments (although not as risky as its common stock), the after-tax cost of debt primarily is a function of three variables: the current yields associated with comparable-maturity risk-free debt, the default risk (or the "spread to Treasuries") associated with the specific company's debt, and the company's income tax rate.

The Spread to Treasuries—A Measure of Default Risk

All taxable debt that is issued and traded in the U.S. capital markets is priced at what is called a *spread to Treasuries.* The spread to Treasuries implies that all corporate debt will have a higher yield (effective interest cost) than yields associated with comparable-maturity U.S. Treasury Bonds. This spread will change over time depending on economic conditions and the relative default risk associated with the specific debt security. The interest rate, or yield, of all debt is vitally dependent on the risk-free rate associated with U.S. Treasury debt. The 30-year risk-free rate is our starting point for the WACC calculation.

The spread to Treasuries is the *measure of default risk* on a specific company's debt, and it is an input into the FCFF approach and the ValuePro 2000 software. For a large company like McDonald's, which has low financial leverage (low percentage of debt in its market capitalization), the spread to Treasuries might be quite small (e.g., 0.75% to 1%). For a company with considerable operating risk or high leverage, the spread to Treasuries might be quite large (e.g., 5% to 9%).

The best way to determine default risk is to see how a particular company's debt is trading in the market and compare it on a spread basis with comparable-maturity Treasury yields. For instance, McDonald's has debt that is traded on the New York Stock Exchange. Quotes for listed, publicly traded debt are available in the finance sector of free Web sites like Yahoo (http://www.yahoo.com/). In a pinch you could always rely on debt quotes from a good financial newspaper like *The Wall Street Journal* or *Investor's Business Daily.*

Many companies will not have outstanding debt that is listed or traded on an exchange. Their debt securities will trade in the dealer-to-dealer market, and trades and quotations may not be available to the general public. Another way to measure default risk and to estimate spreads is to use the default rating systems that are published by the three major rating agencies—Standard & Poor's Corporation, Moody's Investor Services, and Fitch & Company. These rating services publish ratings for many corporate debt issuers. The highest credit ratings, which are earned by companies with very low default risk, are AAA/Aaa and the ratings decline from there.

A viable way of estimating the yield on debt of a company that does not have actively traded bonds is to examine the cost of outstanding traded debt from a default ratings standpoint for a similar company. Then use that yield as a proxy for the cost of debt of the company that you are valuing.

Likewise, it often is difficult to find market value quotes for the outstanding debt of the corporation to determine market capitalization calculations. We've found that the market value of debt usually does not diverge too greatly from the book value of debt. Using the book value of debt does not bias significantly the valuation. That's what we use in our valuation examples.

The After-Tax Cost of Debt

The final adjustment to be made to the cost of debt is to deduct the effect of income taxes. Since interest payments (and interest accruals) are tax-deductible for the company, an adjustment to the WACC is made to reflect this corporate tax saving. The higher the corporate income tax rate, the greater is the tax savings from issuing debt and the lower is the after-tax cost of debt. The deductibility of interest payments reduces the cost of debt financing for the corporation. The equation that represents this deductibility is:

After-Tax Cost of Debt = Pretax Cost of Debt
$$\times\ (1 - \text{Corporate Tax Rate})$$

For example, if the risk-free rate is 5.8% and McDonald's debt trades at a 1% spread to Treasuries and its tax rate is 31.8%, the pretax cost of debt is 5.8% + 1% = 6.8% and the after-tax cost of McDonald's debt is:

McDonald's After-Tax Cost of Debt = 6.8% × (1 – .318) = 4.64%

In summary, the inputs relating to the cost of debt are: (1) an estimate of the current yield on long-term debt of the corporation being valued, represented as a spread to Treasuries; (2) the company's tax rate; and (3) the amount of debt outstanding. For simplicity, use book value of debt if market value isn't available.

The Cost of Preferred Stock and Stock Outstanding

Preferred stock is a specialized financing vehicle that usually represents a very small part of any company's capital structure. Preferred stock is an ownership claim that is senior to that of common stock (hence the adjective *preferred*) but junior to that of debt.

The dividends that are paid by the corporation on preferred stock and common stock, unlike the interest payments on debt, are not tax-deductible to the corporation. However, if a corporation owns stock in another corporation, it is allowed a tax deduction (the *dividends received deduction,* or *DRD*) on the dividends it receives. Thus it is advantageous for a corporation to own stock. This is a long way of saying that there are tax advantages to certain corporate holders for owning preferred or common stock of another corporation.

Over the past 20 years investment bankers and corporate issuers have gotten mighty fancy in the use and structure of preferred stock.

Many options and complex dividend structures may be embedded in a preferred issue. Examples are convertibility into common shares or into debt, redeemability by the corporation after a certain date, and dividend-setting mechanisms designed to keep the market value and par value equal. These esoteric features can make it hard to value preferred stock properly.

Some companies have perpetual preferred stock outstanding that is traded on an exchange. For example, one issue of McDonald's preferred stock listed on the NYSE paid a dividend of $1.93 per year and traded on October 1, 1997 at a price of $25⅚₆ for a yield of 7.6%. McDonald's called that issue for redemption in late 1997 and it no longer is outstanding. We will take that redemption as a signal that McDonald's management currently does not favor preferred stock in its capitalization structure.

Luckily, preferred stock is a very small percentage of the capital structure of most companies. It may be difficult to get a quoted market rate level for the preferred stock of a company. We have found that the current market yield of preferred stock with no fancy convertibility or dividend-setting mechanisms is somewhere between the pretax cost of debt (in the McDonald's example, 6.8%) and the cost of common equity (in the McDonald's example, 8.71%).

When we approach a valuation and cannot find a good quote for preferred stock or a quote for a preferred stock issue of a comparable company, we ballpark the cost by splitting the difference between the pretax cost of debt and the cost of common equity. (In this case, splitting the difference would give a preferred stock yield of 7.75%, if there were any preferred stock outstanding.)

Likewise, it sometimes may be difficult to find market value quotes for the outstanding preferred stock of the corporation to determine market capitalization calculations. We've found that, if there is not a large amount of preferred stock outstanding, using the book value of preferred stock, as opposed to the market value, does not bias significantly the valuation. We use book values for amounts of preferred outstanding in our valuation examples.

The valuation inputs for preferred stock are today's yield level associated with the preferred stock of the company and the amount of preferred stock outstanding. For simplicity, use book value of preferred stock if the market value isn't available.

After the Cost of Capital— The Next Step

In this chapter we explored the estimation of the discount rate that we will use to reduce or adjust the expected free cash flow to the firm. We looked at the calculation of the weighted average cost of capital, and we discussed how to estimate the costs of common equity, debt, and preferred stock. We show the WACC calculation in Exhibit 5-3. We also saw that using market value for common stock and book values for debt and preferred stock was a generally accepted practitioner's way of calculating the WACC of a corporation.

The next step takes us into the realm of putting together all that we have learned so far, as well as finding out where and how we can easily get the information that we need to make informed, intelligent valuations. We examine where and how to get that information in Chapter 6.

Valuation Exercise: Estimating the WACC for McDonald's

The inputs that we discussed above for the ValuePro 2000 software result in the McDonald's weighted average cost of capital screen shown in Exhibit 5-3. McDonald's after-tax WACC is 8.32%. How do we get this number? We calculate the cost of common equity (8.71%) and the after-tax cost of debt (4.64%) and multiply them by their market

	Valuation Date	09/21/98
McDonald's Corporation		
Weighted Average Cost of Capital Screen		

Cost of Common Equity

Long Term Bond Yield	5.80%
Beta	0.97
Equity Risk Premium	3.00%
Cost of Common Equity	8.71%

Market Capitalization and After-Tax Weighted Average Cost of Capital

	Average Yield	After Tax Yield	Market Value	% Capital	After Tax Effect
Long-Term Debt	6.80%	4.64%	4,931	9.6%	0.45%
Preferred Stock	0.00%	0.00%	0	0.0%	0.00%
Common Stock	8.71%	8.71%	46,355	90.4%	7.87%
			51,286	100.0%	8.32%

EXHIBIT 5-3   WACC Screen, McDonald's

McDonald's Corporation
General Pro Forma Screen
7-year Excess Return Period

Discounted Excess Return Period FCFF	$31,412	
Discounted Corporate Residual Value	($4,931)	
Excess Marketable Securities	$0	
Total Corporate Value		

$3,262	Total Corporate Value	
$28,150	Less Debt	
$0.0	Less Preferred Stock	
$31,412	Less Other Senior Claims	
	Total Value to Common Equity	0
	Intrinsic Stock Value	$26,481
		$38.42

(1)	(2)	(3)	(4)	(5)	(6)	(7)	(8)	(9)	(10)	(11)	(12)	(13)
Period	Fiscal Year	Revenues	NOP	Adj. Taxes	NOPAT	Invest.	Deprec.	Net Invest.	Change in Working Capital	FCFF	Discount Factor	Discounted FCFF
0	12/31/97	11,409										
1	12/31/98	12,675	3,194	1,016	2,178	2,611	887	1,724	-13	467	0.9232	431
2	12/31/99	14,082	3,549	1,129	2,420	2,901	986	1,915	-14	519	0.8523	442
3	12/31/2000	15,646	3,943	1,254	2,689	3,223	1,095	2,128	-16	577	0.7869	454
4	12/31/2001	17,382	4,380	1,393	2,987	3,581	1,217	2,364	-17	641	0.7284	465
5	12/31/2002	19,312	4,867	1,548	3,319	3,978	1,352	2,626	-19	712	0.6706	477
6	12/31/2003	21,455	5,407	1,719	3,687	4,420	1,502	2,918	-21	791	0.6191	490
7	12/31/2004	23,837	6,007	1,910	4,097	4,910	1,669	3,242	-24	879	0.5716	502
Residual		23,837	6,007	1,910	4,097	1,669	1,669	0	0	49,248	0.5716	28,150

EXHIBIT 5-4 General Pro Forma Screen, McDonald's

value percentage weightings—9.6% for debt and 90.4% for common stock—to get McDonald's after-tax WACC of 8.32%.

Each of McDonald's estimated free cash flows, shown in column 11 of Exhibit 5-4, is discounted at factors based upon its WACC of 8.32%. The discount factors, shown in column 12 of Exhibit 5-4, range from .9232 for year 1 (equal to 1/1.0832) to .5716 for year 7 (equal to $1/(1.0832)^7$). The discounted free cash flow to the firm for the excess return period is shown in column 13 of Exhibit 5-4.

Recall the calculation of corporate value from Chapter 3:

Corporate Value = Cash Flow Operations
                              + Residual Value + Excess Securities   **(Eq. 1)**

This calculation, shown at the top of Exhibit 5-4, yields a total corporate value of $31,412 million. Also recall from Chapter 3 the calculation of common stock value:

Value to Common Equity = Corporate Value – Senior Claims   **(Eq. 2)**

This calculation, also shown at the top of Exhibit 5-4, yields a value to common equity of $26,481 million, along with the per share **intrinsic stock value of $38.42.**

In the next chapter we explain where and how an investor can quickly get the information needed to use the FCFF approach efficiently and effectively. Armed with this information, our savvy investor will be ready to conquer the investment world!

Notes

1. Aswath Damodaran, *Investment Valuation,* John Wiley & Sons, 1996, pp. 48–49.

2. An economic report by Bill Dudley of Goldman Sachs, "The Equity Risk Premium and the Brave New Business Cycle," *U.S. Economics Analyst,* February 21, 1997, gives a good rationale for nearly 3% as an "equity risk premium that is consistent with fair value for equities versus bonds" (p. 6).

Where and How to Obtain the Information for Valuations

Show Me the Info!

Now that you've finished browsing the first five chapters, you are ready to test-drive the FCFF approach. You want to try your skill at valuation and also see if you can maneuver valuations in the real world. You want to find out whether the FCFF approach and the ValuePro 2000 software are Corvettes or Corvairs! Where and how do you get the inputs that are necessary to take a reasonable stab at valuing a stock? That's a valid question for which there are two answers. You can get the information either through the time-consuming *hard way* or via the almost instantaneous *easy way*.

The Hard Way

The time-consuming hard way involves locating the company's head-quarters, contacting the company's investor relations department, and requesting printed annual and quarterly reports. Since you are not a large institutional investor, you may be referred to the commercial bank that acts as the company's stock transfer agent (and may or may not have a toll-free telephone number).

Within the bowels of the large commercial bank's telephone system you will be routed through a maze of prerecorded messages with various complicated options punctuated by occasional elevator music. Finally, you will be hooked up with the right answering machine through which you will request financial reports and give your mailing address. The company's financial information will then be delivered to you by regular mail through the U.S. Postal Service.

These financial reports will give you the numbers that you need relating to the company's balance sheet, income statement, and cash flow statement. The additional information that you need regarding the company's cost of capital components, its beta, and its projected revenue growth and earnings rates will have to come from other sources.

Some of this additional information can be gleaned from financial newspapers such as *The Wall Street Journal, Barron's, Investor's Business Daily,* or *The New York Times.* You also can go to the local library (assuming that it has a good investment and finance department) to look up back issues of *Value Line* and *Standard & Poor's Stock Guide,* either through hard copy or in the microfilm and microfiche area. The library also may have corporate annual reports. You can then photocopy the relevant material at 10 to 25 cents a page. This is a good exercise to do while you're waiting for annual and quarterly reports to be delivered by regular mail.

Or you can use the almost instantaneous *easy way* to obtain all the information that you need!

The Easy Way

The answer: *the Internet and the World Wide Web!*[1]

If you own or have access to a computer (with a modem of nonglacial speed) that can be hooked into the Internet, consider the possibilities. If you know where and how to look for it, you can get the information that you need almost instantaneously. That's what we discuss in this chapter.

The Internet and the World Wide Web for Investor Information

You've probably heard that the Internet has become very investor-friendly. Recently the Internet has had a tremendous increase in Web sites relating to investments and corporate financial information. Virtually all companies with publicly traded stock have their own corporate Web sites. Companies use their Web sites to market products, to hire employees, and to post annual and quarterly reports, earnings releases, and other financial information.

McDonald's corporate Web site address is http://www.mcdonalds.com/. If you type that exact address into your Web browser, you'll see Ronald McDonald peddling all kinds of McProducts. You'll also see a section relating to stockholder information. Unless you're having a virtual Big Mac attack, this will be the area of the Web site that should be of the greatest interest to you.

The display and format of the financial reports associated with many of these Web sites allow easy downloading of the whole corporate report. They also allow selective printing of separate sections of the report such as the income statement, the balance sheet, and the cash flow schedules. These corporate Web sites should be your primary source of information for most of the corporation-related inputs for your valuations.

Corporate Web Sites

How do you find corporate Web sites on the Internet? You can get to the Internet through America Online or the Microsoft Network, or by using the Netscape browser or the Microsoft Internet Explorer in concert with a local Internet access provider. Each Internet browser, through its *Find* function, is capable of searching the Internet for the uniform resource locator (URL) address of the Web site of McDonald's Corporation or Intel Corporation or almost any publicly traded company.

Once you're connected to the Internet, there are a number of Web sites that function as *search engines*. If your browser can't find the corporate Web site, type in the URL for one of the following search engines. It will take you through its own search procedure to find the Web address that you need:

Yahoo—(http://www.yahoo.com/)

Excite—(http://www.excite.com/)

Lycos—(http://www.lycos.com/)

Altavista—(http://altavista.digital.com/)

Infoseek—(http://guide-p.infoseek.com/)

Hot Bot—(http://www.search.hotbot.com/)

Microsoft Network—(http://www.msn.com/)

America Online—(http://www.aol.com/)

The next best backup source for corporate information is the Web site of the Securities and Exchange Commission (http://www.sec.gov/). The SEC maintains an information service named EDGAR (electronic data gathering, analysis, and retrieval). This service collects submissions by companies that are required to file reports—financial and otherwise—with the SEC.

The purpose of EDGAR is to increase the efficiency and fairness of the securities market by allowing free and immediate access by investors, corporations, and other economic parties to corporate-related information. EDGAR filings are posted to the SEC's Web site no later than 24 hours after their submission. The SEC Web site is well designed and easy to use. However, the SEC-mandated financial reports (10Ks, 10Qs, 8Ks, etc.) are fairly lengthy and contain a lot of legal gobbledygook.

Two great sources for direct links to corporate Web sites are the Yahoo site and Hoover's Online (http://www.hoovers.com/). Yahoo, through its *Finance/Corporate Reports/Profile* link, which uses information provided by Market Guide, Inc., gives a business summary for the corporation plus a section called Company's Web Presence. Under that section are links to both the company's home page and the company's financial report—a quick way to get to the information that you need.

Hoover's maintains detailed financial data, which is available to subscribers on a fee basis, for more than 11,000 corporations. However, Hoover's offers company capsules and minimum financial information at no charge to visitors of its Web site. On each company capsule page is a direct link to the home page of the corporation's Web site.

Web Sites Devoted to Investment Information

There are a number of Web sites relating to the valuation of a corporation's securities. Some Web sites are free or partly free, and some provide information to subscribers only. America Online, through its *Personal Finance/Investment Research* link, allows investors access to certain areas of Disclosure (http://www.disclosure-investor.com/), Morningstar (http://www.morningstar.com/), Bloomberg Finance (http://www.bloomberg.com/), S&P's Comstock (http://www.spcomstock.com/), Zacks (http://www.zacks.com/), and Market Guide (http://www.marketguide.com/). Much of this information may otherwise be available only to subscribers of such services. These types of Web sites have information that is useful for helping you estimate a company's growth rate, a corporation's beta, the 30-year Treasury rate, corporate bond yields, and preferred stock yields.

Yahoo's free site provides a market quote service and extensive fundamental stock information, including estimates of a stock's beta and growth rate. You can access this service through the following Yahoo links *Finance/Corporate Report/(insert stock symbol)/Profile*, which is provided to Yahoo from Market Guide. Also, First Call (http://www1.firstcall.com/) and IBES (http://www.ibes.com/) have areas on investment research that give earnings estimates and growth rates as well as a lot of other information about a company.

For each of the inputs required for the FCFF approach, we point you to the Web site that will give you the best and most easily accessible information. **Warning:** You can burn up a lot of time in cyberspace without realizing it following links from one Web site to another. On the Internet there is more information available about a corporation than almost anyone can absorb. Like Roberto Duran you may find yourself saying, "No mas," as the computer screen keeps filling, files keep downloading, and the printer keeps churning out data.

If you enjoy it, have the time to spare, and have no history of carpel tunnel syndrome—great! Point, click, and be merry! If you're just looking to get info to use for an analysis, you may want to follow our suggestion to minimize Internet time.

In the sections that follow, you'll find all of the info you need to run a valuation. The information and inputs are segmented into three categories: the easy-to-find company inputs; the company inputs requiring estimation; and the economic cost of capital inputs.

Corporate Valuation—
Easy-to-Find Inputs

In this chapter we continue to use McDonald's as our valuation example. Our first order of business is to use our computer to tap into the Internet and, through our America Online, Netscape, or Microsoft Internet Explorer browser, visit the McDonald's Corporation Web site (http://www.mcdonalds.com/).

We enter its main site (Exhibit 6-1) and click on the *Corporate* area of the site. Another click on the *Investor Information* link (Exhibit 6-2) gives us access to the *1997 Annual Report* section. **Warning:** To view this area and some other corporate reports, we had to download the Adobe Acrobat Reader onto our computer. This download is free and relatively painless, but time-consuming.

In the annual report section we downloaded the *text-only version.* (We didn't want to waste valuable computer time downloading pictures of cute kids playing in McDonald's playgrounds.) We printed the following sections: the consolidated statement of income (Exhibit 6-3), the consolidated balance sheet (Exhibit 6-4), and the consolidated statement of cash flows (Exhibit 6-5). Here is how we use those reports.

Income Statement Information

As shown in Table 6-1, to run our FCFF valuation, we need to use information from McDonald's income statement (Exhibit 6-3) for the fiscal year ending December 31, 1997. The income statement has information for three fiscal years—1997, 1996, and 1995. Three years of data (as opposed to one) can help us better understand the corporation, how consistently it has performed, and what trends in revenue growth rate or net operating margin efficiency it has experienced.

Balance Sheet Information

As shown in Table 6-2, we also need information from McDonald's balance sheet (Exhibit 6-4) for the fiscal year ending December 31, 1997. The balance sheet has information for only two fiscal years—1997 and 1996.

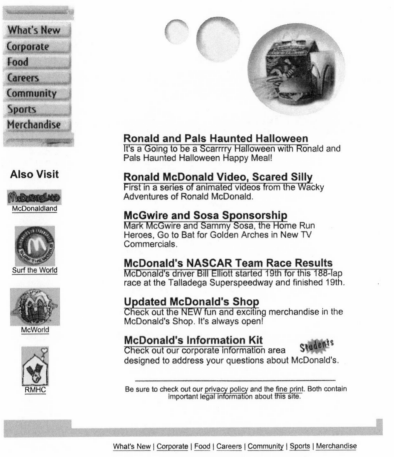

EXHIBIT 6-1   McDonald's Web Site Screen

Cash Flow Statement Information

As shown in Table 6-3, the final information that we need to value McDonald's common stock comes from McDonald's consolidated cash flow statement (Exhibit 6-5) for the fiscal year ending December 31, 1997.

The information that we obtain from the annual or quarterly reports gives us the valuation inputs relating to fiscal year ending, revenues, excess marketable securities, shares outstanding, and (book, not market) value of debt and preferred stock.

What's New

Corporate

Investor Info
Franchising
Our People
Alliances
History
FAQ
Information Kit

Food

Careers

Community

Sports

Merchandise

CORPORATE

McDonald's is a global business that operates in a very decentralized manner, but here we have tried to provide a central source for information about McDonald's business, people and history. Here you can find information about McDonald's as an investment; what we look for in a franchisee; development efforts with our alliance partners; plus the people behind the Golden Arches and our history.

Investor Information

- About McDonald's
- Financial Reports
  - Annual Report
  - Downloadable Financials
  - Edgar Filings
- Financial Press Releases
- Stock Price
- Shareholder Information
  - MCDirect Shares
  - Dividend and Split History
  - Investor Services
  - Contact Information

Franchising

- Franchising Introduction
- Franchising Inside the U.S.
  - Fact Sheet
  - FAQ
  - Inside U.S. Application
- Franchising Outside the U.S.
  - Contacts
  - Outside U.S. Application
  - Requirements

Our People - Learn About the National Black McDonald's Operators Association

- NBMOA
- History
- Community Commitment
- Awards and Honors
- Employment Commitment
- Chapter Locations

Alliances

EXHIBIT 6-2 McDonald's Finance Web Site Screen

McDonald's - Corporate   Page 2 of 2

- Our People Overview
- Featured Franchiser
- NBMOA - National Black McDonald's Operators Association
- MHOA - McDonald's Hispanic Operators Association

Alliances

- Alliances Overview
- Chevron Alliance
- Wal*Mart Alliance
- Amoco Alliance

History

- History of McDonald's and Ray Kroc

Frequently Asked Questions

- FAQ on McDonald's Corporation

Information Kit

- McDonald's Student Information Kit

Investor Info | Franchising | Our People | Alliances | History | FAQ | Information Kit

What's New | Corporate | Food | Careers | Community | Sports | Merchandise

© McDonald's Corporation. All rights reserved.

McDonald's Privacy Policy

EXHIBIT 6-2 *(Cont.)*

These reports also give us the historic information that is helpful in the valuation inputs requiring estimation of revenue growth rate, net operating profit margin, tax rate, depreciation rate, investment rate, and incremental working capital. We discuss where to find the information for our estimation in the next section.

Valuation Inputs Requiring Estimation

The most important cash flow inputs, which drive the intrinsic stock value computation for the FCFF approach, are the estimates for the rev-

FINANCIAL REVIEW

Consolidated Statement of Income

(In millions, except per common share data)	Years ended December 31, 1997	1996	1995
Revenues			
Sales by Company-operated restaurants	$ 8,136.5	$ 7,570.7	$6,863.5
Revenues from franchised and affiliated restaurants	3,272.3	3,115.8	2,931.0
Total revenues	11,408.8	10,686.5	9,794.5
Operating costs and expenses			
Company-operated restaurants			
Food and packaging	2,772.6	2,546.6	2,319.4
Payroll and other employee benefits	2,025.1	1,909.8	1,730.9
Occupancy and other operating expenses	1,851.9	1,706.8	1,497.4
	6,649.6	6,163.2	5,547.7
Franchised restaurants–occupancy expenses	613.9	570.1	514.9
Selling, general and administrative expenses	1,450.5	1,366.4	1,236.3
Other operating (income) expense–net	(113.5)	(45.8)	(105.7)
Total operating costs and expenses	8,600.5	8,053.9	7,193.2
Operating income	2,808.3	2,632.6	2,601.3
Interest expense–net of capitalized interest of $22.7, $22.2 and $22.5	364.4	342.5	340.2
Nonoperating (income) expense–net	36.6	39.1	92.0
Income before provision for income taxes	2,407.3	2,251.0	2,169.1
Provision for income taxes	764.8	678.4	741.8
Net income	$ 1,642.5	$ 1,572.6	$1,427.3
Net income per common share	$ 2.35	$ 2.21	$ 1.97
Net income per common share–diluted	2.29	2.16	1.93
Dividends per common share	$ .32	$ .29	$ .26
Weighted average shares	689.3	698.2	701.5
Weighted average shares–diluted	705.1	716.6	717.7

The accompanying Financial Comments are an integral part of the consolidated financial statements.

EXHIBIT 6-3 McDonald's Consolidated Statement of Income

enue growth rate and the net operating profit margin. On Wall Street, the ability to estimate these numbers is what separates the All-American stock analysts from their lower-paid kin.[2]

In addition, we must estimate the company's tax rate, depreciation, and new investment levels, and the expected change in working capital that's required to support the business. Unless a company has radically changed its operating procedures or has been drastically restructured, most analysts use *an historic averaging process as a first approximation in estimating these inputs.*

As we discussed in Chapter 4, we can estimate these inputs in one of three rational ways: (1) use historic performance of the company as a guide to the likely outcomes in the future; (2) use expectations of analysts or other market participants; or (3) use a mixture of the two blended with our own common sense.

Historic performance of the company usually acts as a fairly good, although far from perfect, indicator of potential future performance. If revenues have been growing at a 5-year compound annual growth rate

FINANCIAL REVIEW

Consolidated Balance Sheet

(In millions, except per share data)	December 31, 1997	1996
Assets		
Current assets		
Cash and equivalents	$ 341.4	$ 329.9
Accounts and notes receivable	483.5	495.4
Inventories, at cost, not in excess of market	70.5	69.6
Prepaid expenses and other current assets	246.9	207.6
Total current assets	1,142.3	1,102.5
Other assets		
Notes receivable due after one year	67.0	85.3
Investments in and advances to affiliates	634.8	694.0
Intangible assets–net	827.5	747.0
Miscellaneous	608.5	405.1
Total other assets	2,137.8	1,931.4
Property and equipment		
Property and equipment, at cost	20,088.2	19,133.9
Accumulated depreciation and amortization	(5,126.8)	(4,781.8)
Net property and equipment	14,961.4	14,352.1
Total assets	$18,241.5	$17,386.0
Liabilities and shareholders' equity		
Current liabilities		
Notes payable	$ 1,293.8	$ 597.8
Accounts payable	650.6	638.0
Income taxes	52.5	22.5
Other taxes	148.5	136.7
Accrued interest	107.1	121.7
Other accrued liabilities	396.4	523.1
Current maturities of long-term debt	335.6	95.5
Total current liabilities	2,984.5	2,135.3
Long-term debt	4,834.1	4,830.1
Other long-term liabilities and minority interests	427.5	726.5
Deferred income taxes	1,063.5	975.9
Common equity put options	80.3	
Shareholders' equity		
Preferred stock, no par value; authorized–165.0 million shares; issued, 1997–none; 1996–7.2 thousand		358.0
Common stock–$.01 par value; authorized–3.5 billion shares; issued–830.3 million	8.3	8.3
Additional paid-in capital	699.2	574.2
Guarantee of ESOP Notes	(171.3)	(193.2)
Retained earnings	12,569.0	11,173.0
Accumulated other comprehensive income	(470.5)	(175.1)
Common stock in treasury, at cost; 144.6 and 135.7 million shares	(3,783.1)	(3,027.0)
Total shareholders' equity	8,851.6	8,718.2
Total liabilities and shareholders' equity	$18,241.5	$17,386.0

The accompanying Financial Comments are an integral part of the consolidated financial statements.

EXHIBIT 6-4   McDonald's Consolidated Balance Sheet

of 8%, an estimated revenue growth rate of 25% may seem a tad aggressive—unless there's a new knock-'em-dead product (like Viagra) or the company has undergone a massive upheaval. As the company matures, the growth rate naturally declines, for reasons that we discussed in Chapter 4.

The trend in movement of historic data may highlight an area of potential concern. For example, McDonald's average NOPM for the past 3 years has been 25.2%, but its downward trend of 26.5%

FINANCIAL REVIEW
Consolidated Statement of Cash Flows

(In millions)	Years ended December 31, 1997	1996	1995
Operating activities			
Net income	$ 1,642.5	$ 1,572.6	$ 1,427.3
Adjustments to reconcile to cash provided by operations			
Depreciation and amortization	793.8	742.9	709.0
Deferred income taxes	(1.1)	32.9	(4.2)
Changes in operating working capital items			
Accounts receivable increase	(57.6)	(77.5)	(49.5)
Inventories, prepaid expenses and other current assets increase	(34.5)	(18.7)	(20.4)
Accounts payable increase	52.8	44.5	52.6
Taxes and other liabilities increase	221.9	121.4	171.3
Refund of U.S. franchisee security deposits	(109.6)		
Other	(65.9)	42.9	10.1
Cash provided by operations	2,442.3	2,461.0	2,296.2
Investing activities			
Property and equipment expenditures	(2,111.2)	(2,375.3)	(2,063.7)
Purchases of restaurant businesses	(113.6)	(137.7)	(110.1)
Sales of restaurant businesses	149.5	198.8	151.6
Property sales	26.9	35.5	66.2
Other	(168.8)	(291.6)	(153.0)
Cash used for investing activities	(2,217.2)	(2,570.3)	(2,109.0)
Financing activities			
Net short-term borrowings (repayments)	1,097.4	228.8	(272.9)
Long-term financing issuances	1,037.9	1,391.8	1,250.2
Long-term financing repayments	(1,133.8)	(841.3)	(532.2)
Treasury stock purchases	(755.1)	(599.9)	(314.5)
Common and preferred stock dividends	(247.7)	(232.0)	(226.5)
Series E preferred stock redemption	(358.0)		
Other	145.7	157.0	63.6
Cash provided by (used for) financing activities	(213.6)	104.4	(32.3)
Cash and equivalents increase (decrease)	11.5	(4.9)	154.9
Cash and equivalents at beginning of year	329.9	334.8	179.9
Cash and equivalents at end of year	$ 341.4	$ 329.9	$ 334.8
Supplemental cash flow disclosures			
Interest paid	$ 401.7	$ 369.0	$ 331.0
Income taxes paid	$ 650.8	$ 558.1	$ 667.6

The accompanying Financial Comments are an integral part of the consolidated financial statements.

EXHIBIT 6-5   McDonald's Consolidated Statement of Cash Flows

to 24.6% may have investors concerned about future declining NOPMs.

Among the profusion of Web sites devoted to investment research and advice, we have found that three of the best sites having free areas of information about revenue and/or earnings estimates for a company are Zacks, IBES, and First Call. New investment-related Web sites spring up often, so keep on the lookout for sites that fit your information needs.

Valuation Inputs for Cost of Capital

The final set of inputs that we will need for the FCFF approach and to run the ValuePro 2000 software relates to the company's weighted average cost of capital.

TABLE 6-1   McDonald's Corporation Income Statement Information (millions of dollars)

	1997	1996	1995
Total revenues	$11,408.8	$10,686.5	$9,794.5
Total operating cost and expenses	8,600.5	8,053.9	7,193.2
Operating income	2,808.3	2,632.6	2,601.3
NOPM (%)	24.6%	24.6%	26.5%
Income before provision for income taxes	2,407.3	2,251.0	2,169.1
Provision for income taxes	764.8	678.4	741.8
Effective income tax rate (%)	31.8%	30.1%	34.2%
Weighted average shares outstanding	689.3	698.2	701.5

Current Stock Price and Shares Outstanding

The current stock price is an important number because it affects the market capitalization value of the corporation and its WACC. As the stock price increases, the percentage of the company's market capitalization that is represented by stock increases. Since common stock is

TABLE 6-2   McDonald's Corporation Balance Sheet Information (millions of dollars)

	1997	1996
Working Capital Data		
Accounts receivable	$483.5	$495.4
+ Inventories	70.5	69.6
− Accounts payable	(650.6)	(638.0)
= Net working capital	(96.6)	(73.0)
Net working capital/revenues (%)	(.85%)	(.68%)
Capital-Related Data		
Excess cash and marketable securities	0	
Long-term debt (book value)	$4,834.1	
Preferred stock (book value)	0	

TABLE 6-3 McDonald's Corporation Cash Flow Information
(millions of dollars)

	1997	1996	1995
Depreciation and amortization	$793.8	$742.9	$709.0
Depreciation/revenues (%)	7.0%	6.9%	7.2%
Property and equipment expenses	2,111.2	2,375.3	2,063.7
Property expense/revenues (%)	18.5%	22.2%	21.1%
3-year average depreciation/revenue (%)		7.0%	
3-year average investment/revenue (%)		20.6%	

the highest yield component of the cost of capital, all else equal, as the company's stock price increases, its cost of capital increases.

Yesterday's stock quotes can be found in many daily newspapers that have a finance section. The Internet can give you more current stock prices. America Online has an easy-to-use stock quote service through its *Personal Finance/Stock Quote* link. When you plug in a company's name or stock symbol you get a current quote (20-minute delay) for the stock. It also will give you the stock's beta and the number of shares outstanding. These quotes are provided to America Online by Comstock, a service of Standard & Poor's Corporation.

Yahoo, the free Web site/search engine, has a similar service through its *Finance/Latest Stock Price* link. These market quotes (on 20-minute delay), along with other information, are provided to Yahoo by Market Guide. There are numerous additional Web sites on which you can get quotes, and your choice of site depends upon your own preferences.

30-Year Treasury Bond Yield

The minimum rate of return, including expectations of inflation, from any investment should be at least as great as the yield available from a risk-free investment. For common stocks, we use as a base rate the yield associated with long-term, 30-year U.S. Treasury Bonds.

The current yield on the 30-year Treasury can be found in any newspaper with a good financial section or through numerous financial Web sites, of which the easiest for us to use is America Online. AOL's *Per-*

sonal Finance/The Markets/Bond&Money/U.S. Treasury Yields link takes you to Bloomberg Online. The Web site of Bloomberg Online (http://www.bloomberg.com/) is great for finding information on the U.S. debt market and other financial markets.

Perhaps the most official Web site for U.S. Treasury Bond yields is that of the Federal Reserve Board of Governors, which posts a daily form H15 release. On September 18, 1998, the 30-year constant-maturity Treasury yield was 5.18%. The length of the Fed's Web address is its biggest drawback (http://www.bog.frb.fed.us/releases/H15/update/).

Company Bond Yield Spread to Treasury

Also on the Fed H15 release are the current bond yields for Moody's Aaa-rated and Baa-rated corporate bonds, and A-rated utility bonds. The indicative yields for these three types of bonds on September 18, 1998 were 6.43%, 7.12%, and 6.93% respectively.

The H15 release should give you a good feel for what the company's yield spread to Treasury should be. For instance, we would consider McDonald's to be close to a Aaa-rated company. On the basis of the H15 release, McDonald's bond yield spread to Treasury would be 6.43% − 5.18% = 1.25%, and we round up to 1.5% to be conservative.

Another debt-related Web site is Bonds-Online (http://www.bonds-online.com/). Through its *Treasuries* link a current complete yield curve is displayed, along with 10 years of year-end rates. The historic data provide a great perspective on what can realistically happen to interest rate movements over the excess return period. Also, the *Corporates* link of Bonds-Online gives spread to Treasuries data by year of maturity and rating category for five classifications of corporate bonds: banks, financials, industrials, transportation, and utilities—a good source for corporate bond information.

Company Preferred Stock Yield

If the company has preferred stock outstanding that is traded on an exchange, the Internet-related quote services that we described above will give you preferred stock prices for the company. To get the preferred stock yield (for a preferred stock that has no stated maturity), simply divide the dividend rate by the preferred stock price. For example, one issue of preferred stock of Consolidated Edison had a dividend of $1.94 per year and was trading on December 31, 1997 at a price of $25.53. Its yield is calculated by dividing $1.94 by $25.53: $1.94/25.53 = 7.60\%$.

The Equity Risk Premium

The equity risk premium is an estimate of the excess return an investor expects to earn on a "risky" stock relative to a risk-free asset. We use the yield on the 30-year U.S. Treasury Bond as a measure of the return on a risk-free asset. This item is not one that you typically stumble upon while surfing the Web.[3]

We have developed a computer model based on a Goldman Sachs discounted cash flow model that calculates an implied equity risk premium based upon observed stock market variables. We calculate the equity risk premium and show it on our Web site (http://www.valuepro.net/).

Company-Specific Beta

As we have discussed, a company's beta is the risk measure used in the CAPM, the model most frequently used by market professionals in assessing a stock's risk. Several Web sites that specialize in financial information list a stock's beta estimate in their free area. For example, on July 22, 1998, a beta estimate of 0.97 was listed for McDonald's in the business summary section of Yahoo's *Finance/Corporate Reports/Profiles* link. S&P's Comstock, accessed through America Online's *Personal Finance/Quotes* link, listed a beta of 0.94. Why the difference and which one should you use?

A company's beta is estimated by running a statistical test (known as a *regression analysis*) relating the price movement of the stock and the price movement of the stock market in general. Various market participants use different time periods and measurement techniques in performing this calculation, so slightly different beta estimates may result.

When a difference arises, the most conservative approach, which results in a higher WACC and lower stock value, is to use the higher beta. Another approach is to use the average of the betas for the analysis. For the valuations that we perform in this book, we use the higher value of beta.

Value of Debt and Preferred Stock Outstanding

The book values of debt and preferred stock are listed in the balance sheet section of the corporation's annual reports. The best (and to our knowledge, only) way to get an accurate reading of total market value of debt and preferred stock is the old-fashioned way—price each separate issue and aggregate the values.

For companies like Microsoft, which has no debt and only one issue of preferred stock outstanding, this exercise is easy. For corporations like Consolidated Edison, which has 38 issues of various types of debt outstanding, the procedure can be tedious. What is a rational way of handling this potentially time-consuming problem?

Here's how we do it. If we're doing a quick and dirty valuation to see how a company is trading by comparing it with its rough intrinsic value, we use the book value of debt and preferred stock as reported in the company's annual or quarterly report. If we are being employed under a consulting contract on a grossly overpaid hourly basis to perform a valuation, we will do an in-depth analysis of every feature and option embedded in the debt or preferred stock so that we can value the company to the penny (and maximize our billing time).

It's fortunate that the market value of debt and preferred stock generally does not vary too much from book value. With the exception of valuing a highly leveraged company for which debt and preferred stock make up a large percentage of the market capitalization, the use of book value does not significantly bias the analysis of the common stock's intrinsic value.

Custom Valuations—The Next Step

In Chapter 4 we discussed how to estimate the future cash flows of a company, using McDonald's as an example. In Chapter 5 we saw how to estimate the company's WACC, again using McDonald's as our example. In this chapter we discussed where to get the various inputs needed to perform a valuation for McDonald's, and we gave you suggestions as to how to get the info while minimizing your online computer time.

The exercise that follows pulls together all the inputs that we gathered in this chapter. In Chapter 7 we get a bit fancier and vary our assumptions regarding revenue growth rates, net operating profit margins, and WACCs. First, we finish our McDonald's valuation example.

Valuation Exercise: McDonald's

Let's put our McDonald's valuation together using the categories of inputs that we classified above. On the ValuePro 2000 general input screen (Exhibit 6-6) the *easy-to-find* inputs are given in **bold,** the inputs *requiring estimation* are in *italics,* and the *cost of capital* inputs are underlined.

		Valuation Date	10/14/98
General Input Screen			
Intrinsic Stock Value $38.42			

General Inputs

Company Name **McDonald's Corporation**

Fiscal Year	**12/31/97**	Depreciation Rate (% of Rev.)	*7.00%*
Excess Return Period (years)	*7*	Investment Rate (% of Rev)	*20.60%*
Revenues ($mil)	**$11,409**	Working Capital (% of change in Rev.)	*-1.00%*
Revenue Growth Rate (%)	*11.10%*	Excess Marketable Securities ($mil)	**0**
Net Operating Profit Margin (%)	*25.20%*	Other Senior Claims	**0**
Tax Rate (%)	*31.80%*		

Cost of Capital Inputs

Current Stock Price	$67.25
Annual Dividend Per Share (e.g. $1.00)	**$0.36**
Shares Outstanding (mil)	689.3
30-year Treasury Bond Yield (e.g 6.50%)	5.80%
Bond Yield Spread to Treasury (e.g. 1.00%)	1.00%
Preferred Stock Yield (e.g. 8.00%)	0.00%
Equity Risk Premium (e.g. 3.00%)	*3.00%*
Company Specific Beta (e.g. 1.00)	0.97
Value of Debt Outstanding ($mil)	$4,931.0
Value of Preferred Stock ($mil)	$0.0
Weighted Average Cost of Capital	8.32%

EXHIBIT 6-6 General Input Screen, McDonald's

	Valuation Date	09/21/98
McDonald's Corporation		
Weighted Average Cost of Capital Screen		

Cost of Common Equity

Long Term Bond Yield	5.80%
Beta	0.97
Equity Risk Premium	3.00%
Cost of Common Equity	8.71%

Market Capitalization and After-Tax Weighted Average Cost of Capital

	Average Yield	After Tax Yield	Market Value	% Capital	After Tax Effect
Long-Term Debt	6.80%	4.64%	4,931	9.6%	0.45%
Preferred Stock	0.00%	0.00%	0	0.0%	0.00%
Common Stock	8.71%	8.71%	46,355	90.4%	7.87%
			51,286	100.0%	8.32%

EXHIBIT 6-7 WACC Screen, McDonald's

McDonald's Corporation
General Pro Forma Screen
7-year Excess Return Period

Discounted Excess Return Period FCFF	$31,412
Discounted Corporate Residual Value	($4,931)
Excess Marketable Securities	$0
Total Corporate Value	0

$3,262	Total Corporate Value
$28,150	Less Debt
$0.0	Less Preferred Stock
$31,412	Less Other Senior Claims
	Total Value to Common Equity

Total Value to Common Equity $26,481

Intrinsic Stock Value $38.42

(1) Period	(2) Fiscal Year	(3) Revenues	(4) NOP	(5) Adj. Taxes	(6) NOPAT	(7) Invest.	(8) Deprec.	(9) Net Invest.	(10) Change in Working Capital	(11) FCFF	(12) Discount Factor	(13) Discounted FCFF
0	12/31/97	11,409										
1	12/31/98	12,675	3,194	1,016	2,178	2,611	887	1,724	-13	467	0.9232	431
2	12/31/99	14,082	3,549	1,129	2,420	2,901	986	1,915	-14	519	0.8523	442
3	12/31/2000	15,646	3,943	1,254	2,689	3,223	1,095	2,128	-16	577	0.7869	454
4	12/31/2001	17,382	4,380	1,393	2,987	3,581	1,217	2,364	-17	641	0.7264	465
5	12/31/2002	19,312	4,867	1,548	3,319	3,978	1,352	2,626	-19	712	0.6706	477
6	12/31/2003	21,455	5,407	1,719	3,687	4,420	1,502	2,918	-21	791	0.6191	490
7	12/31/2004	23,837	6,007	1,910	4,097	4,910	1,669	3,242	-24	879	0.5716	502
Residual		23,837	6,007	1,910	4,097	1,669	1,669	0	0	49,248	0.5716	28,150

EXHIBIT 6-8 General Pro Forma Screen, McDonald's

Placing those inputs into the program, we get a cost of capital screen (Exhibit 6-7) showing a WACC of 8.32%. The general pro forma screen (Exhibit 6-8) shows a total corporate value of $31,412 million, a total value to common equity of $26,481 million, and a per share intrinsic stock value of $38.42.

We fine-tune our skills and use of the ValuePro 2000 software in more complex, custom valuations and see *valuations in action* in the next chapter.

Notes

1. A seminal book on using the Internet for investing is Ted Allrich, *The On-Line Investor: How to Find the Best Stocks Using Your Computer,* St. Martin's Press, New York, 1995.

2. *Institutional Investor* magazine polls institutional investors and creates an annual listing of the best analysts in different sectors of the stock market. The winners of each sector receive the title All-American, and this designation is worth an additional several hundred thousand per year in compensation to the analyst.

3. Aswath Damodaran calculates an implied equity risk premium on a yearly basis from 1960 until 1998 on his Web page (http://www.stern.nyu.edu/~adamodar/).

CHAPTER 7

Valuations in Action

Overview

In this chapter we value five different large cap companies—Microsoft, Intel, AT&T, Consolidated Edison, and McDonald's. For each company we initially take a "baseline" valuation, in which our cash flow and cost of capital estimates are based upon historic assumptions and our growth estimates are based upon analysts' consensus expectations. This valuation approach gives us a good initial estimate of a company's intrinsic stock value.

Valuation is an *art*—you should be realistic about your assumptions and inputs. Varying your inputs will give you a *range* of value for a stock rather than a point. Herein, we introduce various reasonable assumptions regarding growth rates, NOPMs, net investment, and cost of capital to see how those changes affect intrinsic value. Some of these changes—for instance, for AT&T and McDonald's—reflect previously stated goals of corporate management. This "valuation sensitivity approach" will give us a sense of which cash flows and cost of capital estimates are most important to which types of companies.

Some of the results are surprising. For instance, a change in interest rates and cost of capital will affect the intrinsic value of a growth stock such as Intel much more significantly on a percentage basis than it will affect the intrinsic value of a utility like Consolidated Edison—whose investors are current-dividend, current-income conscious.

The market price of the stock reacts in *anticipation of a change or the announcement of a change in the operating aspects of a company*—rather than waiting to see the change reflected in the corporate income statements, balance sheets, and cash flow statements a quarter or a year hence.

So let's get started by looking at one of the preeminent growth stocks of the 1990s—Microsoft Corporation.

Valuation of Microsoft

General Description of Microsoft— The Quintessential Growth Company

Microsoft, incorporated in 1981, is the dominant player in the personal computer (PC) software market. Its operating systems software programs, which include MS-DOS (Microsoft disk operating system), Windows 95, Windows NT, and Windows 98, run over 85% of the PCs currently in use.

Microsoft also developed and markets the top-selling application software package in the world—Office 97, which includes Word (word processing), Excel (spreadsheet), and Power Point (graphics) software. Finally, Microsoft develops and sells software relating to interactive media, games, reference works, and information products.

Microsoft is also the dominant provider of services and software for the Internet. Its Explorer is the number one Internet browser and has been at the heart of an antitrust suit brought against Microsoft by the U.S. Department of Justice and a number of states.

Microsoft's market capitalization makes it the number one company in the world (General Electric is number two), with a total market value of approximately $277 billion. That market value is a huge 19 times 1998 sales of $14.48 billion and 61 times 1998 earnings of $4.49 billion. Its stock has split many times—most recently in early 1998. Microsoft pays no dividends but actively repurchases shares in the open market and repurchased 38.8 million shares in 1998.

Bill Gates, the CEO and founder of Microsoft, owns about 22% of the company and he is the richest person in the world. He has been and continues to be an outstanding manager with a singular intensity and focus. Several years ago he married a Microsoft coworker. Competitors are fervently hoping that he produces numerous progeny, gets involved in attending T-ball games and coaching kids' soccer, and lightens up on his workaholic and fiercely competitive business style.

Baseline Valuation of Microsoft—August 27, 1998
Growth Rate—25%; Excess Return Period—10 Years;
NOPM—45.87%; WACC—9.12%

No valuation is timeless. The intrinsic value of a company changes as its prospects, product mix, and competitive position, and the product market in general changes to adjust to new technologies, consumer needs, capital demands, and "market psychology." This valuation was made on a date that by historical standards was volatile. The Dow Jones Industrial Average declined 357.36 points (4.2%) that day and the 30-year bond declined in yield to 5.35%, an historic low at that point in time.

In any valuation it's important to incorporate the latest available information. For Microsoft the business year ends on June 30. The latest audited information that was publicly available at the time of this valuation is for the fiscal year ending June 30, 1997—quite stale in the rapidly changing world of high-tech. In this situation it is important to look at quarterly earnings releases (which are not audited) to help assess the most recent performance of the corporation. Microsoft, on July 16, 1998, issued an earnings release, which it posted on its Web site, for the quarter and year ending June 30, 1998.

The earnings release is the source of much of the information incorporated in this valuation. We have included the income statement and balance sheet associated with the earnings release as Exhibits 7-1 and 7-2, respectively. Since there was no cash flow statement associated with the earnings release, we have included the cash flow statement associated with Microsoft's 1997 annual report as Exhibit 7-3.

After taking the information provided from the earnings release, Microsoft's 1997 annual report, and Web sites relating to investments, we came up with the following valuation estimates.

Microsoft Corporation
Income Statements
(In millions, except earnings per share)

	Three Months Ended June 30		Year Ended June 30	
	1997	1998	1997	1998
Revenue	$3,175	$3,995	$11,358	$14,484
Operating expenses:				
Cost of revenue	242	314	1,085	1,197
Research and development	516	711	1,925	2,502
Acquired in-process technology	0	0	0	296
Sales and marketing	744	919	2,856	3,412
General and administrative	94	128	362	433
Total operating expenses	1,596	2,072	6,228	7,840
Operating income	1,579	1,923	5,130	6,644
Interest income	127	214	443	703
Other expenses	(80)	(49)	(259)	(230)
Income before income taxes	1,626	2,088	5,314	7,117
Provision for income taxes	569	731	1,860	2,627
Net income	1,057	1,357	3,454	4,490
Preferred stock dividends	7	7	15	28
Net income available for common shareholders	$1,050	$1,350	$ 3,439	$ 4,462
Earnings per share (1):				
Basic	$ 0.44	$ 0.55	$ 1.44	$ 1.83
Diluted	$ 0.40	$ 0.50	$ 1.32	$ 1.67

(1) Earnings per share for the three months and year ended June 30, 1997
    have been restated to reflect a two-for-one stock split in February 1998.

EXHIBIT 7-1   Microsoft Income Statement, 4Q 1998

Revenue Growth Rate.   The historic revenue growth of Microsoft has been nothing short of spectacular. As we discussed previously, Microsoft's CAGR for the 10-year period ending in 1997 is 41.78%. However, Microsoft's growth rate has been decelerating as that of all growth companies must. Its CAGR for the 3-year period ending in 1997 is 34.48%—still very healthy. According to the earnings release, revenues grew from $11,358 million in 1997 to $14,484 million in 1998—an increase of 27.5%. Operating income grew from $5,130 million in 1997 to $6,644 in 1998—an increase of 29.5%.

As we noted above, Microsoft is trading at a market capitalization level of 61 times earnings and 19 times annual sales—very lofty levels

Microsoft Corporation
Balance Sheets
(In millions)

	June 30, 1997	June 30, 1998
Assets		
Current assets:		
Cash and short-term investments	$ 8,966	$13,927
Accounts receivable	980	1,460
Other	427	502
Total current assets	10,373	15,889
Property, plant, and equipment	1,465	1,505
Equity investments	2,346	4,703
Other assets	203	260
Total assets	$14,387	$22,357
Liabilities and stockholders' equity		
Current liabilities:		
Accounts payable	$ 721	$ 759
Accrued compensation	336	359
Income taxes payable	466	915
Unearned revenue	1,418	2,888
Other	669	809
Total current liabilities	3,610	5,730
Stockholders' equity:		
Convertible preferred stock	980	980
Common stock and paid-in capital	4,509	8,025
Retained earnings	5,288	7,622
Total stockholders' equity	10,777	16,627
Total liabilities and stockholders' equity	$14,387	$22,357

EXHIBIT 7-2   Microsoft Balance Sheet, 4Q 1998

for any stock. Clearly impounded in Microsoft's market price are expectations of market participants for very high continued future growth. Let's see what those expectations are.

Zacks Investment Research (http://www.zacks.com/) conducts research relating to earnings estimates and stock recommendations among stock market analysts. Zacks, which looks at earnings per share growth, not revenue growth, over periods out to 5 years, polled 23 analysts who cover Microsoft. It found expectations of earnings per share growth over the next 5 years for Microsoft that ranged from 30% to 19.5%, with the median being 25%. Other investment-related Web sites

Microsoft Corporation Cash Flows Statements
(In millions)

	Year ended June 30		
	1995	1996	1997
Cash flows from operations			
Net income	$ 1,453	$ 2,195	$ 3,454
Depreciation and amortization	269	480	557
Unearned revenue	69	983	1,601
Recognition of unearned revenue			
from prior periods	(54)	(477)	(743)
Other current liabilities	404	584	321
Accounts receivable	(91)	(71)	(336)
Other current assets	(60)	25	(165)
Net cash from operations	1,990	3,719	4,689
Cash flows used for financing			
Common stock issued	332	504	744
Common stock repurchased	(698)	(1,385)	(3,101)
Put warrant proceeds	49	124	95
Preferred stock issued			980
Preferred stock dividends			(15)
Stock option income tax benefits	179	352	796
Net cash used for financing	(138)	(405)	(501)
Cash flows used for investments			
Additions to property, plant, and equipment	(495)	(494)	(499)
Equity investments and other	(230)	(625)	(1,669)
Short-term investments	(651)	(1,551)	(921)
Net cash used for investments	(1,376)	(2,670)	(3,089)
Net change in cash and equivalents	476	644	1,099
Effect of exchange rates on cash and equivalents	9	(5)	6
Cash and equivalents, beginning of year	1,477	1,962	2,601
Cash and equivalents, end of year	1,962	2,601	3,706
Short-term investments	2,788	4,339	5,260
Cash and short-term investments	$ 4,750	$ 6,940	$ 8,966

See accompanying notes.

EXHIBIT 7-3   Microsoft Cash Flow Statement

that include earnings growth estimates are IBES (http://www.ibes .com/) and First Call (http://www1.firstcall.com/).

For our base-case valuation of Microsoft, we use the 25% EPS growth assumption from the analysts polled by Zacks as our revenue growth rate for the 10-year excess return period. In our model, embedding growth in revenue as opposed to operating income or earnings (which are a function of revenue and NOPM) will not greatly affect a stock's intrinsic value. In the valuation following our base case, we look at a two-stage growth model in which we reduce the growth rate to 15% in years 6 through 10.

Excess Return Period.   We previously have discussed the 1-5-7-10 Rule for boring, decent, good, and great companies. It would be hard to find anyone who does not consider Microsoft a well run, "great" company with a huge competitive advantage that it will continue to exploit. Microsoft is a powerful company.

However, new technologies replace older ones and competitive advantages fade—sometimes much faster than anyone can anticipate. When we're putting our hard-earned money on the line, 10 years into the future is the max that we're willing to discount in the way of an excess return period. That's what we use in our valuation of Microsoft.

NOPM Estimate. NOPM is the second of The Five Chinese Brothers. Microsoft's NOPM has increased steadily over time. According to the earnings release, operating income for 1998 was $6,644 million, which when divided by revenue of $14,484 million ($6,644/$14,484) yields an NOPM of 45.87%. This is slightly above the 1997 NOPM of 45.1%. We use the 45.87% 1998 NOPM number for our base-case valuation.

Income Tax Rates. According to the earnings release, provision for income taxes for 1998 was $2,627 million, based on income before income taxes of $7,117 million, resulting in an income tax rate for 1998 of 36.9%. This rate is significantly greater than the 35% effective rate paid by Microsoft in 1996 and 1997. We use the 36.9% rate in our base-line valuation.

New Investment, Depreciation, and Net Investment. The earnings release does not have the information that we need for valuation relating to net investment for 1998. We use the information that is available in the 1997 annual report and adjust it for the additional revenue associated with 1998.

Additions to property, plant, and equipment ($495, $494, and $499 million, respectively, in 1995, 1996, and 1997) averaged $496 million per year, or 5.7% of yearly revenue. We use that 5.7% ratio for our new investment rate. This is a relatively low new investment rate—compared with the new investment rates associated with Intel or McDonald's, for example. It shows that Microsoft is **not** a very capital-intensive corporation.

Depreciation of $269, $480, and $557 million, respectively, in 1995, 1996, and 1997, averaged $435 million per year, or 5% of yearly revenue. We use that 5% ratio as our depreciation rate input. The net investment ratio simply is the new investment ratio minus the depreciation ratio.

Incremental Working Capital. As the last of The Five Chinese Brothers, incremental working capital is a very minor expense to Microsoft. Microsoft has no inventory to speak of. According to the earnings release, accounts receivable in 1998 totaled $1,460 million, while accounts payable totaled $759 million, resulting in a net out of pocket of $1,460 − $759 = $701 million, or 4.84% of revenue.

Cost of Capital Inputs. We took the information that we need for the cost of capital inputs from two investment-related Web sites: S&P Comstock through America Online and Yahoo! Finance. The closing price on August 27, 1998, for Microsoft was $109.25 per share. America Online, through its S&P Comstock *Market Quotes* link, reported that there were 2,464 million shares of Microsoft outstanding and that the beta of those shares was 1.25. Yahoo! Finance, through its Market Guide–affiliated link, reported Microsoft's beta to be 1.26. We use the higher 1.26 beta figure in an effort to be more conservative in our stock valuation.

We used America Online's link to the Bloomberg Finance Web site to give us the most recent yield, 5.35%, on the 30-year Treasury Bond. Microsoft has no debt outstanding, so its bond yield spread is unimportant. According to its 1997 annual report and 1998 earnings release, it does have $980 million of preferred stock outstanding—an insignificant sum compared with Microsoft's market capitalization. We estimated a cost to the preferred stock at 7.5%—over 2 percentage points higher than the 30-year Treasury rate.

We also note on the earnings release that Microsoft had $13,927 million in cash and short-term investments that were not subject to operating risks. We use that amount for our excess marketable securities entry. Also according to the earnings release, assuming the dilution associated with its stock option program, Microsoft effectively had 2,706 million shares outstanding—236 million more than the 2,470 million shares that actually were outstanding at the time. **That's a dilution factor of 9.4%.** Again for conservatism, we use the higher figure for effective shares outstanding in our valuation.

Finally, we use an equity risk premium of 3%, consistent with the most recent Goldman Sachs estimate of this figure. It is also the estimate that we use on our associated Web site (http://www.valuepro .net/).

Microsoft's Baseline Valuation. We plug all these figures neatly into the ValuePro 2000 general input screen (Exhibit 7-4). The resulting

	Valuation Date	10/14/98
General Input Screen		
Intrinsic Stock Value $104.03		

General Inputs

Company Name	Microsoft Corporation		
Fiscal Year	06/30/98	Depreciation Rate (% of Rev.)	5.00%
Excess Return Period (years)	10	Investment Rate (% of Rev)	5.70%
Revenues ($mil)	$14,484	Working Capital (% of change in Rev.)	4.84%
Revenue Growth Rate (%)	25.00%	Excess Marketable Securities ($mil)	13927
Net Operating Profit Margin (%)	45.87%	Other Senior Claims	0
Tax Rate (%)	36.90%		

Cost of Capital Inputs

Current Stock Price	$109.25
Annual Dividend Per Share (e.g. $1.00)	$0.00
Shares Outstanding (mil)	2706
30-year Treasury Bond Yield (e.g 6.50%)	5.35%
Bond Yield Spread to Treasury (e.g. 1.00%)	0.00%
Preferred Stock Yield (e.g. 8.00%)	7.50%
Equity Risk Premium (e.g. 3.00%)	3.00%
Company Specific Beta (e.g. 1.00)	1.26
Value of Debt Outstanding ($mil)	$0.0
Value of Preferred Stock ($mil)	$980.0
Weighted Average Cost of Capital	9.12%

EXHIBIT 7-4   General Input Screen, Microsoft

cost of capital screen (Exhibit 7-5) shows Microsoft to have a WACC of 9.12%, and the general pro forma screen (Exhibit 7-6) shows Microsoft stock to have an intrinsic value of $104.03—roughly 4% lower than its closing price of $109.25.

At current price levels, we believe that Microsoft is fully valued and are not in a hurry to buy the stock. We're more inclined to buy when a stock's market price falls 10% to 20% below what we estimate to be its intrinsic value. The benefit of the valuation is that we know more about

	Valuation Date	09/21/98
Microsoft Corporation		
Weighted Average Cost of Capital Screen		

Cost of Common Equity

Long Term Bond Yield	5.35%
Beta	1.26
Equity Risk Premium	3.00%
Cost of Common Equity	9.13%

Market Capitalization and After-Tax Weighted Average Cost of Capital

	Average Yield	After Tax Yield	Market Value	% Capital	After Tax Effect
Long-Term Debt	5.35%	3.38%	0	0.0%	0.00%
Preferred Stock	7.50%	7.50%	980	0.3%	0.02%
Common Stock	9.13%	9.13%	295,630	99.6%	9.10%
			296,610	100.0%	9.12%

EXHIBIT 7-5   WACC Screen, Microsoft

Microsoft Corporation
General Pro Forma Screen
10-year Excess Return Period

		Discounted Excess Return Period FCFF	$282,496
		Discounted Corporate Residual Value	$0
		Excess Marketable Securities	($980)
		Total Corporate Value	0

$89,877	Total Corporate Value
$178,692	Less Debt
$13,927.0	Less Preferred Stock
$282,496	Less Other Senior Claims
	Total Value to Common Equity $281,516
	Intrinsic Stock Value $104.03

(1)	(2)	(3)	(4)	(5)	(6)	(7)	(8)	(9)	(10)	(11)	(12)	(13)
Period	Fiscal Year	Revenues	NOP	Adj. Taxes	NOPAT	Invest.	Deprec.	Net Invest.	Change in Working Capital	FCFF	Discount Factor	Discounted FCFF
0	06/30/98	14,484										
1	06/30/99	18,105	8,305	3,064	5,240	1,032	905	127	175	4,938	0.9164	4,525
2	06/30/2000	22,631	10,381	3,831	6,550	1,290	1,132	158	219	6,173	0.8398	5,184
3	06/30/2001	28,289	12,976	4,788	8,188	1,612	1,414	198	274	7,716	0.7695	5,938
4	06/30/2002	35,361	16,220	5,985	10,235	2,016	1,768	248	342	9,645	0.7052	6,802
5	06/30/2003	44,202	20,275	7,482	12,794	2,519	2,210	309	428	12,056	0.6462	7,791
6	06/30/2004	55,252	25,344	9,352	15,992	3,149	2,763	387	535	15,071	0.5922	8,925
7	06/30/2005	69,065	31,680	11,690	19,990	3,937	3,453	483	669	18,838	0.5427	10,223
8	06/30/2006	86,331	39,600	14,612	24,988	4,921	4,317	604	836	23,548	0.4973	11,710
9	06/30/2007	107,914	49,500	18,266	31,235	6,151	5,396	755	1,045	29,435	0.4557	13,414
10	06/30/2008	134,893	61,875	22,832	39,043	7,689	6,745	944	1,306	36,793	0.4176	15,365
Residual		134,893	61,875	22,832	39,043	6,745	6,745	0	0	427,890	0.4176	178,692

EXHIBIT 7-6 General Pro Forma Screen, Microsoft

Microsoft now and we're in a position to actively monitor its price and purchase it when it comes into our buying range. Next we see how its stock price is affected if revenue growth falls short of the expectations discussed above.

Microsoft Valuation—Two-Stage Growth
Lower Estimated Revenue Growth Rates in Years 6 to 10

Let's look at what happens to the valuation of a growth stock like Microsoft if and when its projected growth rate begins to decrease. Assume that the market expects Microsoft's growth rate to be 25% for the next 5 years and expects growth to drop to 15% for years 6 to 10.

The ValuePro 2000 custom valuation input screen (Exhibit 7-7) allows an investor to change assumptions about growth rates, NOPMs, new investment and depreciation rates, income tax rates, incremental working capital rates, and WACC rates on a year-to-year basis over the excess return period—up to 30 years. If we plug the 15% assumption into the revenue growth rate area of the custom valuation input screen for years 6 to 10, we see the result of that exercise on the custom pro forma screen (Exhibit 7-8).

The new per share intrinsic value of Microsoft, based on reduced growth rate assumptions, is $76.59—a decrease of 26.5% from its $104.03 per share intrinsic value under a constant 25% growth assumption. If Microsoft underperforms current market expectations, there is a potential for significant downside price movement. Histori-

Valuation Date   09/21/98
Custom Valuation Input Screen
Microsoft Corporation
Intrinsic Stock Value $76.59

Period	Fiscal Year	Revenue Growth Rate	Net Operating Margin	Tax Rate	Invest. Rate	Dep. Rate	Increm. Working Capital	WACC
0	06/30/98							
1	06/30/99	25.00%	45.87%	36.90%	5.70%	5.00%	4.84%	9.12%
2	06/30/2000	25.00%	45.87%	36.90%	5.70%	5.00%	4.84%	9.12%
3	06/30/2001	25.00%	45.87%	36.90%	5.70%	5.00%	4.84%	9.12%
4	06/30/2002	25.00%	45.87%	36.90%	5.70%	5.00%	4.84%	9.12%
5	06/30/2003	25.00%	45.87%	36.90%	5.70%	5.00%	4.84%	9.12%
6	06/30/2004	15.00%	45.87%	36.90%	5.70%	5.00%	4.84%	9.12%
7	06/30/2005	15.00%	45.87%	36.90%	5.70%	5.00%	4.84%	9.12%
8	06/30/2006	15.00%	45.87%	36.90%	5.70%	5.00%	4.84%	9.12%
9	06/30/2007	15.00%	45.87%	36.90%	5.70%	5.00%	4.84%	9.12%
10	06/30/2008	15.00%	45.87%	36.90%	5.70%	5.00%	4.84%	9.12%
Residual								9.12%

EXHIBIT 7-7   Custom Valuation Input Screen, Microsoft

Microsoft Corporation
Custom Pro Forma Screen
10-year Excess Return Period

Discounted Excess Return Period FCFF							$208,223 Total Corporate Value					
Discounted Corporate Residual Value							$117,773 Less Debt					
Excess Marketable Securities							$13,927.0 Less Preferred Stock		$0			
Total Corporate Value							$208,223 Less Other Senior Claims		($980)			
								Total Value to Common Equity	0			
									$207,243			
								Intrinsic Stock Value	$76.59			

(1)	(2)	(3)	(4)	(5)	(6)	(7)	(8)	(9)	(10)	(11)	(12)	(13)
Period	Fiscal Year	Revenues	NOP	Adj. Taxes	NOPAT	Invest.	Deprec.	Net Invest.	Change in Working Capital	FCFF	Discount Factor	Discounted FCFF
0	06/30/98	14,484										
1	06/30/99	18,105	8,305	3,064	5,240	1,032	905	127	175	4,938	0.9164	4,525
2	06/30/2000	22,631	10,381	3,831	6,550	1,290	1,132	158	219	6,173	0.8398	5,184
3	06/30/2001	28,289	12,976	4,788	8,188	1,612	1,414	198	274	7,716	0.7695	5,938
4	06/30/2002	35,361	16,220	5,985	10,235	2,016	1,768	248	342	9,645	0.7052	6,802
5	06/30/2003	44,202	20,275	7,482	12,794	2,519	2,210	309	428	12,056	0.6462	7,791
6	06/30/2004	50,832	23,317	8,604	14,713	2,897	2,542	356	321	14,036	0.5922	8,312
7	06/30/2005	58,457	26,814	9,894	16,920	3,332	2,923	409	369	16,141	0.5427	8,760
8	06/30/2006	67,225	30,836	11,379	19,458	3,832	3,361	471	424	18,563	0.4973	9,231
9	06/30/2007	77,309	35,462	13,085	22,376	4,407	3,865	541	488	21,347	0.4557	9,728
10	06/30/2008	88,905	40,781	15,048	25,733	5,068	4,445	622	561	24,549	0.4176	10,252
Residual		88,905	40,781	15,048	25,733	4,445	4,445	0	0	282,014	0.4176	117,773

EXHIBIT 7-8 Custom Pro Forma Screen, Microsoft

cally, Microsoft has regularly exceeded expectations and we have no reason to assume that this time things will be different. We would be very hesitant to short a stock like Microsoft, which consistently has performed very well.

Valuation of Intel

General Description of Intel—A "Great" Growth Company

Intel is the leader in sales of microprocessors for personal computers. A microprocessor is the central processing unit (the "brains") of a PC. It processes system data and controls other devices in the computer. Intel was incorporated in 1968 and introduced the first microprocessor to the world in 1971. Its most popular microprocessors are the Pentium and Pentium II with MMX media enhancement.

Intel offers original equipment manufacturers (OEMs) of computers—among them, Compaq, Gateway, Dell, and IBM—a wide range of PC building block components (microprocessors, chip sets, graphics ports, etc.) to meet their manufacturing needs. Also, Intel offers PC users products that expand the capability of their systems and networks.

Intel is the world's leading semiconductor manufacturer and dominates the market (with more than a 90% share) for the microprocessors used in PCs. As such, its growth and success is closely tied to the growth of the computer industry. It partners closely with PC makers, software developers, and PC users to develop processor, network and communications, and computer enhancement products that meet their needs.

According to *Business Week*,[1] Intel is tenth in the world in terms of market capitalization, with a total market value of $144 billion, and fourth in the world in terms of 1997 profits. The market value of Intel is approximately 6 times annual sales of $25 billion and approximately 21 times 1997 earnings of $6.9 billion. Intel's common stock pays a quarterly dividend of 3 cents per share. Intel is heavily dependent upon its international sales and has approximately 60% of its revenue from non-U.S. sources.

The common stock of Intel, although faltering in 1998, historically has performed very well. According to Intel's 1996 annual report, "a purchase of 100 shares for $2,350 at the initial public offering in 1971 would have grown to 15,188 shares (reflecting 10 splits) worth more than $2 million by the end of fiscal 1996."[2] That's not a shabby return!

How do we value Intel's shares?

Baseline Valuation of Intel—August 28, 1998
Growth Rate—20%; Excess Return Period—10 Years;
NOPM—35%; WACC—8.9%

Let's first take a look at market estimates of cash flow parameters for Intel, based on its fiscal year ending December 27, 1997. On July 14, 1998 Intel issued an earnings release for the 6 months ended June 27, 1998. We downloaded the most recent annual report for 1997 and most recent earnings release from Intel's corporate Web site.

We have included the audited 1997 income statement, 1997 balance sheet, and 1997 cash flow statement as Exhibits 7-9, 7-10, and 7-11. We include the income statement and balance sheet associated with the 1998 6-month earnings release as Exhibits 7-12 and 7-13. Here are our baseline valuation estimates using the most recent publicly available information.

Revenue Growth Rate. The historic revenue growth rate for Intel has been strong. Market Guide (http://www.marketguide.com/), which we accessed through our America Online *Stock Reports* link, reports 5-year revenue growth and earnings growth for Intel of 33.8% and

Consolidated statements of income   intel.

Three years ended December 27, 1997

(in millions—except per share amounts)	1997	1996	1995
Net revenues	$ 25,070	$ 20,847	$ 16,202
Cost of sales	9,945	9,164	7,811
Research and development	2,347	1,808	1,296
Marketing, general and administrative	2,891	2,322	1,843
Operating costs and expenses	15,183	13,294	10,950
Operating income	9,887	7,553	5,252
Interest expense	(27)	(25)	(29)
Interest income and other, net	799	406	415
Income before taxes	10,659	7,934	5,638
Provision for taxes	3,714	2,777	2,072
Net income	$ 6,945	$ 5,157	$ 3,566
Basic earnings per common share	$ 4.25	$ 3.13	$ 2.16
Diluted earnings per common share	$ 3.87	$ 2.90	$ 2.02
Weighted average common shares outstanding	1,635	1,645	1,650
Dilutive effect of:			
Employee stock options	102	94	96
1998 Step-Up Warrants	58	37	22
Weighted average common shares outstanding, assuming dilution	1,795	1,776	1,768

See accompanying notes.

EXHIBIT 7-9   Intel Consolidated Statement of Income

Consolidated balance sheets
December 27, 1997 and December 28, 1996

int͡el.

(In millions—except per share amounts)

	1997	1996
Assets		
Current assets:		
Cash and cash equivalents	$ 4,102	$ 4,165
Short-term investments	5,630	3,742
Trading assets	195	87
Accounts receivable, net of allowance for doubtful accounts of $65 ($68 in 1996)	3,438	3,723
Inventories	1,697	1,293
Deferred tax assets	676	570
Other current assets	129	104
Total current assets	**15,867**	**13,684**
Property, plant and equipment:		
Land and buildings	5,113	4,372
Machinery and equipment	10,577	8,729
Construction in progress	2,437	1,161
	18,127	14,262
Less accumulated depreciation	7,461	5,775
Property, plant and equipment, net	**10,666**	**8,487**
Long-term investments	**1,839**	**1,353**
Other assets	**508**	**211**
Total assets	**$ 28,880**	**$ 23,735**
Liabilities and stockholders' equity		
Current liabilities:		
Short-term debt	$ 212	$ 389
Long-term debt redeemable within one year	110	-
Accounts payable	1,407	969
Accrued compensation and benefits	1,268	1,128
Deferred income on shipments to distributors	516	474
Accrued advertising	500	410
Other accrued liabilities	842	507
Income taxes payable	1,165	986
Total current liabilities	**6,020**	**4,863**
Long-term debt	**448**	**728**
Deferred tax liabilities	**1,076**	**997**
Put warrants	**2,041**	**275**
Commitments and contingencies		
Stockholders' equity:		
Preferred Stock, $.001 par value, 50 shares authorized; none issued	-	-
Common Stock, $.001 par value, 4,500 shares authorized; 1,628 issued and outstanding (1,642 in 1996) and capital in excess of par value	3,311	2,897
Retained earnings	15,984	13,975
Total stockholders' equity	**19,295**	**16,872**
Total liabilities and stockholders' equity	**$ 28,880**	**$ 23,735**

See accompanying notes.

EXHIBIT 7-10   Intel Consolidated Balance Sheet

34.5%, respectively. The 1997 income statement for Intel shows net revenues of $16,202 million in 1995, increasing by 28.7% to $20,847 in 1996, and further increasing by 20.26% to $25,070 in 1997. Over the same 3-year period, operating income of $5,252 million in 1995 increased by 43.8% to $7,553 million in 1996, and by 30.9% to $9,887 million in 1997.

Now for the bad news! According to the earnings release, **net revenue** for the 6-month period ended June 27, 1998 **declined 4%,** from $12,408 million to $11,928 million. During the same period, operating income declined by 35%, from $5,625 million to $3,731 million. Clearly, these 6-month results are a concern for a growth company like Intel. What happened?

Consolidated balance sheets
December 27, 1997 and December 28, 1996

int_el.

(In millions—except per share amounts)

	1997	1996
Assets		
Current assets:		
Cash and cash equivalents	$ 4,102	$ 4,165
Short-term investments	5,630	3,742
Trading assets	195	87
Accounts receivable, net of allowance for doubtful accounts		
of $65 ($68 in 1996)	3,438	3,723
Inventories	1,697	1,293
Deferred tax assets	676	570
Other current assets	129	104
Total current assets	**15,867**	**13,684**
Property, plant and equipment:		
Land and buildings	5,113	4,372
Machinery and equipment	10,577	8,729
Construction in progress	2,437	1,161
	18,127	14,262
Less accumulated depreciation	7,461	5,775
Property, plant and equipment, net	**10,666**	**8,487**
Long-term investments	**1,839**	**1,353**
Other assets	**508**	**211**
Total assets	**$ 28,880**	**$ 23,735**
Liabilities and stockholders' equity		
Current liabilities:		
Short-term debt	$ 212	$ 389
Long-term debt redeemable within one year	110	-
Accounts payable	1,407	969
Accrued compensation and benefits	1,268	1,128
Deferred income on shipments to distributors	516	474
Accrued advertising	500	410
Other accrued liabilities	842	507
Income taxes payable	1,165	986
Total current liabilities	**6,020**	**4,863**
Long-term debt	**448**	**728**
Deferred tax liabilities	**1,076**	**997**
Put warrants	**2,041**	**275**
Commitments and contingencies		
Stockholders' equity:		
Preferred Stock, $.001 par value, 50 shares authorized; none issued	-	-
Common Stock, $.001 par value, 4,500 shares authorized; 1,628 issued and outstanding		
(1,642 in 1996) and capital in excess of par value	3,311	2,897
Retained earnings	15,984	13,975
Total stockholders' equity	**19,295**	**16,872**
Total liabilities and stockholders' equity	**$ 28,880**	**$ 23,735**

See accompanying notes.

EXHIBIT 7-11   Intel Consolidated Statement of Cash Flow

It appears that Intel with its global reach, like much of the computer industry, is being adversely affected by a shaky international business climate that has been nicknamed the "Asian Contagion." Whether this affliction is permanent, or is temporary and will blow over without lasting economic damage to U.S. multinational corporations like Intel, remains to be seen.

Intel's market is being further eroded by the rapid growth of low-cost PCs. According to *Business Week*,[3] Intel has been slow to respond to a consumer shift to the sub-$1,000 PC market. According to Dataquest Inc., Intel has a 99% share of the microprocessors associated with the $1,500 and up PC market, a 72% share of the $1,000 to $1,500

INTEL CORPORATION
CONSOLIDATED SUMMARY FINANCIAL STATEMENTS
(In millions, except per share amounts)

INCOME	Three Months Ended		Six Months Ended	
	June 27, 1998	June 28, 1997	June 27, 1998	June 28, 1997
NET REVENUE	$ 5,927	$ 5,960	$ 11,928	$ 12,408
Cost of sales	3,027	2,343	5,776	4,650
Research and development	623	575	1,218	1,156
Marketing, general and administrative	671	704	1,382	1,397
Purchased in-process research and development	–	–	165	–
Operating costs and expenses	4,321	3,622	8,541	7,203
OPERATING INCOME	1,606	2,338	3,387	5,205
Interest and other	144	212	344	420
INCOME BEFORE TAXES	1,750	2,550	3,731	5,625
Income taxes	578	905	1,286	1,997
NET INCOME	$ 1,172	$ 1,645	$ 2,445	$ 3,628
BASIC EARNINGS PER SHARE	$ 0.69	$ 1.01	$ 1.47	$ 2.22
DILUTED EARNINGS PER SHARE	$ 0.66	$ 0.92	$ 1.38	$ 2.02
COMMON SHARES OUTSTANDING	1,691	1,635	1,666	1,636
COMMON SHARES ASSUMING DILUTION	1,769	1,797	1,772	1,798

EXHIBIT 7-12   Intel Consolidated Income Statement, June 1998

market, and only a 45% market share of the $1,000 and below market—which is by far the fastest-growing market segment.

The problem at hand is to estimate what revenue growth rate to incorporate in our baseline analysis of Intel. We pulled up Zacks EPS estimates and recommendations for Intel. We found that the 22 ana-

BALANCE SHEET	At June 27, 1998	At March 28, 1998	At Dec. 27, 1997
CURRENT ASSETS			
Cash and short-term investments	$ 7,698	$ 10,609	$ 9,927
Accounts receivable	3,126	3,092	3,438
Inventories:			
Raw materials	250	254	255
Work in process	988	1,035	928
Finished goods	465	532	514
	1,703	1,821	1,697
Deferred tax assets and other	841	750	805
Total current assets	13,368	16,272	15,867
Property, plant and equipment, net	12,003	11,137	10,666
Long-term investments	2,040	2,082	1,839
Other assets	1,007	738	508
TOTAL ASSETS	$ 28,418	$ 30,229	$ 28,880
CURRENT LIABILITIES			
Short-term debt	$ 242	$ 365	$ 322
Accounts payable and accrued liabilities	3,445	3,454	4,017
Deferred income on shipments to distributors	391	516	516
Income taxes payable	176	1,519	1,165
Total current liabilities	4,254	5,854	6,020
LONG-TERM DEBT	472	441	448
DEFERRED TAX LIABILITIES	1,248	1,164	1,076
PUT WARRANTS	711	1,185	2,041
STOCKHOLDERS' EQUITY			
Common Stock and capital in excess of par value	4,853	4,955	3,311
Retained earnings	16,880	16,630	15,984
Total stockholders' equity	21,733	21,585	19,295
TOTAL LIABILITIES AND STOCKHOLDERS' EQUITY	$ 28,418	$ 30,229	$ 28,880

EXHIBIT 7-13 Intel Consolidated Balance Sheet, June 1998

lysts polled on Intel estimate that Intel's 5-year earnings growth rate will range from a high of 39% to a low of 10% with a median of 20%. The poll participants are knowledgeable, and many of them have direct access to Intel's corporate finance and investor relations departments. The *Business Week* article probably didn't come as a surprise to many of the analysts, nor has it lowered their projected 5-year growth rate.

This relatively high growth rate indicates that most analysts think Intel will weather the Asian Contagion quite well and will suffer only a temporary hiatus in its growth. We use the 20% median growth rate for our baseline valuation of Intel.

Excess Return Period.   It would be hard to argue against the position that Intel, like Microsoft, is a "great" company and is worthy of our maximum excess return period of 10 years. That is what we use for our baseline valuation of Intel.

NOPM Estimate.   According to Intel's 1997 income statement, NOPM has increased yearly over the 1995–1997 period. In 1995, operating income equaled $5,252 million, which when divided by net revenues of $16,202 yielded an NOPM of 32.41%. Likewise, with operating income of $7,553 million and net revenues of $20,847 million, 1996 NOPM equaled 36.23%; and with operating income of $9,887 million and net revenues of $25,070, 1997 NOPM equaled 39.44%.

However, the subpar performance associated with the first 6 months of 1998 shows operating income of $3,387 million, based on net revenue of $11,928 million, and an NOPM of 28.4%. What should we use for our valuation?

We assume that the Asian Contagion will be successfully handled in some way, shape, or form by Intel and that it will be relatively brief. We use an NOPM of 35%, which is 1% lower than the 36% average of the NOPMs from 1995, 1996, and 1997. In the valuation that follows the baseline case, we reduce the NOPM to the 28.4% level and see how that affects intrinsic value.

Income Tax Rates.   For the income tax rate for Intel, we take the provision for income taxes of $3,714 million from the 1997 income statement and divide it by 1997 income before taxes of $10,659 million to get an income tax rate of 34.84%. This is what we use for our baseline valuation case.

New Investment, Depreciation, and Net Investment.   From the 1997 cash flow statement, we see that additions to property, plant, and equipment totaled $4,501 million in 1997, $3,024 million in 1996, and $3,550 million in 1995—very substantial investments that equaled 17.9%, 14.5%, and 21.9% of net revenues in 1997, 1996, and 1995, respectively. The average new investment as a percentage of revenue over the 3-year period was 18.1%, which is what we use in our valuation example.

Also from the 1997 cash flow statement, we see that depreciation totaled $2,192 million in 1997, $1,888 million in 1996, and $1,371 million in 1995—figures that equaled 8.74%, 9.06%, and 8.46% of net revenues in 1997, 1996, and 1995, respectively. The depreciation rate averaged 8.75% for the period, and that's what we use in the baseline valuation. The difference between new investment and depreciation gives net investment.

Incremental Working Capital.   Whereas incremental working capital was insignificant to Microsoft, it is quite significant to Intel. On December 27, 1997, accounts receivable were $3,438 million, inventories were $1,697 million, and accounts payable were $1,407 million, resulting in a net working capital cost of $3,438 + $1,697 − $1,407 = $3,728 million, or 14.87% of net revenue. This is the number we use for our incremental working capital input in the baseline valuation.

Cost of Capital Inputs.   We follow the same general procedures that we described under the Microsoft cost of capital inputs section. The closing price for Intel's stock on August 28, 1998 was $77 per share. S&P Comstock estimated Intel's beta to be 1.18, while Market Guide estimated it to be 1.19, which is the number we use in the valuation. The 30-year U.S. Treasury Bond yield was 5.35%, while the yield associated with the Dow Jones Industrial Bond Average was 6.68%, resulting in a spread to Treasuries of 1.33% for Intel's debt. We continue to use an equity risk premium of 3%.

We use the 1998 6-month earnings release to get the excess marketable securities number of $7,698 million, long-term debt outstanding of $472 million, and common shares outstanding of 1,769 million, assuming the dilution associated with Intel's stock option and outstanding warrants program.

Intel's Baseline Valuation.   We plug these numbers into the Value-Pro general input screen (Exhibit 7-14). The program churns out the cost of capital screen (Exhibit 7-15), which shows Intel to have a WACC of 8.9%. The general pro forma screen (Exhibit 7-16) shows Intel to

	Valuation Date	10/14/98

General Input Screen

Intrinsic Stock Value $127.43

General Inputs

Company Name	Intel Corporation		
Fiscal Year	12/27/97	Depreciation Rate (% of Rev.)	8.75%
Excess Return Period (years)	10	Investment Rate (% of Rev)	18.10%
Revenues ($mil)	$25,070	Working Capital (% of change in Rev.)	14.87%
Revenue Growth Rate (%)	20.00%	Excess Marketable Securities ($mil)	7698
Net Operating Profit Margin (%)	35.00%	Other Senior Claims	0
Tax Rate (%)	34.84%		

Cost of Capital Inputs

Current Stock Price	$77.00
Annual Dividend Per Share (e.g. $1.00)	$0.12
Shares Outstanding (mil)	1769
30-year Treasury Bond Yield (e.g 6.50%)	5.35%
Bond Yield Spread to Treasury (e.g. 1.00%)	1.33%
Preferred Stock Yield (e.g. 8.00%)	0.00%
Equity Risk Premium (e.g. 3.00%)	3.00%
Company Specific Beta (e.g. 1.00)	1.19
Value of Debt Outstanding ($mil)	$472.0
Value of Preferred Stock ($mil)	$0.0
Weighted Average Cost of Capital	8.90%

EXHIBIT 7-14 General Input Screen, Intel

have an intrinsic value of $127.43, or roughly 66% greater than the market price of $77 per share.

At a price level of $77 per share, and if our valuation assumptions continue to hold, Intel is significantly undervalued and represents a great buying opportunity. Before we call our broker or place our order over the Internet with an on-line brokerage firm, let's play some what-if games to look at how certain variables can affect Intel's intrinsic value.

	Valuation Date	09/21/98

Intel Corporation
Weighted Average Cost of Capital Screen

Cost of Common Equity

Long Term Bond Yield	5.35%
Beta	1.19
Equity Risk Premium	3.00%
Cost of Common Equity	8.92%

Market Capitalization and After-Tax Weighted Average Cost of Capital

	Average Yield	After Tax Yield	Market Value	% Capital	After Tax Effect
Long-Term Debt	6.68%	4.35%	472	0.3%	0.02%
Preferred Stock	0.00%	0.00%	0	0.0%	0.00%
Common Stock	8.92%	8.92%	136,213	99.6%	8.89%
			136,685	100.0%	8.90%

EXHIBIT 7-15 WACC Screen, Intel

Intel Corporation
General Pro Forma Screen
10-year Excess Return Period

Discounted Excess Return Period FCFF									$225,890			
Discounted Corporate Residual Value									($472)			
Excess Marketable Securities									$0			
Total Corporate Value									0			

$48,769	Total Corporate Value									
$169,423	Less Debt									
$7,698.0	Less Preferred Stock									
$225,890	Less Other Senior Claims									
	Total Value to Common Equity								$225,418	
	Intrinsic Stock Value								**$127.43**	

(1)	(2)	(3)	(4)	(5)	(6)	(7)	(8)	(9)	(10)	(11)	(12)	(13)
Period	Fiscal Year	Revenues	NOP	Adj. Taxes	NOPAT	Invest.	Deprec.	Net Invest.	Change in Working Capital	FCFF	Discount Factor	Discounted FCFF
0	12/27/97	25,070										
1	12/27/98	30,084	10,529	3,668	6,861	5,445	2,632	2,813	746	3,303	0.9182	3,033
2	12/27/99	36,101	12,635	4,402	8,233	6,534	3,159	3,375	895	3,963	0.8432	3,341
3	12/27/2000	43,321	15,162	5,283	9,880	7,841	3,791	4,051	1,074	4,756	0.7742	3,682
4	12/27/2001	51,985	18,195	6,339	11,856	9,409	4,549	4,861	1,288	5,707	0.7109	4,057
5	12/27/2002	62,382	21,834	7,607	14,227	11,291	5,458	5,833	1,546	6,848	0.6528	4,470
6	12/27/2003	74,859	26,201	9,128	17,072	13,549	6,550	6,999	1,855	8,218	0.5994	4,926
7	12/27/2004	89,830	31,441	10,954	20,487	16,259	7,860	8,399	2,226	9,861	0.5504	5,428
8	12/27/2005	107,796	37,729	13,145	24,584	19,511	9,432	10,079	2,672	11,834	0.5054	5,981
9	12/27/2006	129,356	45,274	15,774	29,501	23,413	11,319	12,095	3,206	14,200	0.4641	6,590
10	12/27/2007	155,227	54,329	18,928	35,401	28,096	13,582	14,514	3,847	17,040	0.4261	7,262
Residual		155,227	54,329	18,928	35,401	13,582	13,582	0	0	397,576		169,423

EXHIBIT 7-16   General Pro Forma Screen, Intel

Intel Valuation—What If There Are Lower NOPMs?

Let's look at what happens to the intrinsic value of Intel if the NOPM is reduced from 35% in the baseline valuation example to 28.4%, which is equal to the NOPM associated with the 6-month period ended June 27, 1998, as described in the earnings release.

If we plug 28.4% into the NOPM slot of the general input screen (Exhibit 7-17), the program creates the general pro forma screen, (Exhibit 7-18), which shows an intrinsic value of $98.57 per share. This is well above the $77 current price range. Intel still looks like a good buying opportunity.

Let's play one more what-if game.

Intel Valuation—What If There Are Lower NOPMs and Lower Growth Rates?

Let's piggyback on the valuation above and assume that Intel's NOPM runs at the lower 28.4% level, and that its revenue growth will not be 20% per year, but will be equal to 15% per year. With Intel's dominant position in the computer industry, these assumptions appear to be reasonable worst-case scenarios.

If we plug 15% into the revenue growth rate slot of the general input screen for Intel (Exhibit 7-19), the general pro forma screen (Exhibit

		Valuation Date	10/14/98
General Input Screen			
Intrinsic Stock Value $98.57			

General Inputs

Company Name	Intel Corporation		
Fiscal Year	12/27/97	Depreciation Rate (% of Rev.)	8.75%
Excess Return Period (years)	10	Investment Rate (% of Rev)	18.10%
Revenues ($mil)	$25,070	Working Capital (% of change in Rev.)	14.87%
Revenue Growth Rate (%)	20.00%	Excess Marketable Securities ($mil)	7698
Net Operating Profit Margin (%)	28.40%	Other Senior Claims	0
Tax Rate (%)	34.84%		

Cost of Capital Inputs

Current Stock Price	$77.00
Annual Dividend Per Share (e.g. $1.00)	$0.12
Shares Outstanding (mil)	1769
30-year Treasury Bond Yield (e.g 6.50%)	5.35%
Bond Yield Spread to Treasury (e.g. 1.00%)	1.33%
Preferred Stock Yield (e.g. 8.00%)	0.00%
Equity Risk Premium (e.g. 3.00%)	3.00%
Company Specific Beta (e.g. 1.00)	1.19
Value of Debt Outstanding ($mil)	$472.0
Value of Preferred Stock ($mil)	$0.0
Weighted Average Cost of Capital	8.90%

EXHIBIT 7-17 General Input Screen: Lower NOPM, Intel

Intel Corporation
General Pro Forma Screen
10-year Excess Return Period

Discounted Excess Return Period FCFF	$174,836		$29,664	Total Corporate Value			
Discounted Corporate Residual Value	($472)		$137,475	Less Debt			
Excess Marketable Securities	$0		$7,698.0	Less Preferred Stock			
Total Corporate Value	0		$174,836	Less Other Senior Claims			
				Total Value to Common Equity	$174,364		
				Intrinsic Stock Value	$98.57		

(1)	(2)	(3)	(4)	(5)	(6)	(7)	(8)	(9)	(10)	(11)	(12)	(13)
Period	Fiscal Year	Revenues	NOP	Adj. Taxes	NOPAT	Invest.	Deprec.	Net Invest.	Change in Working Capital	FCFF	Discount Factor	Discounted FCFF
0	12/27/97	25,070										
1	12/27/98	30,084	8,544	2,977	5,567	5,445	2,632	2,813	746	2,009	0.9182	1,845
2	12/27/99	36,101	10,253	3,572	6,681	6,534	3,159	3,375	895	2,410	0.8432	2,032
3	12/27/2000	43,321	12,303	4,286	8,017	7,841	3,791	4,051	1,074	2,893	0.7742	2,240
4	12/27/2001	51,985	14,764	5,144	9,620	9,409	4,549	4,861	1,288	3,471	0.7109	2,468
5	12/27/2002	62,382	17,717	6,172	11,544	11,291	5,458	5,833	1,546	4,165	0.6528	2,719
6	12/27/2003	74,859	21,260	7,407	13,853	13,549	6,550	6,999	1,855	4,998	0.5994	2,996
7	12/27/2004	89,830	25,512	8,888	16,624	16,259	7,860	8,399	2,226	5,998	0.5504	3,301
8	12/27/2005	107,796	30,614	10,666	19,948	19,511	9,432	10,079	2,672	7,198	0.5054	3,638
9	12/27/2006	129,356	36,737	12,799	23,938	23,413	11,319	12,095	3,206	8,637	0.4641	4,008
10	12/27/2007	155,227	44,084	15,359	28,725	28,096	13,582	14,514	3,847	10,365	0.4261	4,417
Residual		155,227	44,084	15,359	28,725	13,582	13,582	0	0	322,604	0.4261	137,475

EXHIBIT 7-18   General Pro Forma Screen: Lower NOPM, Intel

				Valuation Date	10/14/98
		General Input Screen			
		Intrinsic Stock Value $68.83			

General Inputs

Company Name	Intel Corporation		
Fiscal Year	12/27/97	Depreciation Rate (% of Rev.)	8.75%
Excess Return Period (years)	10	Investment Rate (% of Rev)	18.10%
Revenues ($mil)	$25,070	Working Capital (% of change in Rev.)	14.87%
Revenue Growth Rate (%)	15.00%	Excess Marketable Securities ($mil)	7698
Net Operating Profit Margin (%)	28.40%	Other Senior Claims	0
Tax Rate (%)	34.84%		

Cost of Capital Inputs

Current Stock Price	$77.00
Annual Dividend Per Share (e.g. $1.00)	$0.12
Shares Outstanding (mil)	1769
30-year Treasury Bond Yield (e.g 6.50%)	5.35%
Bond Yield Spread to Treasury (e.g. 1.00%)	1.33%
Preferred Stock Yield (e.g. 8.00%)	0.00%
Equity Risk Premium (e.g. 3.00%)	3.00%
Company Specific Beta (e.g. 1.00)	1.19
Value of Debt Outstanding ($mil)	$472.0
Value of Preferred Stock ($mil)	$0.0
Weighted Average Cost of Capital	8.90%

EXHIBIT 7-19   General Input Screen: Lower NOPM and Lower Growth Rate, Intel

7-20) shows the cash flows that justify an intrinsic stock value of $68.83—not all that much less than the current $77 market price of Intel. In other words, the downside risk from investing in Intel at this level is not great—a good characteristic for an investment. Intel still looks like a "strong buy" candidate to us.

Valuation of Consolidated Edison

General Description of ConEd—A "Decent" Utility

Consolidated Edison Inc. ("ConEd") is one of the largest publicly owned gas and electric utilities in the United States. It is the holding company for the Consolidated Edison Company, which provides electric power to most of New York City and Westchester County. It also provides gas in Manhattan, the Bronx, and parts of Queens and Westchester County, and steam in parts of the borough of Manhattan.

The company also has subsidiaries that provide wholesale and retail power to customers in the northeastern parts of the United States. It is expanding its coverage into New Jersey and Pennsylvania through the purchase of Orange and Rockland Utilities.

Intel Corporation
General Pro Forma Screen
10-year Excess Return Period

Discounted Excess Return Period FCFF		$122,229
Discounted Corporate Residual Value		($472)
Excess Marketable Securities		$0
Total Corporate Value		0

$24,708	Total Corporate Value	
$89,823	Less Debt	
$7,698.0	Less Preferred Stock	
$122,229	Less Other Senior Claims	
	Total Value to Common Equity	$121,757
	Intrinsic Stock Value	**$68.83**

(1)	(2)	(3)	(4)	(5)	(6)	(7)	(8)	(9)	(10)	(11)	(12)	(13)
Period	Fiscal Year	Revenues	NOP	Adj. Taxes	NOPAT	Invest.	Deprec.	Net Invest.	Change in Working Capital	FCFF	Discount Factor	Discounted FCFF
0	12/27/97	25,070										
1	12/27/98	28,830	8,188	2,853	5,335	5,218	2,523	2,696	559	2,080	0.9182	1,910
2	12/27/99	33,155	9,416	3,281	6,135	6,001	2,901	3,100	643	2,392	0.8432	2,017
3	12/27/2000	38,128	10,828	3,773	7,056	6,901	3,336	3,565	740	2,751	0.7742	2,130
4	12/27/2001	43,848	12,453	4,339	8,114	7,936	3,837	4,100	850	3,164	0.7109	2,249
5	12/27/2002	50,425	14,321	4,989	9,331	9,127	4,412	4,715	978	3,639	0.6528	2,375
6	12/27/2003	57,988	16,469	5,738	10,731	10,496	5,074	5,422	1,125	4,184	0.5994	2,508
7	12/27/2004	66,687	18,939	6,598	12,341	12,070	5,835	6,235	1,293	4,812	0.5504	2,649
8	12/27/2005	76,690	21,780	7,588	14,192	13,881	6,710	7,170	1,487	5,534	0.5054	2,797
9	12/27/2006	88,193	25,047	8,726	16,321	15,963	7,717	8,246	1,711	6,364	0.4641	2,953
10	12/27/2007	101,422	28,804	10,035	18,769	18,357	8,874	9,483	1,967	7,318	0.4261	3,119
Residual		101,422	28,804	10,035	18,769	8,874	8,874	0	0	210,783	0.4261	89,823

EXHIBIT 7-20 General Pro Forma Screen: Lower NOPM and Lower Growth Rate, Intel

146

ConEd's utility rates are among the highest in the nation, and the company is considering the sale of at least half of its electric-generating capacity in New York. With the recent deregulation of the utilities industry in the United States, it is preparing to make the transition to a more competitive, less regulated environment.

The stocks of utility companies, like ConEd, are known as defensive stocks. Defensive stocks are the stocks of companies that sell food, beverages, power, water, and other staples that must be bought by consumers in bad times as well as good. The revenues and profits of companies with defensive stocks are fairly unaffected by changing economic conditions. In fact, when the prices of many cyclical stocks fall with a decline in the business cycle, investors frequently reallocate their portfolios, selling off growth and high-tech stocks and buying defensive stocks.

The stock of ConEd will not be mistaken for the stock of a growth company like Microsoft or Intel, and its market capitalization ratios reflect this characterization. For example, in 1997 ConEd's operating revenues were $7,121 million. Microsoft's 1997 figure of $11,358 was only 1.6 times greater. ConEd's operating income was $1,427 million. Microsoft's $5,130 operating income figure was only 3.6 times greater. Microsoft's market capitalization on August 20, 1998 was $277 billion—a very large 26 times greater than the market capitalization of ConEd on that same date.

However, the market performance of August 31, 1998, the date of this valuation, reflects the downside of high-tech growth stocks compared with defensive stocks like ConEd. On that date, the DJIA dropped 512.61 points (–6.4%) to 7,539.07. The NASDAQ Index dropped 140.43 points (–8.6%) to 1,449.25. Microsoft dropped $9\frac{9}{16}$ points to 95\frac{15}{16}$, Intel dropped $5\frac{13}{16}$ to $71\frac{3}{16}$, and ConEd dropped only $\frac{1}{4}$ to $47\frac{5}{16}$. The yield on the 30-year Treasury Bond dropped to an all-time low of 5.26%. To say that the U.S. domestic stock market was in a state of disarray at this time is a gross understatement.

On the plus side, ConEd has little exposure to the "Asian Contagion" or political and economic unrest in Russia. ConEd also pays a healthy current dividend per share of $2.12 per year. For many stock investors, ConEd represents a safe haven in a stock market that, otherwise, reflects a sea of international economic turmoil. With that in mind, let's get into our valuation of ConEd.

Baseline Valuation of ConEd—August 31, 1998
Growth Rate—2%; Excess Return Period—5 Years;
NOPM—20.8%; WACC—6.75%

Let's first look at the cash flow estimates for ConEd. We have included the audited 1997 income statement, balance sheet, and cash flow statement, which we downloaded from ConEd's corporate Web site (http://www.coned.com/), as Exhibits 7-21, 7-22, and 7-23, respectively. On July 28, 1998, ConEd issued its second-quarter earnings release, which we also downloaded. The consolidated income statement for the 6 months ended June 30, 1998 and 1997 is shown in Exhibit 7-24.

Revenue Growth Rate. The historical revenue growth for ConEd has been meek. The 1997 income statement (Exhibit 7-21) shows operating revenues of $6,536 million in 1995, increasing 6.4% to $6,959 million in 1996, and further increasing 2.3% to $7,121 in 1997. The 2-year CAGR for the 1995–1997 period is 4.4%. According to the earnings release, ConEd's most recent operating revenues decreased slightly—$3,414 million for the 6 months ended June 30, 1998 versus $3,423 million for the 6 months ended June 30, 1997. The bad news is that operating income stayed flat for that entire 3-year period.

Warning: The operating income on an income statement of a utility, such as ConEd, has federal income taxes already included as part of operating expenses. This is not the way operating expenses are reported for U.S. industrial corporations. In our analysis and in the calculation of operating income and NOPM, we reduce ConEd's reported operating expenses by the amount of its federal income taxes, which increases ConEd's reported operating income. We then subtract federal income taxes before our calculation of FCFF.

Using the adjustment described above, we calculate operating income for 1995, 1996, and 1997 as $1,437.7 million, $1,410.7 million, and $1,428.3 million, respectively—**an absolutely flat operating income curve with no growth.** According to the earnings release and incorporating our adjustment described above, operating income did step up significantly, from $489.1 million for the 6 months ended June 30, 1998 to $530.6 million for the 6 months ended June 30, 1997, an increase of 8.5%.

What are the pros saying about growth? Again, we consulted Zacks for its 5-year earnings per share growth estimates. We found that

CONSOLIDATED INCOME STATEMENT CONSOLIDATED EDISON, INC.

Year Ended December 31 (Thousands of Dollars)	1997	1996	1995
Operating revenues (Note A)			
Electric	**$5,635,575**	$5,541,117	$5,389,408
Gas	**1,093,880**	1,015,070	813,356
Steam	**391,799**	403,549	334,133
Total operating revenues	**7,121,254**	6,959,736	6,536,897
Operating expenses			
Purchased power	**1,349,421**	1,272,854	1,107,223
Fuel	**596,824**	573,275	504,104
Gas purchased for resale	**479,218**	418,271	259,789
Other operations	**1,108,845**	1,163,159	1,139,732
Maintenance	**474,788**	458,815	512,102
Depreciation and amortization (Note A)	**502,779**	496,412	455,776
Taxes, other than federal income tax	**1,181,081**	1,166,199	1,120,232
Federal income tax (Notes A and I)	**382,910**	397,160	396,560
Total operating expenses	**6,075,866**	5,946,145	5,495,518
Operating income	**1,045,388**	1,013,591	1,041,379
Other income (deductions)			
Investment income (Note A)	**11,554**	8,327	16,966
Allowance for equity funds used during construction (Note A)	**4,448**	3,468	3,763
Other income less miscellaneous deductions	**(18,696)**	(8,749)	(8,149)
Federal income tax (Notes A and I)	**3,190**	970	(1,060)
Total other income	**496**	4,016	11,520
Income before interest charges	**1,045,884**	1,017,607	1,052,899
Interest on long-term debt	**318,158**	307,820	301,917
Other interest	**17,083**	17,331	28,954
Allowance for borrowed funds used during construction (Note A)	**(2,180)**	(1,629)	(1,822)
Net interest charges	**333,061**	323,522	329,049
Net income	**712,823**	694,085	723,850
Preferred stock dividend requirements	**(18,344)**	(19,859)	(35,565)
Gain on refunding of preferred stock (Note B)	**-**	13,943	-
Net income for common stock	**$694,479**	$688,169	$688,285
Basic and diluted earnings per common share	**$2.95**	$2.93	$2.93

Average number of shares outstanding during each year (235,082,063; 234,976,697 and 234,930,301)

The accompanying notes are an integral part of these financial statements.

EXHIBIT 7-21 Con Edison Consolidated Income Statement

among the 10 analysts that Zacks polled for ConEd, earnings growth rates ranged from 1% to 4%, with a median of 2%. For our initial valuation of ConEd, the 2% growth rate is the one we use. Next, we see what growth rate is needed to justify ConEd's current market price, all else being held constant.

CONSOLIDATED BALANCE SHEET CONSOLIDATED EDISON, INC.
ASSETS

At December 31 (Thousands of Dollars)	1997	1996
Utility plant, at original cost (Note A)		
Electric	$11,743,745	$11,588,344
Gas	1,741,562	1,642,231
Steam	576,206	536,672
General	1,203,427	1,152,001
Total	15,264,940	14,919,248
Less: Accumulated depreciation	4,392,377	4,285,732
Net	10,872,563	10,633,516
Construction work in progress	292,218	332,333
Nuclear fuel assemblies and components, less accumulated amortization	102,321	101,461
Net utility plant	11,267,102	11,067,310
Current assets		
Cash and temporary cash investments (Note A)	183,458	106,882
Funds held for refunding of debt	328,874	-
Accounts receivable - customer, less allowance for uncollectible accounts of $21,600 in 1997 and 1996	581,163	544,004
Other receivables	60,759	42,056
Regulatory accounts receivable (Note A)	(1,682)	45,397
Fuel, at average cost	53,697	64,709
Gas in storage, at average cost	37,209	44,979
Materials and supplies, at average cost	191,759	204,801
Prepayments	75,516	64,492
Other current assets	16,457	15,167
Total current assets	1,527,210	1,132,487
Investments and nonutility property (Note A)	292,397	177,224
Deferred charges (Note A)		
Enlightened Energy program costs	117,807	133,718
Unamortized debt expense	126,085	130,786
Recoverable fuel costs (Note A)	98,301	101,462
Power contract termination costs	80,978	58,835
Other deferred charges	239,559	271,081
Total deferred charges	662,730	695,882
Regulatory asset - future federal income taxes (Notes A and I)	973,079	984,282
Total	$14,722,518	$14,057,185

CAPITALIZATION AND LIABILITIES At December 31 (Thousands of Dollars)	1997	1996

Capitalization (see Consolidated Statement of Capitalization)

EXHIBIT 7-22   Con Edison Consolidated Balance Sheet

Common shareholders' equity	**$5,930,079**	$5,727,568
Preferred stock subject to mandatory redemption (Note B)	**84,550**	84,550
Other preferred stock (Note B)	**233,468**	238,098
Long-term debt	**4,188,906**	4,238,622
Total capitalization	**10,437,003**	10,288,838
Noncurrent liabilities		
Obligations under capital leases	**39,879**	42,661
Other noncurrent liabilities	**106,137**	80,499
Total noncurrent liabilities	**146,016**	123,160
Current liabilities		
Long-term debt due within one year (Note B)	**529,385**	106,256
Accounts payable	**440,114**	431,115
Customer deposits	**161,731**	159,616
Accrued taxes	**65,736**	27,342
Accrued interest	**85,613**	83,090
Accrued wages	**82,556**	80,225
Other current liabilities	**183,122**	147,968
Total current liabilities	**1,548,257**	1,035,612
Provisions related to future federal income taxes and other deferred credits (Notes A and I)		
Accumulated deferred federal income tax	**2,307,835**	2,289,092
Accumulated deferred investment tax credits	**163,680**	172,510
Other deferred credits	**119,727**	147,973
Total deferred credits	**2,591,242**	2,609,575
Contingencies (Note F)		
Total	**$14,722,518**	$14,057,185

The accompanying notes are an integral part of these financial statements.

EXHIBIT 7-22 *(Cont.)*

Excess Return Period. We don't have anything against ConEd. It has operated in a highly regulated, monopolistic industry. Competition is being introduced into the utility industry, and ConEd's managers will have to cope with a whole new set of concerns. How they will cope, and what actions they will take and their competitors will take, remains to be seen. With this uncertainty and pending future developments and performance, we believe that we should be conservative

CONSOLIDATED STATEMENT OF CASH FLOWS CONSOLIDATED EDISON, INC.
Year Ended December 31 (Thousands of Dollars)

	1997	1996	1995
Operating activities			
Net income	$712,823	$694,085	$723,850
Principal non-cash charges (credits) to income			
Depreciation and amortization	502,779	496,412	455,776
Deferred recoverable fuel costs	3,161	(42,008)	(61,937)
Federal income tax deferred	22,620	40,600	69,020
Common equity component of allowance for funds used during construction	(4,321)	(3,274)	(3,546)
Other non-cash charges	17,268	9,602	14,382
Changes in assets and liabilities			
Accounts receivable - customer, less allowance for uncollectibles	(37,159)	(46,789)	(56,719)
Regulatory accounts receivable	47,079	(51,878)	32,827
Materials and supplies, including fuel and gas in storage	31,824	(26,505)	43,341
Prepayments, other receivables and other current assets	(31,017)	5,117	4,566
Enlightened Energy program costs	15,911	10,564	25,919
Power contract termination costs	11,551	30,827	55,387
Accounts payable	8,999	10,263	46,383
Other - net	(62,978)	(19,679)	(72,785)
Net cash flows from operating activities	1,238,540	1,107,337	1,276,464
Investing activities including construction			
Construction expenditures	(654,221)	(675,233)	(692,803)
Nuclear fuel expenditures	(14,579)	(48,705)	(12,840)
Contributions to nuclear decommissioning trust	(21,301)	(21,301)	(18,893)
Common equity component of allowance for funds used during construction	4,321	3,274	3,546
Net cash flows from investing activities including construction	(685,780)	(741,965)	(720,990)
Financing activities including dividends			
Issuance of long-term debt	480,000	525,000	228,285
Retirement of long-term debt	(106,256)	(183,524)	(10,889)
Advance refunding of preferred stock and long-term debt	-	(412,311)	(155,699)
Issuance and refunding costs	(8,930)	(18,480)	(5,269)
Funds held for refunding of debt	(328,874)	-	-
Common stock dividends	(493,711)	(488,756)	(479,262)
Preferred stock dividends	(18,413)	(22,711)	(35,569)
Net cash flows from financing activities including dividends	(476,184)	(600,782)	(458,403)
Net increase (decrease) in cash and temporary cash investments	76,576	(235,410)	97,071
Cash and temporary cash investments at January 1	106,882	342,292	245,221
Cash and temporary cash investments at December 31	$183,458	$106,882	$342,292
Supplemental disclosure of cash flow information			
Cash paid during the period for:			
Interest	$310,310	$309,279	$309,953
Income taxes	335,631	346,755	344,754

The accompanying notes are an integral part of these financial statements.

EXHIBIT 7-23   Con Edison Consolidated Statement of Cash Flow

Consolidated Edison, Inc.
Consolidated Income Statement
for the Six Months Ended June 30, 1998 and 1997

	1998	1997
	(Thousands of Dollars)	
Operating revenues		
Electric	$ 2,577,643	$ 2,497,316
Gas	595,732	668,396
Steam	192,801	224,450
Non-utility	47,912	33,481
Total operating revenues	3,414,088	3,423,643
Operating expenses		
Purchased power	682,676	666,929
Fuel	258,424	273,780
Gas purchased for resale	276,341	341,205
Other operations	565,218	566,956
Maintenance	250,684	261,022
Depreciation and amortization	257,523	248,797
Taxes, other than federal income tax	592,634	575,811
Federal income tax	127,976	115,931
Total operating expenses	3,011,476	3,050,431
Operating income	402,612	373,212
Other income (deductions)		
Investment income	5,984	3,978
Allowance for equity funds used during construction	1,087	3,320
Other income less miscellaneous deductions	535	(726)
Federal income tax	(454)	(1,599)
Total other income	7,152	4,973
Income before interest charges	409,764	378,185
Interest on long-term debt	156,043	157,944
Other interest	11,313	7,701
Allowance for borrowed funds used during construction	(557)	(1,627)
Net interest charges	166,799	164,018
Preferred stock dividend requirements	(9,072)	(9,207)
Net Income for common stock	$ 233,893	$ 204,960
Common shares outstanding - average (000)	235,205	235,009
Basic and diluted earnings per share	$ 0.99	$ 0.87
Con Edison Sales		
Electric (Thousands of kilowatthours)		
Con Edison customers	17,790,466	17,213,254
Delivery service to NYPA and others	4,360,230	4,250,306
Service for municipal agencies	465,482	510,591
Total sales in service territory	22,616,178	21,974,151
Off-system and ESCO sales	760,433	1,012,848
Gas (dekatherms)		
Firm (A)	54,285,625	59,021,742
Off-peak firm/interruptible	11,187,254	13,419,753
Total sales to Con Edison customers	65,472,879	72,441,495
Transportation of customer-owned gas		

	1998	1997
NYPA	1,725,535	7,368,630
Other	7,186,264	3,453,753
Off-system sales	9,932,608	4,760,561
Total sales and transportation	84,317,286	88,024,439
Steam (Thousands of pounds)	13,526,399	14,937,516

(A) Includes firm sales and transportation volumes.

EXHIBIT 7-24   Con Edison Consolidated Income Statement, June 1998

from a valuation perspective and assign a 5-year "decent" excess return period to ConEd. That's what we use.

NOPM Estimate. According to ConEd's 1997 income statement and incorporating the federal tax adjustment described above, ConEd had NOPMs in 1995, 1996, and 1997 of 22.0%, 20.3%, and 20.1%, respectively, for an average of 20.8% over the 3-year period. This 20.8% NOPM rate is what we use in our valuation.

Income Tax Rates. From the 1997 income statement for ConEd, we take the federal income tax figure of $382.9 million and add it to the 1997 net income figure of $712.8 million to get income before taxes of $1,095.7 million. We divide those numbers ($382.9/$1.095.7) to get an income tax rate of 34.9% for use in our valuation.

New Investment, Depreciation, and Net Investment. From the 1997 cash flow statement (Exhibit 7-23), we see that additions to property, plant, and equipment totaled $685.8 million in 1997, $741.9 million in 1996, and $721 million in 1995—or 9.6%, 10.7%, and 11.0% of net revenues in 1997, 1996, and 1995 respectively. The average new investment as a percentage of revenue over the 3-year period was 10.4%, which is the new investment rate that we use in our valuation example.

Also from the 1997 cash flow statement, we see that depreciation was $502.8 million in 1997, $496.4 million in 1996, and $455.8 million in 1995—or 7.1%, 7.1%, and 7.1% of net revenues in 1997, 1996, and 1995, respectively. The depreciation rate averaged 7.1% for the period and that's what we use in the baseline valuation. The difference between new investment and depreciation gives net investment.

Incremental Working Capital. Incremental working capital is insignificant for ConEd. According to the 1997 balance sheet (Exhibit 7-24), accounts receivable minus accounts payable plus customer's deposits were negative for ConEd at the end of both fiscal 1997 (–0.2) and fiscal 1996 (–0.6), for an average of –0.4 of revenue. This is the number we use for our incremental working capital input in our baseline valuation.

Cost of Capital Inputs. The closing price for ConEd's stock on August 31, 1998 was $47⅚ per share. S&P Comstock reported that 235.488 million shares of ConEd were outstanding and estimated ConEd's beta to be .80, while Market Guide estimated it to be .81, which is the number we use in the valuation. There is no significant stock option program for ConEd, as opposed to Microsoft and Intel, so we need not worry about earnings dilution problems.

The 30-year U.S. Treasury Bond yield was 5.26%, and we continue to use an equity risk premium of 3%. However, with the recent volatility and global meltdown increasing investor's *fear*, a higher equity risk premium may be embedded into equity pricing.

From the 1997 balance sheet, we get the long-term debt outstanding of $4,718 million, and $318 million of preferred stock outstanding. There does not seem to be a lot of excess marketable securities and cash on hand for ConEd. We use the yield associated with the Dow Jones Utilities Bond Average of 6.9%, available in the New York Exchange Bonds section of *The Wall Street Journal,* as our rate associated with the bonds of ConEd. This gives us a yield spread to Treasuries of 6.90% − 5.26% = 1.64%, which is what we use for our valuation. We also use a preferred stock yield of 7.5%.

ConEd's Baseline Valuation. We plug these figures into the general input screen in Exhibit 7-25. ValuePro 2000 churns out the cost of capital screen, which shows ConEd to have a WACC of 6.75% (Exhibit 7-26), and the general pro forma screen (Exhibit 7-27), which shows ConEd stock to have an intrinsic value of $40.44—roughly 14.5% less than the August 31, 1998 closing price of $47.31 per share.

		Valuation Date	10/14/98
	General Input Screen		
	Intrinsic Stock Value $40.44		

General Inputs

Company Name	Consolidated Edison		
Fiscal Year	12/31/97	Depreciation Rate (% of Rev.)	7.10%
Excess Return Period (years)	5	Investment Rate (% of Rev)	10.40%
Revenues ($mil)	$7,121	Working Capital (% of change in Rev.)	-0.40%
Revenue Growth Rate (%)	2.00%	Excess Marketable Securities ($mil)	0
Net Operating Profit Margin (%)	20.80%	Other Senior Claims	0
Tax Rate (%)	34.90%		

Cost of Capital Inputs

Current Stock Price	$47.31
Annual Dividend Per Share (e.g. $1.00)	$2.12
Shares Outstanding (mil)	235.488
30-year Treasury Bond Yield (e.g 6.50%)	5.26%
Bond Yield Spread to Treasury (e.g. 1.00%)	1.64%
Preferred Stock Yield (e.g. 8.00%)	7.50%
Equity Risk Premium (e.g. 3.00%)	3.00%
Company Specific Beta (e.g. 1.00)	0.81
Value of Debt Outstanding ($mil)	$4,718.0
Value of Preferred Stock ($mil)	$318.0
Weighted Average Cost of Capital	6.75%

EXHIBIT 7-25   General Input Screen, Con Ed

			Valuation Date		09/21/98

Consolidated Edison
Weighted Average Cost of Capital Screen

Cost of Common Equity

Long Term Bond Yield	5.26%
Beta	0.81
Equity Risk Premium	3.00%
Cost of Common Equity	7.69%

Market Capitalization and After-Tax Weighted Average Cost of Capital

	Average Yield	After Tax Yield	Market Value	% Capital	After Tax Effect
Long-Term Debt	6.90%	4.49%	4,718	29.2%	1.31%
Preferred Stock	7.50%	7.50%	318	2.0%	0.15%
Common Stock	7.69%	7.69%	11,142	68.9%	5.30%
			16,178	100.0%	6.75%

EXHIBIT 7-26 WACC Screen, Con Ed

Needless to say, we are not thrilled about buying ConEd stock at current levels. If rates continue to go down or ConEd's earnings start to show some real growth, the current stock price in our opinion could be justified.

ConEd Valuation—What Growth Rate Is Needed to Justify $47.31 per Share?

What growth rate, all other inputs being held constant (a tough thing to do in today's markets), is needed to justify ConEd's current stock price of $47.31 per share? If we pull up the general input screen to our ConEd valuation and plug 4.4% into the revenue growth rate slot (Exhibit 7-28), we get $47.36 per share. This is the growth rate *implied* by today's market price for ConEd.

Amazingly, this 4.4% implied growth rate is exactly equal to ConEd's observed compound annual growth rate of operating revenue associated with the 1995–1997 period. What a coincidence! Or is it?

ConEd Valuation—What If There Are Higher Interest Rates and WACCs?

Let's now go back to our baseline 2% revenue growth, $40.44 valuation of ConEd. A significant concern for an investor in purchasing a utility is how the stock price will react if interest rates rise. We pose that scenario to the ValuePro 2000 software by assuming that interest rates increase ¼ percent per year during years 2 through 5, for a total increase of 1% over the excess return period.

Consolidated Edison
General Pro Forma Screen
5-year Excess Return Period

	Discounted Excess Return Period FCFF	$3,190
	Discounted Corporate Residual Value	$11,369
	Excess Marketable Securities	$0.0
	Total Corporate Value	$14,559

Total Corporate Value	$14,559	
Less Debt	($4,718)	
Less Preferred Stock	($318)	
Less Other Senior Claims	0	
Total Value to Common Equity	$9,523	
Intrinsic Stock Value	$40.44	

(1)	(2)	(3)	(4)	(5)	(6)	(7)	(8)	(9)	(10)	(11)	(12)	(13)
Period	Fiscal Year	Revenues	NOP	Adj. Taxes	NOPAT	Invest.	Deprec.	Net Invest.	Change in Working Capital	FCFF	Discount Factor	Discounted FCFF
0	12/31/97	7,121										
1	12/31/98	7,263	1,511	527	984	755	516	240	-1	744	0.9367	697
2	12/31/99	7,409	1,541	538	1,003	771	526	244	-1	759	0.8775	666
3	12/31/2000	7,557	1,572	549	1,023	786	537	249	-1	774	0.8220	637
4	12/31/2001	7,708	1,603	560	1,044	802	547	254	-1	790	0.7700	608
5	12/31/2002	7,862	1,635	571	1,065	818	558	259	-1	806	0.7213	581
Residual		7,862	1,635	571	1,065	558	558	0	0	15,763	0.7213	11,369

EXHIBIT 7-27 General Pro Forma Screen, Con Ed

		Valuation Date	10/14/98
General Input Screen			
Intrinsic Stock Value $47.36			

General Inputs

Company Name Consolidated Edison

Fiscal Year	12/31/97	Depreciation Rate (% of Rev.)	7.10%
Excess Return Period (years)	5	Investment Rate (% of Rev)	10.40%
Revenues ($mil)	$7,121	Working Capital (% of change in Rev.)	-0.40%
Revenue Growth Rate (%)	4.40%	Excess Marketable Securities ($mil)	0
Net Operating Profit Margin (%)	20.80%	Other Senior Claims	0
Tax Rate (%)	34.90%		

Cost of Capital Inputs

Current Stock Price	$47.31
Annual Dividend Per Share (e.g. $1.00)	$2.12
Shares Outstanding (mil)	235.488
30-year Treasury Bond Yield (e.g 6.50%)	5.26%
Bond Yield Spread to Treasury (e.g. 1.00%)	1.64%
Preferred Stock Yield (e.g. 8.00%)	7.50%
Equity Risk Premium (e.g. 3.00%)	3.00%
Company Specific Beta (e.g. 1.00)	0.81
Value of Debt Outstanding ($mil)	$4,718.0
Value of Preferred Stock ($mil)	$318.0
Weighted Average Cost of Capital	6.75%

EXHIBIT 7-28   General Input Screen, Con Ed

How do we do this? Using the custom valuation input screen, in the WACC column we input 7% in year 2, 7.25% in year 3, 7.5% in year 4, and 7.75% in year 5 and the residual period, as shown in Exhibit 7-29. What is the result? The custom valuation pro forma screen (Exhibit 7-30) shows an intrinsic value for ConEd, given the assumed increase in interest rates, of $32.09—a drop of 20.6% over the base-case value of $40.44. Once again, at the $47.31 level, we are not excited enough to buy ConEd.

Valuation of AT&T

General Description of AT&T—A "Good" Value Company

AT&T, with more than 90 million customers, is the number one long-distance telephone carrier in the United States. AT&T provides voice, data, and video telecommunications services to businesses, individuals, and governments. It provides local and regional, domestic and international communications/transmission services, along with cellular telephone and other wireless services to its customers. It also offers billing, directory assistance, and calling card services.

In July 1997, AT&T hired a new chairman, C. Michael Armstrong, and its stock soared over the ensuing year from $34⅜ into the high-$60s

		Revenue	Net				Increm.	
	Fiscal	Growth	Operating	Tax	Invest.	Dep.	Working	
Period	Year	Rate	Margin	Rate	Rate	Rate	Capital	WACC
0	12/31/97							
1	12/31/98	2.00%	20.80%	34.90%	10.40%	7.10%	-0.40%	6.75%
2	12/31/99	2.00%	20.80%	34.90%	10.40%	7.10%	-0.40%	7.00%
3	12/31/2000	2.00%	20.80%	34.90%	10.40%	7.10%	-0.40%	7.25%
4	12/31/2001	2.00%	20.80%	34.90%	10.40%	7.10%	-0.40%	7.50%
5	12/31/2002	2.00%	20.80%	34.90%	10.40%	7.10%	-0.40%	7.75%
Residual		2.00%						7.75%

Valuation Date 09/21/98
Custom Valuation Input Screen
Consolidated Edison
Intrinsic Stock Value $32.09

EXHIBIT 7-29 Custom Valuation Input Screen, Con Ed

in mid-1998, and closed on August 31, 1998 at $50⅛, down 5¹¹⁄₁₆—because the stock market was having a bad hair day. Why did AT&T soar to such heights earlier in 1998?

Under Armstrong, an AT&T outsider that came from another corporation, it has sold units like its credit card business, that are tangential to its business of providing communications services. It also is in the process of acquiring Tele-Communications Inc. (TCI), the leading cable TV company in the United States.

However, Armstrong's most important initiative, at least from the perspective of an increase in stock value, is his initiative to reduce AT&T's selling, general, and administrative expenses from 29% of revenue to 22% of revenue, according to the February 9, 1998, issue of *Business Week*. The huge effect that this change in NOPM presents for AT&T's stock value will become clear as we get into the valuation. AT&T currently pays an annual dividend of $1.32 per share.

Baseline Valuation of AT&T—August 31, 1998
Growth Rate—11.5%; Excess Return Period—7 Years;
NOPM—13.58%; WACC—6.84%

Once again, we start our valuation with the most recent financial reports of AT&T. We downloaded its audited 1997 annual report and its unaudited earnings commentary dated July 23, 1998, from AT&T's corporate Web site. We have included the 1997 income statement as Exhibit 7-31, the 1997 balance sheet as Exhibit 7-32, and the 1997 cash flow statement as Exhibit 7-33.

Here is our valuation.

Consolidated Edison
Custom Pro Forma Screen
5-year Excess Return Period

		Discounted Excess Return Period FCFF	$3,135	Total Corporate Value	$12,593
		Discounted Corporate Residual Value	$9,458	Less Debt	($4,718)
		Excess Marketable Securities	$0.0	Less Preferred Stock	($318)
		Total Corporate Value	$12,593	Less Other Senior Claims	0
				Total Value to Common Equity	$7,557
				Intrinsic Stock Value	$32.09

(1)	(2)	(3)	(4)	(5)	(6)	(7)	(8)	(9)	(10)	(11)	(12)	(13)
Period	Fiscal Year	Revenues	NOP	Adj. Taxes	NOPAT	Invest.	Deprec.	Net Invest.	Change in Working Capital	FCFF	Discount Factor	Discounted FCFF
0	12/31/97	7,121										
1	12/31/98	7,263	1,511	527	984	755	516	240	-1	744	0.9367	697
2	12/31/99	7,409	1,541	538	1,003	771	526	244	-1	759	0.8734	663
3	12/31/2000	7,557	1,572	549	1,023	786	537	249	-1	774	0.8106	628
4	12/31/2001	7,708	1,603	560	1,044	802	547	254	-1	790	0.7488	592
5	12/31/2002	7,862	1,635	571	1,065	818	558	259	-1	806	0.6885	555
Residual		7,862	1,635	571	1,065	558	558	0	0	13,737	0.6885	9,458

EXHIBIT 7-30 Custom Pro Forma Screen, Con Ed

Consolidated Statements of Income
AT&T Corp. and Subsidiaries

For the Years Ended December 31 *Dollars in Millions (except per share amounts)*	1997	1996	1995
Revenues	51,319	50,546	48,445
Operating Expenses			
Access and other interconnection	16,306	16,332	17,618
Network and other communications services	9,316	7,918	7,757
Depreciation and amortization	3,827	2,740	3,520
Selling, general and administrative	14,902	14,793	14,366
Total operating expenses	44,351	41,783	43,261
Operating income	6,968	8,763	5,184
Other income – net	416	390	284
Interest expense	191	343	490
Income from continuing operations before income taxes	7,193	8,810	4,978
Provision for income taxes	2,721	3,237	1,943
Income from continuing operations	4,472	5,573	3,035
Discontinued Operations			
Income (loss) from discontinued operations (net of taxes of $50 in 1997,$(353) in 1996 and $(1,147) in 1995)	100	173	(2896.00)
Gain on sale of discontinued operations (net of taxes of $43 in 1997 and $138 in 1996)	66	162	
Net income	4,638	5,908	139.00
Weighted-average common shares and potential common shares (millions)*	1,630	1,616	1592.00
Per Common Share – Basic:			
Income from continuing operations	$2.75	$3.46	1.92
Income(loss) from discontinued operations	0.06	0.11	(1.83)
Gain on sale of discontinued operations	0.04	0.1	–
Net income	$2.85	$3.67	$0.09
Per Common Share – Diluted:			
Income from continuing operations	$2.74	$3.45	$1.91
Income(loss) from discontinued operations	0.06	0.11	(1.82)
Gain on sale of discontinued operations	0.04	0.1	–
Net income	$2.84	$3.66	$0.09

Amounts represent the weighted-average shares assuming dilution from the potential exercise of outstanding stock options. Amounts are reduced by 5 million, 6 million and 8 million shares for 1997, 1996 and 1995, respectively, assuming no dilution.

*The notes on pages 44 through 55 are an integral part of the consolidated financial statements.

EXHIBIT 7-31 AT&T Consolidated Statement of Income

Revenue Growth Rate. According to the 1997 income statement, the recent revenue growth performance of AT&T has been anemic. Revenues, which totaled $48,445 million in 1995, grew 4.3% to $50,546 million in 1996, further growing only 1.5% to $51,319 million in 1997. According to the earnings commentary, revenues grew only 0.8% in the 6 months ended June 30, 1998.

Operating income has performed erratically over the 3-year period, growing by 69% from $4,978 million in 1995 to $8,810 million in 1996, and then falling by 20.5% to $6,968 million in 1997. According to the earnings commentary, operating income for the 6-month period ending June 30, 1998, was negatively affected by a $3,344 million "asset impairment and restructuring charge." Absent this charge, operating

Consolidated Balance Sheets
AT&T Corp. and Subsidiaries

At December 31 *Dollars in Millions*	1997	1996
Assets		
Cash and cash equivalents	$ 145.00	$ –
Receivables, less allowances of $977 and $942		
Accounts receivable	8,573	8,969
Other receivables	5,684	6,140
Deferred income taxes	1,252	1,266
Other current assets	525	698
Total current assets	16,179	17,073
Property, plant and equipment – net	22,710	19,736
Licensing costs, net of accumulated amortization of $1,076 and $913	8,329	8,071
Investments	3,857	3,875
Long-term receivables	1,794	872
Prepaid pension costs	2,156	1,933
Other assets	2,509	2,312
Net assets of discontinued operations	1,101	1,510
Total assets	$ 58,636	$ 55,382
Liabilities		
Accounts payable	$ 6,243	$ 6,157
Payroll and benefit-related liabilities	2,348	2,614
Debt maturing within one year	3,998	2,449
Dividends payable	538	536
Other current liabilities	3,815	4,395
Total current liabilities	16,942	16,151
Long-term debt	6,826	7,883
Long-term benefit-related liabilities	3,142	3,037
Deferred income taxes	5,711	4,827
Other long-term liabilities and deferred credits	3,367	3,189
Total liabilities	35,988	35,087
Shareowners' Equity		
Common shares, par value $1 per share	1,624	1,623
Authorized shares: 2,000,000,000		
Outstanding shares: 1,624,213,505 at December 31, 1997, 1,623,487,646 at December 31, 1996 1,623,487,646 at December 31, 1996		
Additional paid-in capital	15,751	15,697
Guaranteed ESOP obligation	(70)	(96)
Foreign currency translation adjustments	(28)	(7)
Retained earnings	5,370	3,078
Total shareowners' equity	22,647	20,295
Total liabilities and shareowners' equity	$ 58,635	$ 55,382

*The notes on pages 44 through 55 are an integral part of the consolidated financial statements.

EXHIBIT 7-32   AT&T Consolidated Balance Sheet

income for the period would have been $4,231 million—a 34.3% increase over the period ended June 30, 1997.

We checked with Zacks to see what Wall Street thought about AT&T's earnings growth potential—which was last updated on August 14, 1998. Of the 20 analysts polled, 5-year earnings per share growth ranged from a low of 5% to a high of 20% and a median of 11.5%. It is our belief that Mr. Armstrong is going to be very concerned about the bottom line and will try very hard to perform up to or even exceed

Consolidated Statements of Cash Flows
AT&T Corp. and Subsidiaries

For the Years Ended December 31 *Dollars in Millions*	1997	1996	1995
Operating Activities			
Net income	4,638	5,908	139
Add: (Income)loss from discontinued operations	(100)	(173)	2,896
Gain on sale of discontinued operations	(66)	(162)	–
Income from continuing operations	4,472	5,573	3,035
Adjustments to reconcile net income to net cash provided by operating activities of continuing operations:			
Restructuring and other charges	–	–	3,023
Depreciation and amortization	3,627	2,740	2,586
Provision for uncollectibles	1,957	1,938	1,613
Increase in accounts receivable	(1,431)	(2,165)	(2,220)
Increase in accounts payable	16	513	872
Net increase in other operating assets and liabilities	(787)	(1,079)	(87)
Other adjustments for noncash items – net	383	355	(624)
Net cash provided by operating activities of continuing operations	8,437	7,875	8,198
Investing Activities			
Capital expenditures	(7,143)	(6,334)	(4,597)
Proceeds from sale or disposal of property, plant and equipment	169	145	204
(Increase)decrease in finance assets	(465)	3,499	1,845
Acquisitions of licenses	(436)	(267)	(1,978)
Net decrease(increase) in investments	109	(140)	9
Dispositions(acquisitions), net of cash acquired	1,513	2,145	(3,406)
Other investing activities – net	(156)	(23)	(240)
Net cash used in investing activities of continuing operations	(6,407)	(975)	(8,163)
Financing Activities			
Proceeds from long-term debt issuances	–	–	2,392
Retirements of long-term debt	(662)	(1,236)	(2,137)
(Acquisition)issuance of common shares	(163)	1,293	1,214
Dividends paid	(2,142)	(2,122)	(2,088)
Increase(decrease) in short-term borrowings – net	1,114	(5,301)	1,976
Other financing activities – net	52	1,986	100
Net cash (used in) provided by financing activities of continuing operations	(1,801)	(5,380)	1,457
Net cash used in discontinued operations	(84)	(1,595)	(1,544)
Net increase (decrease) in cash and cash equivalents	145	(75)	(52)
Cash and cash equivalents at beginning of year	–	75	127
Cash and cash equivalents at end of year	$ 145	$ –	$ 75

*The notes on pages 44 through 55 are an integral part of the consolidated financial statements.

EXHIBIT 7-33 AT&T Consolidated Statement of Cash Flow

expectations. So we use the 11.5% ratio as our revenue growth rate in the baseline valuation.

Excess Return Period. The excess return period is difficult to estimate. AT&T has a lot going for it in terms of brand name and market share and reputation. However, its performance in the past has been erratic, its recent labor union relationships have been a question, and the competition in the communications industry and the rapidly changing technologies have been a concern. We use a 7-year excess return period for the baseline valuation, pending further analysis of AT&T's performance under CEO Armstrong.

NOPM Estimate.   For AT&T, NOPM is the area of real concern to us. The historical NOPM for AT&T has gone from 10.7% in 1995, to 17.34% in 1996, to 13.58% in 1997. For the baseline valuation we use 13.58% to find AT&T's intrinsic value if the company continues to operate as it has been recently. For a what-if scenario, we see how the intrinsic value is affected if Mr. Armstrong meets his goal of reducing AT&T's SG&A expenses from 29% of revenue to 22% of revenue. Presently, however, we use 13.58%.

Income Tax Rates.   From the 1997 income statement for AT&T, we take the federal income tax figure of $2,721 million and divide it by the 1997 income from continuing operations before income taxes figure of $7,193 million ($2,721/$7,193) to get an income tax rate of 37.8%. That ratio is what we use for our valuation.

New Investment, Depreciation, and Net Investment.   From the 1997 cash flow statement (Exhibit 7-33), we see that capital expenditures totaled $7,143 million in 1997, $6,334 million in 1996, and $4,597 million in 1995—or 13.9%, 12.5%, and 9.5% of revenues in 1997, 1996, and 1995, respectively. The average new investment as a percentage of revenue over the 3-year period was 12%, which is the new investment rate that we use in our valuation example.

Also from the 1997 cash flow statement, we see that depreciation and amortization totaled $3,827 million in 1997, $2,740 million in 1996, and $2,586 million in 1995—or 7.5%, 5.4%, and 5.3% of net revenues in 1997, 1996, and 1995, respectively. The depreciation rate averaged 6.1% for the period, and that's what we use in the baseline valuation. The difference between new investment and depreciation gives net investment.

Incremental Working Capital.   Incremental working capital is very significant for AT&T. According to its 1997 balance sheet, accounts receivable plus other receivables were $14,257 million in 1997 and $15,109 million in 1996. Accounts payable were $6,243 million in 1997 and $6,157 million in 1996, yielding net receivables of $8,014 million, or 15.6% of revenues in 1997 and $8,952, or 17.7% of revenues in 1996. The average is 16.65% of revenues for the 2 years. This is the number we use for our incremental working capital input in the baseline valuation.

Cost of Capital Inputs.   The closing price for AT&T's stock on August 31, 1998, was $50⅛ per share. S&P Comstock reported that

1,806.338 million shares of AT&T were outstanding and estimated AT&T's beta to be 0.59, while Market Guide estimated it to be 0.58. We use the higher 0.59 estimate of beta, which will result in a lower, more conservative valuation. The 30-year U.S. Treasury Bond yield was 5.26%, and we continue to use an equity risk premium of 3%.

We use the 1997 balance sheet (Exhibit 7-32) to get the long-term debt outstanding of $6,826 million. AT&T does not have preferred stock outstanding. Since there is not much excess marketable securities and cash on hand for AT&T, we make that input equal to zero. We use the yield associated with the Dow Jones Utilities Bond Average of 6.9%, available in the New York Exchange Bonds section of *The Wall Street Journal,* as our rate associated with the bonds of AT&T. This gives us a yield spread to Treasuries of 6.90% – 5.26% = 1.64%, which is what we use for our valuation.

AT&T's Baseline Valuation.   We plug these figures into the Value-Pro 2000 general input screen in Exhibit 7-34. The program churns out the cost of capital screen (Exhibit 7-35), which shows AT&T to have a WACC of 6.84%. The general pro forma screen (Exhibit 7-36) shows AT&T stock to have an intrinsic value of $45.52. That is roughly 9.2% less than the August 31, 1998, closing price of $50⅛ per share.

			Valuation Date	10/14/98
	General Input Screen			
	Intrinsic Stock Value $45.52			

		General Inputs		
Company Name	AT&T			
Fiscal Year	12/31/97	Depreciation Rate (% of Rev.)		6.10%
Excess Return Period (years)	7	Investment Rate (% of Rev)		12.00%
Revenues ($mil)	$51,319	Working Capital (% of change in Rev.)		16.65%
Revenue Growth Rate (%)	11.50%	Excess Marketable Securities ($mil)		0
Net Operating Profit Margin (%)	13.58%	Other Senior Claims		0
Tax Rate (%)	37.80%			

	Cost of Capital Inputs
Current Stock Price	$50.12
Annual Dividend Per Share (e.g. $1.00)	$1.32
Shares Outstanding (mil)	1806
30-year Treasury Bond Yield (e.g 6.50%)	5.26%
Bond Yield Spread to Treasury (e.g. 1.00%)	1.64%
Preferred Stock Yield (e.g. 8.00%)	0.00%
Equity Risk Premium (e.g. 3.00%)	3.00%
Company Specific Beta (e.g. 1.00)	0.59
Value of Debt Outstanding ($mil)	$6,826.0
Value of Preferred Stock ($mil)	$0.0
Weighted Average Cost of Capital	6.84%

EXHIBIT 7-34 General Input Screen, AT&T

			Valuation Date	09/21/98
		AT&T		
	Weighted Average Cost of Capital Screen			

Cost of Common Equity	
Long Term Bond Yield	5.26%
Beta	0.59
Equity Risk Premium	3.00%
Cost of Common Equity	7.03%

Market Capitalization and After-Tax Weighted Average Cost of Capital

	Average Yield	After Tax Yield	Market Value	% Capital	After Tax Effect
Long-Term Debt	6.90%	4.29%	6,826	7.0%	0.30%
Preferred Stock	0.00%	0.00%	0	0.0%	0.00%
Common Stock	7.03%	7.03%	90,526	93.0%	6.54%
			97,352	100.0%	6.84%

EXHIBIT 7-35 WACC Screen, AT&T

AT&T Valuation—What If There Are Increased NOPMs?

Let's look at the intrinsic value of AT&T as if the planned decrease in SG&A expenses from 29% of revenue to 22% of revenue actually occurs—keeping in mind that this type of adjustment could be wrenching and could take a long time. In this valuation we assume that AT&T's NOPM increases by 2% per year for years 1, 2, and 3 and 1% in year 4, for a total increase of 7% over 4 years. The progression that AT&T's NOPM takes for our valuation is 13.58% in 1998, 15.38% in 1999, 17.58% in 2000, 19.58% in 2001, and 20.58% in 2002 and thereafter. See the custom valuation input screen in Exhibit 7-37.

With the insertion of those increasing NOPMs, all else being held equal, the program creates the custom valuation pro forma screen in Exhibit 7-38. This shows an intrinsic value for AT&T stock of $77.16, a premium of $27.04 or 54% over its current $50.12 price. Now, AT&T management has to accomplish these efficiency goals while maintaining revenue and earnings growth. Should this happen, CEO Armstrong and his top lieutenants will have earned a very substantial option and bonus package. Based on our belief that AT&T will increase significantly its NOPM, we would buy AT&T.

Valuation of McDonald's

In Chapters 4, 5 and 6, we provide an in-depth description and baseline valuation of McDonald's—so we won't waste your time and our publisher's paper costs by reproducing it here. We will, however, introduce the most recent earnings release and see how the baseline

AT&T
General Pro Forma Screen
7-year Excess Return Period

Discounted Excess Return Period FCFF $89,031 Total Corporate Value
Discounted Corporate Residual Value   ($6,826) Less Debt
Excess Marketable Securities $0 Less Preferred Stock
Total Corporate Value $3,548   0 Less Other Senior Claims

$85,484 $82,205 Total Value to Common Equity
$0.0 $45.52 Intrinsic Stock Value
$89,031

(1) Period	(2) Fiscal Year	(3) Revenues	(4) NOP	(5) Adj. Taxes	(6) NOPAT	(7) Invest.	(8) Deprec.	(9) Net Invest.	(10) Change in Working Capital	(11) FCFF	(12) Discount Factor	(13) Discounted FCFF
0	12/31/97	51,319										
1	12/31/98	57,221	7,771	2,937	4,833	6,866	3,490	3,376	983	475	0.9360	444
2	12/31/99	63,801	8,664	3,275	5,389	7,656	3,892	3,764	1,096	529	0.8761	464
3	12/31/2000	71,138	9,661	3,652	6,009	8,537	4,339	4,197	1,222	590	0.8200	484
4	12/31/2001	79,319	10,772	4,072	6,700	9,518	4,838	4,680	1,362	658	0.7675	505
5	12/31/2002	88,441	12,010	4,540	7,470	10,613	5,395	5,218	1,519	734	0.7184	527
6	12/31/2003	98,611	13,391	5,062	8,329	11,833	6,015	5,818	1,693	818	0.6724	550
7	12/31/2004	109,952	14,931	5,644	9,287	13,194	6,707	6,487	1,888	912	0.6294	574
Residual		109,952	14,931	5,644	9,287	6,707	6,707	0	0	135,820	0.6294	85,484

EXHIBIT 7-36 General Pro Forma Screen, AT&T

		Revenue	Net				Increm.	
	Fiscal	Growth	Operating	Tax	Invest.	Dep.	Working	
Period	Year	Rate	Margin	Rate	Rate	Rate	Capital	WACC
0	12/31/97							
1	12/31/98	11.50%	13.58%	37.80%	12.00%	6.10%	16.65%	6.84%
2	12/31/99	11.50%	15.58%	37.80%	12.00%	6.10%	16.65%	6.84%
3	12/31/2000	11.50%	17.58%	37.80%	12.00%	6.10%	16.65%	6.84%
4	12/31/2001	11.50%	19.58%	37.80%	12.00%	6.10%	16.65%	6.84%
5	12/31/2002	11.50%	20.58%	37.80%	12.00%	6.10%	16.65%	6.84%
6	12/31/2003	11.50%	20.58%	37.80%	12.00%	6.10%	16.65%	6.84%
7	12/31/2004	11.50%	20.58%	37.80%	12.00%	6.10%	16.65%	6.84%
Residual								6.84%

Valuation Date 10/09/98
Custom Valuation Input Screen
AT&T
Intrinsic Stock Value $77.16

EXHIBIT 7-37 Custom Valuation Input Screen, AT&T

valuation of McDonald's is affected by changing NOPM assumptions.

As we have said before, no valuation is timeless. September 1, 1998, when we valued McDonald's, was another volatile day in the stock market. The DJIA had a positive 288.36 point snap back from a 512.61 point loss a day earlier. To many participants, the recent stock market volatility, both up and down, was reminiscent of the Space Mountain ride at Disney World. McDonald's was up $3¹¹⁄₁₆ to $60¹⁄₁₆ on the day of the valuation. That rise partly offset its $6⁵⁄₁₆ per share drop a day earlier.

Baseline Valuation of McDonald's—September 1, 1998
Growth Rate—13%; Excess Return Period—7 Years;
NOPM—25.2%; WACC—7.85%

Since our last valuation, in which we came up with a value of $38.42 based on an historic growth rate of 11.1%, McDonald's announced the institution of the "home office productivity initiative" to reduce SG&A expenses (sound familiar?).

On July 20, 1998, McDonald's issued a press release in which it announced results for the 6 months ended June 30, 1998. McDonald's reported an increase in revenues of 10% and an increase of operating income, excluding special charges, of 7% over the similar 6-month period in 1997. Further, it announced that as a result of the productivity initiative, McDonald's expects to save approximately $100 million in SG&A expenses per year.

First, let's review the bidding for our McDonald's valuation. We start with variables that have not changed since our last valuation of

AT&T
Custom Pro Forma Screen
7-year Excess Return Period

			Discounted Excess Return Period FCFF	$16,633	Total Corporate Value					$146,180		
			Discounted Corporate Residual Value	$129,547	Less Debt					($6,826)		
			Excess Marketable Securities	$0.0	Less Preferred Stock					$0		
			Total Corporate Value	$146,180	Less Other Senior Claims					0		
					Total Value to Common Equity					$139,354		
					Intrinsic Stock Value					$77.16		

(1)	(2)	(3)	(4)	(5)	(6)	(7)	(8)	(9)	(10)	(11)	(12)	(13)
Period	Fiscal Year	Revenues	NOP	Adj. Taxes	NOPAT	Invest.	Deprec.	Net Invest.	Change in Working Capital	FCFF	Discount Factor	Discounted FCFF
0	12/31/97	51,319										
1	12/31/98	57,221	7,771	2,937	4,833	6,866	3,490	3,376	983	475	0.9360	444
2	12/31/99	63,801	9,940	3,757	6,183	7,656	3,892	3,764	1,096	1,323	0.8761	1,159
3	12/31/2000	71,138	12,506	4,727	7,779	8,537	4,339	4,197	1,222	2,360	0.8200	1,935
4	12/31/2001	79,319	15,531	5,871	9,660	9,518	4,838	4,680	1,362	3,618	0.7675	2,777
5	12/31/2002	88,441	18,201	6,880	11,321	10,613	5,395	5,218	1,519	4,584	0.7184	3,293
6	12/31/2003	98,611	20,294	7,671	12,623	11,833	6,015	5,818	1,693	5,112	0.6724	3,437
7	12/31/2004	109,952	22,628	8,553	14,075	13,194	6,707	6,487	1,888	5,699	0.6294	3,587
Residual		109,952	22,628	8,553	14,075	6,707	6,707	0	0	205,830	0.6294	129,547

EXHIBIT 7-38 Custom Pro Forma Screen, AT&T

169

June 1, 1998. We keep the following variables the same: revenues—$11,409; excess return period—7 years; net operating profit margin—25.2%; income tax rate—31.8%; investment rate—20.6%; depreciation rate—7%; incremental working capital rate (–1.0%); equity risk premium—3%; and value of debt outstanding—$4,931 million.

Variables that have changed are as follows. We pulled up the McDonald's median 5-year EPS growth rate from Zacks. We found that Zacks surveyed 17 analysts and found growth rates for McDonald's ranging from 9% to 15%, with a median of 13%—which is the revenue growth rate that we use in our valuation.

S&P Comstock gave us an updated number of 687.43 million shares outstanding, which reflects the results of the stock buyback program actively instituted by McDonald's. McDonald's repurchased $516 million in common shares during the 6 months ended June 30, 1998. S&P Comstock also gave us a beta estimate of 0.95 as compared with the Market Guide beta estimate of 0.96. We use the 0.96 beta in our valuation.

We also use the current 30-year U.S. Treasury Bond yield of 5.35%, down from the 5.8% rate of our previous valuation. And our bond yield spread to Treasury has been changed to 1.55%, giving a debt cost to McDonald's of 6.9%.

We plug all these numbers into the Value Pro 2000 general input screen shown in Exhibit 7-39. The weighted average cost of capital screen in Exhibit 7-40 shows a WACC for McDonald's of 7.85%. The general pro forma screen in Exhibit 7-41 shows an intrinsic value of $48.39.

Our value of $48.39 is still well short of—in fact, 19.5% below—the $60.06 closing price for McDonald's. What does the market know or believe that we don't?

McDonald's Valuation—What If There Are Increased NOPMs?

After looking a little further at the earnings press release to quantify the potential impact of the "home office productivity initiative," we found that the company expects to save $100 million in SG&A expenses per year as a result of the initiative. That number sounds reasonable for a company that had $1,450 million in SG&A expenses in 1997. But what exactly does that mean in terms of the stock's intrinsic value? We take it to mean that, all other things equal, SG&A will decrease by $100 million per year and net operating profits will increase by $100 million per year, thereby increasing McDonald's NOPM.

Valuation Date 10/14/98

General Input Screen
Intrinsic Stock Value $48.39

General Inputs
Company Name McDonald's Corporation

Fiscal Year	12/31/97	Depreciation Rate (% of Rev.)	7.00%
Excess Return Period (years)	7	Investment Rate (% of Rev)	20.60%
Revenues ($mil)	$11,409	Working Capital (% of change in Rev.)	-1.20%
Revenue Growth Rate (%)	13.00%	Excess Marketable Securities ($mil)	0
Net Operating Profit Margin (%)	25.20%	Other Senior Claims	0
Tax Rate (%)	31.80%		

Cost of Capital Inputs

Current Stock Price	$60.06
Annual Dividend Per Share (e.g. $1.00)	$0.36
Shares Outstanding (mil)	687.4
30-year Treasury Bond Yield (e.g 6.50%)	5.35%
Bond Yield Spread to Treasury (e.g. 1.00%)	1.55%
Preferred Stock Yield (e.g. 8.00%)	0.00%
Equity Risk Premium (e.g. 3.00%)	3.00%
Company Specific Beta (e.g. 1.00)	0.96
Value of Debt Outstanding ($mil)	$4,931.0
Value of Preferred Stock ($mil)	$0.0
Weighted Average Cost of Capital	7.85%

EXHIBIT 7-39 General Input Screen, McDonald's

How much will that $100 million initiative increase NOPM? The answer is **not very much.** If we look back at Table 4-4, which calculates a 25.2% average NOPM for McDonald's, we find that the addition of $100 million per year in NOP will increase NOPM to 26.2%—an increased NOPM of only 1%. What does that 1% increase do for McDonald's intrinsic stock value? Very little! When we plug 26.2% into the NOPM slot for McDonald's, the program churns out the ValuePro 2000 general pro forma screen shown in Exhibit 7-42. The intrinsic stock value for McDonald's is now $51.35, an increase in value of about $3.

Valuation Date 09/21/98

McDonald's Corporation
Weighted Average Cost of Capital Screen

Cost of Common Equity

Long Term Bond Yield	5.35%
Beta	0.96
Equity Risk Premium	3.00%
Cost of Common Equity	8.23%

Market Capitalization and After-Tax Weighted Average Cost of Capital

	Average Yield	After Tax Yield	Market Value	% Capital	After Tax Effect
Long-Term Debt	6.90%	4.71%	4,931	10.7%	0.50%
Preferred Stock	0.00%	0.00%	0	0.0%	0.00%
Common Stock	8.23%	8.23%	41,285	89.3%	7.35%
			46,216	100.0%	7.85%

EXHIBIT 7-40 WACC Screen, McDonald's

McDonald's Corporation
General Pro Forma Screen
7-year Excess Return Period

Valuation Date 09/21/98

	Discounted Excess Return Period FCFF	$3,600	Total Corporate Value	$38,197
	Discounted Corporate Residual Value	$34,597	Less Debt	($4,931)
	Excess Marketable Securities	$0.0	Less Preferred Stock	$0
	Total Corporate Value	$38,197	Less Other Senior Claims	0
			Total Value to Common Equity	$33,266
			Intrinsic Stock Value	$48.39

(1)	(2)	(3)	(4)	(5)	(6)	(7)	(8)	(9)	(10)	(11)	(12)	(13)
Period	Fiscal Year	Revenues	NOP	Adj. Taxes	NOPAT	Invest.	Deprec.	Net Invest.	Change in Working Capital	FCFF	Discount Factor	Discounted FCFF
0	12/31/97	11,409										
1	12/31/98	12,892	3,249	1,033	2,216	2,656	902	1,753	-18	480	0.9272	445
2	12/31/99	14,568	3,671	1,167	2,504	3,001	1,020	1,981	-20	543	0.8597	466
3	12/31/2000	16,462	4,148	1,319	2,829	3,391	1,152	2,239	-23	613	0.7971	489
4	12/31/2001	18,602	4,688	1,491	3,197	3,832	1,302	2,530	-26	693	0.7390	512
5	12/31/2002	21,020	5,297	1,684	3,613	4,330	1,471	2,859	-29	783	0.6852	536
6	12/31/2003	23,753	5,986	1,903	4,082	4,893	1,663	3,230	-33	885	0.6353	562
7	12/31/2004	26,841	6,764	2,151	4,613	5,529	1,879	3,650	-37	999	0.5890	589
Residual		26,841	6,764	2,151	4,613	1,879	1,879	0	0	58,734	0.5890	34,597

EXHIBIT 7-41   General Pro Forma Screen, McDonald's

172

McDonald's Corporation
General Pro Forma Screen
7-year Excess Return Period

Discounted Excess Return Period FCFF						$40,229						
Discounted Corporate Residual Value						($4,931)						
Excess Marketable Securities						$0						
Total Corporate Value												

$4,259 Total Corporate Value
$35,970 Less Debt
$0.0 Less Preferred Stock
$40,229 Less Other Senior Claims
Total Value to Common Equity   0
$35,298
Intrinsic Stock Value   **$61.35**

(1)	(2)	(3)	(4)	(5)	(6)	(7)	(8)	(9)	(10)	(11)	(12)	(13)
Period	Fiscal Year	Revenues	NOP	Adj. Taxes	NOPAT	Invest.	Deprec.	Net Invest.	Change in Working Capital	FCFF	Discount Factor	Discounted FCFF
0	12/31/97	11,409										
1	12/31/98	12,892	3,378	1,074	2,304	2,656	902	1,753	-18	568	0.9272	527
2	12/31/99	14,568	3,817	1,214	2,603	3,001	1,020	1,981	-20	642	0.8597	552
3	12/31/2000	16,462	4,313	1,372	2,941	3,391	1,152	2,239	-23	725	0.7971	578
4	12/31/2001	18,602	4,874	1,550	3,324	3,832	1,302	2,530	-26	820	0.7390	606
5	12/31/2002	21,020	5,507	1,751	3,756	4,330	1,471	2,859	-29	926	0.6852	635
6	12/31/2003	23,753	6,223	1,979	4,244	4,893	1,663	3,230	-33	1,047	0.6353	665
7	12/31/2004	26,841	7,032	2,236	4,796	5,529	1,879	3,650	-37	1,183	0.5890	697
Residual		26,841	7,032	2,236	4,796	1,879	1,879	0	0	61,065		35,970

EXHIBIT 7-42 General Pro Forma Screen: Increased NOPM, McDonald's

Where does NOPM for McDonald's have to be, all else being equal, to justify its current price of $60.06? After playing around with the NOPM input in the ValuePro general input screen, we found that McDonald's stock price *implied* an NOPM of approximately 29.2% to justify a stock value of $60.06. Once again, we are not in a hurry to buy McDonald's stock at current price levels.

Where Do We Go from Here?

We hope that, in going over our examples, you see a pattern in our approach to valuation. We start with the most recent audited financial statements and the most recent quarterly earnings release of the corporation that we're going to value to get a sense of its revenues, growth potential, NOPMs, investment and working capital requirements, and tax rates.

Then we look at capital structure and market capitalization. We find risk parameters by getting estimates of the company's beta and costs of debt and preferred stock. We forecast the company's free cash flows, discount them at the company's weighted average cost of capital, net out other claims, and calculate the intrinsic value of the stock.

The calculations involved in making the valuation by hand are easy but tedious. A better way to value stocks under the discounted cash flow method is to use a spreadsheet program like ValuePro 2000, or to write your own integrated spreadsheet computer program similar to ValuePro 2000. In Chapter 8 we describe a method by which you can do just that. If writing software is not your strength, we'll show you how and where to find the ValuePro 2000 software.

Notes

1. "The Year of the Deal," *Business Week,* July 13, 1998, pp. 53–54. Information was provided to *Business Week* for the ranking of the Global 1000 by Geneva-based Morgan Stanley Capital International.

2. 1996 annual report of Intel Corporation, p. 17.

3. A. Reinhardt and P. Burrows, "It's Not Easy Being Cheap," *Business Week,* August 17, 1998, pp. 61–62.

A Spreadsheet Valuation Approach

The discounted cash flow valuation method consists of a set of simple calculations that allow an investor to value a stock. Throughout the text we have shown in detail the calculations required to derive cost of capital, cash flows, and an intrinsic stock value. In this chapter we outline the steps necessary to develop a valuation model based on the DCF method. The valuation model can be written using a spreadsheet program such as Excel or Lotus.

A valuation model enables the investor to perform scenario analysis and monitor changes in stock values as expectations change. As we have discussed, the value of any stock can be traced to five *cash flow measures*. Since the valuation model is only as accurate as its inputs, it is helpful for the investor to be able to test the sensitivity of inputs. It is useful to calculate implied levels of cash flow measures necessary to generate a current stock price. A powerful valuation model will allow the investor to determine, for example, the implied revenue growth rate that supports the current stock price.

In this chapter, we begin by outlining the inputs necessary to generate valuations. Using these inputs, we develop a cost of capital screen, a pro forma screen with annual cash flows over the excess return period, and a stock valuation. As an example we value Intel Corporation over a 10-year excess return period.

Layout of the Model

The first and most important step in developing a valuation model is to determine screen layout. It is important to set up the model with a minimum number of screens and a logical sequence of movement between screens. Separating input and output screens is generally a good starting point. Our valuation model is segmented into five major screens—two input screens and three output screens. The starting point of a valuation is the general input screen, in which the user inputs several basic data entries sufficient to value the company. The information from the general input screen is used to generate values on the weighted average cost of capital screen. The general inputs and resulting WACC are used to develop a general pro forma screen for the excess return period.

A second input screen, the custom valuation input screen, contains custom inputs. This screen is used to generate a detailed valuation and is used in conjunction with the pro forma screen to generate a custom pro forma screen. The valuation generated from the general inputs assumes static cash flow measures over the excess return period, whereas the valuation generated from the custom input screen allows for different cash flow measures in each period. Exhibit 8-1 displays a flowchart for an easy-to-use valuation model.

General Input Screen

In Chapter 6, we discussed information sources that can be tapped when starting a valuation. The inputs necessary to generate the intrinsic value of most stocks can be found in company financial statements, most of which are available on the Internet. The general inputs are used to calculate cost of capital and to generate a pro forma screen. In our valuation model, we have condensed on one input screen the necessary inputs to generate a basic valuation. We subdivide the inputs into two

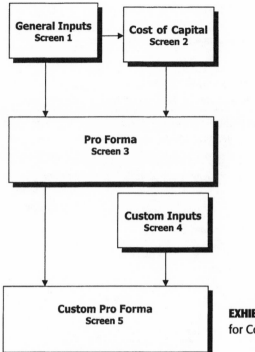

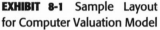

EXHIBIT 8-1 Sample Layout for Computer Valuation Model

categories: general inputs, which are used to compute cash flows or are descriptive, and cost-of-capital inputs, which are used to compute a discount factor. The basic inputs are listed in detail in Exhibit 8-2.

Exhibit 8-3 depicts a sample layout for the ValuePro 2000 general input screen for Intel Corporation. All the necessary inputs for valuing a stock are on the general input screen. Separating the input screen into general inputs and cost of capital inputs simplifies data entry. The intrinsic stock value at the top of the screen comes from the general pro forma screen described later in the chapter.

Weighted Average Cost of Capital Screen

The second step in the layout is to create a screen that calculates market capitalization and a weighted average cost of capital (WACC). This screen requires no inputs. All the information necessary to generate the screen has been entered on the general input screen.

EXHIBIT 8-2 Required Inputs for a Basic Valuation

General Inputs		
Input	**Description**	**Format**
Company name	Used to identify the valuation on all output pages so that printouts can be easily identified	Text
Fiscal year	Nearest fiscal year reporting date used as a starting point for generating annual pro forma numbers	Date: dd/mm/yy
Excess return period	Determines the number of annual periods for the pro forma	Number rounded to the nearest year
Revenues	Most recent fiscal year revenues	$ millions
Revenue growth rate	Estimated annual revenue growth rate over the excess return period	Percent
Net operating profit margin	Most recent net operating profit margin	Percent
Tax rate	Current corporate income tax rate	Percent
Depreciation rate	Most recent annual depreciation rate as a percent of revenues	Percent
Investment rate	Fixed capital investment rate as a percent of revenues	Percent
Working capital	Change in working capital investment as a percent of change in revenue	Percent
Excess marketable securities	Cash and securities in excess of that needed for operations	$ millions
Other senior claims	Unfunded pension liabilities, etc.	$ millions
Cost-of-Capital Inputs		
Current stock price	Most recent market price	Dollars, two decimal places
Shares outstanding	Total common shares outstanding	Millions
30-year Treasury Bond yield	Current yield on 30-year Treasury Bond	Percent
Bond yield spread to Treasuries	Corporate bond spread as a spread to the 30-year Treasury yield	Percent

EXHIBIT 8-2   Required Inputs for a Basic Valuation (Continued)

Input	Description	Format
Preferred stock yield	Yield on preferred stock	Percent
Equity risk premium	Current equity risk premium required by the market	Percent
Company-specific beta	Estimated beta	Two decimal places
Value of debt outstanding	Value of debt outstanding	$ millions
Value of preferred stock	Value of preferred stock outstanding	$ millions

Exhibit 8-4 shows a sample WACC screen for Intel Corporation. The screen is split between the cost of common equity and the market capitalization and after-tax weighted average cost of capital. The cost of common equity is generated from the capital asset pricing model described in Chapter 5. The cost of common equity is calculated as follows:

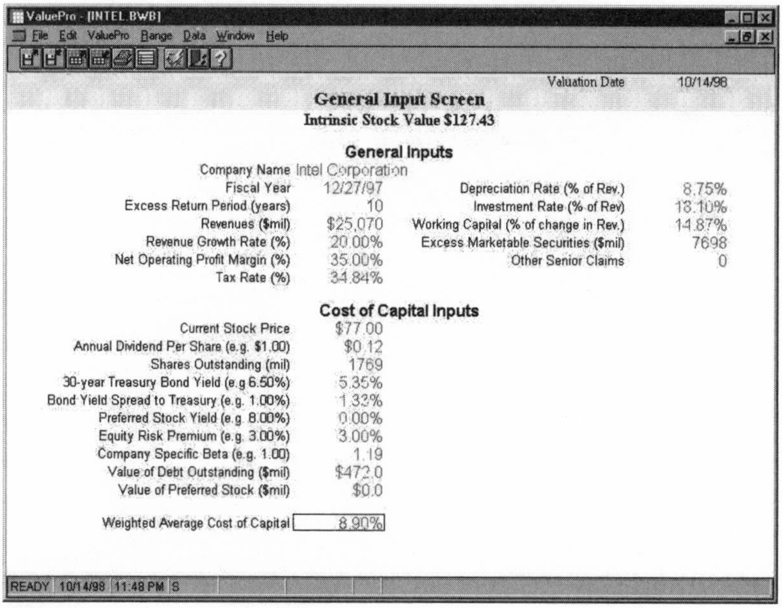

EXHIBIT 8-3   General Input Screen

Cost of Common Equity = Long-Term Bond Yield
+ (Beta × Equity Risk Premium)

For Intel Corporation, the cost of common equity is calculated
from the number on the general input screen as:

Cost of Common Equity = 5.35% + (1.19 × 3%) = 8.92%

The after-tax weighted average cost of capital is derived using the cost
of common equity from the top of the screen and inputs from the general
input screen. Recall that the WACC is weighted by the amounts of debt,
preferred stock, and common stock and adjusted by the tax benefits of
the debt. We calculate the WACC using five columns of numbers for each
type of capital—long-term debt, preferred stock, and common stock.

Average yield is taken directly from the general inputs screen.

After-tax yield is the long-term debt yield adjusted by the tax rate.
For Intel Corporation, the income tax rate is 34.84%; therefore, the
after-tax yield on the long-term debt is 6.68% × (1 − .3484) = 4.35%.
Since preferred stock and common stock have no tax benefits, the
yields are simply carried over from the previous column.

				Valuation Date	10/08/98
		Intel Corporation			
		Weighted Average Cost of Capital Screen			
Cost of Common Equity					
Long-Term Bond Yield	5.35%				
Beta	1.19				
Equity Risk Premium	3.00%				
Cost of Common Equity	8.92%				

Market Capitalization and After-Tax Weighted Average Cost of Capital

	Average Yield	After-Tax Yield	Market Value	% Capital	After-Tax Effect
Long-Term Debt	6.68%	4.35%	472	0.3%	0.02%
Preferred Stock	0.00%	0.00%	0	0.0%	0.00%
Common Stock	8.92%	8.92%	136,213	99.6%	8.89%
			136,685	100.0%	8.90%

READY   10/8/98   9:14 PM   S

EXHIBIT 8-4   WACC Screen

Market value is taken directly from the general inputs screen.

% capital represents the appropriate weight for each capitalization. Intel Corporation has 0.3% long-term debt, 0.0% preferred stock, and 99.6% common stock.

After-tax effect is found by multiplying the after-tax yield by the appropriate % capital. The final step is to sum the After-Tax Effect column to arrive at a WACC. For Intel Corporation, the WACC is 8.9%.

General Pro Forma Screen

Using the WACC and the general inputs, we have enough information to produce a general pro forma and stock valuation. In the general pro forma screen, we lay out cash flows for each year in the excess return period and calculate a residual value. Exhibit 8-5 shows the general pro forma screen for Intel Corporation based on the general inputs in Exhibit 8-3. The screen is divided into a valuation summary and the cash flows per annum and residual value that support that value.

Intel Corporation
General Pro Forma Screen
10-year Excess Return Period

Valuation Date 10/08/98

		Discounted Excess Return Period FCFF	$48,769	Total Corporate Value	$225,890
		Discounted Corporate Residual Value	$169,423	Less Debt	($472)
		Excess Marketable Securities	$7,698.0	Less Preferred Stock	$0
		Total Corporate Value	$225,890	Less Other Senior Claims	0
				Total Value to Common Equity	$225,418
				Intrinsic Stock Value	**$127.43**

(1)	(2)	(3)	(4)	(5)	(6)	(7)	(8)	(9)	(10)	(11)	(12)	(13)
Period	Fiscal Year	Revenues	NOP	Adj. Taxes	NOPAT	Invest.	Deprec.	Net Invest.	Change in Working Capital	FCFF	Discount Factor	Discounted FCFF
0	12/27/97	25,070										
1	12/27/98	30,084	10,529	3,668	6,861	5,445	2,632	2,813	746	3,303	0.9182	3,033
2	12/27/99	36,101	12,635	4,402	8,233	6,534	3,159	3,375	895	3,963	0.8432	3,341
3	12/27/2000	43,321	15,162	5,283	9,880	7,841	3,791	4,051	1,074	4,756	0.7742	3,682
4	12/27/2001	51,985	18,195	6,339	11,856	9,409	4,549	4,861	1,288	5,707	0.7109	4,057
5	12/27/2002	62,382	21,834	7,607	14,227	11,291	5,458	5,833	1,546	6,846	0.6528	4,470
6	12/27/2003	74,859	26,201	9,128	17,072	13,549	6,550	6,999	1,855	8,218	0.5994	4,926
7	12/27/2004	89,830	31,441	10,954	20,487	16,259	7,860	8,399	2,226	9,861	0.5504	5,428
8	12/27/2005	107,796	37,729	13,145	24,584	19,511	9,432	10,079	2,672	11,834	0.5054	5,981
9	12/27/2006	129,356	45,274	15,774	29,501	23,413	11,319	12,095	3,206	14,200	0.4641	6,590
10	12/27/2007	155,227	54,329	18,928	35,401	28,096	13,582	14,514	3,847	17,040	0.4261	7,262
Residual		155,227	54,329	18,928	35,401	13,582	13,582	0	0	397,576	0.4261	169,423

EXHIBIT 8-5 General Pro Forma Screen

The cash flows on the bottom of the screen are necessary to calculate the intrinsic stock value. The necessary steps to derive the discounted FCFF and residual value are given in the 13 columns running across the bottom of the screen. Exhibit 8-6 shows the calculations for the excess return period and the residual value by column.

Once the discounted FCFF and residual value are calculated following the steps outlined in Exhibit 8-6, the final valuation step is to

EXHIBIT 8-6 Calculations in the General Pro Forma Screen

Column	Title	Excess Return Period*	Residual Value
(1)	Period	Year in excess return period	Residual
(2)	Fiscal year	Fiscal year end associated with period	—
(3)	Revenues	Revenues for each fiscal year adjusted by revenue growth rate in each period	Revenues from final year in excess return period
(4)	NOP	(3) × Net operating profit margin	NOP from final year in excess return period
(5)	Adjusted taxes	(4) × tax rate	Adjusted taxes from final year in excess return period
(6)	NOPAT	(4) – (5)	NOPAT from final year in excess return period
(7)	Investment	Investment rate × (3)	Depreciation from final year in excess return period
(8)	Depreciation	Depreciation rate × (3)	Depreciation from final year in excess return period
(9)	Net investment	(7) – (8)	0
(10)	Change in working capital	Working capital rate × change in (3) in each fiscal year	0
(11)	FCFF	(6) – (9) – (10)	NOPAT/WACC
(12)	Discount factor	Discount factor for each period using WACC as discount rate	Discount factor from final year in excess return period
(13)	Discounted FCFF	(11) × (12)	(11) × (12)

*numbers in parenthesis refer to columns.

calculate intrinsic stock value. In our valuation model, we have broken the final valuation step into total corporate value and total value to common equity. Total corporate value is found by taking the sum of the discounted FCFF over the excess return period, the discounted corporate residual value, and excess marketable securities (from the general input screen). The second step is to subtract (from the total corporate value) debt, preferred stock, and other senior claims, all of which come from the general input screen. The resulting value is total value to common equity. This value divided by shares outstanding results in intrinsic stock value. For Intel Corporation the intrinsic stock value based on the inputs in the general input screen is $127.43.

Custom Valuation Screens

The general pro forma screen generates stock values on the basis of the simplified assumption of constant WACC and cash flow measures over the excess return period. In many cases, however, more detailed information is available and an investor will want to generate stock values under changing assumptions.

The revenue growth rate for Intel Corporation is assumed to be constant at 20% over the 10-year excess return period in the general pro forma screen shown in Exhibit 8-5. If revenue growth is expected to change over that time period, a more detailed valuation screen is necessary to account for that change. A custom valuation input screen allows for adjustments in WACC and cash flow measures over the entire excess return period.

Exhibit 8-7 depicts a custom valuation input screen for Intel Corporation. There are seven ratios or rates that affect the valuation of a stock over the excess return period—revenue growth rate, net operating profit margin, tax rate, investment rate, depreciation rate, incremental working capital rate, and WACC. The custom valuation input screen allows changes to be made in any of these measures.

In Exhibit 8-7, the default rates from the general inputs screen are shown and the resulting intrinsic stock value at the top of the screen is the same as the value generated on the general pro forma screen. Exhibit 8-8 presents a custom valuation input screen with the revenue growth rate increasing in each fiscal year by 0.5%. The resulting intrinsic stock value is $148.65.

ValuePro - [INTEL.BWB]

File Edit ValuePro Range Data Window Help

Valuation Date 10/08/98

Custom Valuation Input Screen
Intel Corporation
Intrinsic Stock Value $127.43

Period	Fiscal Year	Revenue Growth Rate	Net Operating Margin	Tax Rate	Invest. Rate	Dep. Rate	Increm. Working Capital	WACC
0	12/27/97							
1	12/27/98	20.00%	35.00%	34.84%	18.10%	8.75%	14.87%	8.90%
2	12/27/99	20.00%	35.00%	34.84%	18.10%	8.75%	14.87%	8.90%
3	12/27/2000	20.00%	35.00%	34.84%	18.10%	8.75%	14.87%	8.90%
4	12/27/2001	20.00%	35.00%	34.84%	18.10%	8.75%	14.87%	8.90%
5	12/27/2002	20.00%	35.00%	34.84%	18.10%	8.75%	14.87%	8.90%
6	12/27/2003	20.00%	35.00%	34.84%	18.10%	6.75%	14.87%	6.90%
7	12/27/2004	20.00%	35.00%	34.84%	18.10%	8.75%	14.87%	8.90%
8	12/27/2005	20.00%	35.00%	34.84%	18.10%	8.75%	14.87%	8.90%
9	12/27/2006	20.00%	35.00%	34.84%	18.10%	8.75%	14.87%	8.90%
10	12/27/2007	20.00%	35.00%	34.84%	18.10%	8.75%	14.87%	8.90%
Residual								8.90%

READY 10/8/98 9:24 PM F(V)

EXHIBIT 8-7 Custom Valuation Input Screen

ValuePro - [INTEL.BWB]

File Edit ValuePro Range Data Window Help

Valuation Date 10/08/98

Custom Valuation Input Screen
Intel Corporation
Intrinsic Stock Value $148.65

Period	Fiscal Year	Revenue Growth Rate	Net Operating Margin	Tax Rate	Invest. Rate	Dep. Rate	Increm. Working Capital	WACC
0	12/27/97							
1	12/27/98	20.00%	35.00%	34.84%	18.10%	8.75%	14.87%	8.90%
2	12/27/99	20.50%	35.00%	34.84%	18.10%	8.75%	14.87%	8.90%
3	12/27/2000	21.00%	35.00%	34.84%	18.10%	8.75%	14.87%	8.90%
4	12/27/2001	21.50%	35.00%	34.84%	18.10%	8.75%	14.87%	8.90%
5	12/27/2002	22.00%	35.00%	34.84%	18.10%	8.75%	14.87%	8.90%
6	12/27/2003	22.50%	35.00%	34.84%	18.10%	8.75%	14.87%	8.90%
7	12/27/2004	23.00%	35.00%	34.84%	18.10%	8.75%	14.87%	8.90%
8	12/27/2005	23.50%	35.00%	34.84%	18.10%	8.75%	14.87%	8.90%
9	12/27/2006	24.00%	35.00%	34.84%	13.10%	8.75%	14.87%	8.90%
10	12/27/2007	24.50%	35.00%	34.84%	18.10%	8.75%	14.87%	8.90%
Residual								8.90%

READY 10/8/98 9:22 PM F(V)

EXHIBIT 8-8 Custom Valuation Input Screen: Changes in Revenue Growth Rate

ValuePro - [INTEL.BWB]

File Edit ValuePro Range Data Window Help

Valuation Date   10/08/98

Intel Corporation
Custom Pro Forma Screen
10-year Excess Return Period

Discounted Excess Return Period FCFF	$51,861 Total Corporate Value	$263,427
Discounted Corporate Residual Value	$203,868 Less Debt	($472)
Excess Marketable Securities	$7,698.0 Less Preferred Stock	$0
Total Corporate Value	$263,427 Less Other Senior Claims	0
	Total Value to Common Equity	$262,955
	Intrinsic Stock Value	$148.65

(1)	(2)	(3)	(4)	(5)	(6)	(7)	(8)	(9)	(10)	(11)	(12)	(13)
Period	Fiscal Year	Revenues	NOP	Adj. Taxes	NOPAT	Invest.	Deprec.	Net Invest.	Change in Working Capital	FCFF	Discount Factor	Discounted FCFF
0	12/27/97	25,070										
1	12/27/98	30,084	10,529	3,668	6,861	5,445	2,632	2,813	746	3,303	0.9182	3,033
2	12/27/99	36,251	12,688	4,420	8,267	6,561	3,172	3,389	917	3,961	0.8432	3,340
3	12/27/2000	43,864	15,352	5,349	10,004	7,939	3,838	4,101	1,132	4,770	0.7742	3,693
4	12/27/2001	53,295	18,653	6,499	12,154	9,646	4,663	4,983	1,402	5,769	0.7109	4,101
5	12/27/2002	65,020	22,757	7,928	14,828	11,769	5,689	6,079	1,743	7,006	0.6528	4,573
6	12/27/2003	79,649	27,877	9,712	18,165	14,416	6,969	7,447	2,175	8,542	0.5994	5,120
7	12/27/2004	97,968	34,289	11,946	22,343	17,732	8,572	9,160	2,724	10,459	0.5504	5,758
8	12/27/2005	120,991	42,347	14,754	27,593	21,899	10,587	11,313	3,423	12,857	0.5054	6,498
9	12/27/2006	150,029	52,510	18,294	34,216	27,155	13,127	14,028	4,318	15,870	0.4641	7,365
10	12/27/2007	186,786	65,375	22,777	42,598	33,808	16,344	17,464	5,466	19,668	0.4261	8,381
Residual		186,786	65,375	22,777	42,598	16,344	16,344	0	0	478,405	0.4261	203,868

READY 10/8/98 9:27 PM F(V)

EXHIBIT 8-9   Custom Pro Forma Screen

The resulting stock value must be generated on an additional pro forma screen, which we refer to as a custom pro forma screen and present in Exhibit 8-9. The custom pro forma screen is set up in the same format as the general pro forma screen; however, the appropriate WACC and cash flow measures are incorporated in each valuation step. For example, in column 3 revenues must be adjusted by the growth rate on the custom valuation input screen for the appropriate year in the excess return period.

How to Purchase the ValuePro 2000 Software

The valuation model outlined in this book can be applied most efficiently through a computer and spreadsheet software. When a valuation model is developed on the computer, the most important step is proper planning and layout. You should be able to enter data simply and move between screens in a logical sequence.

With the steps outlined in this chapter, you can create a simple and powerful investment valuation tool. The software allows you to avoid simplifying assumptions such as constant growth rates. Custom valuation screens will accomplish this goal. Other features can be added to the program, such as measures of sensitivity to key value determinants. Additional time spent with the computer model will yield more accurate valuations and a more successful investment strategy.

The ValuePro 2000 software, which is used throughout this book, can be purchased on our Internet site at http://www.valuepro.net/, or you can call us at 215-283-5250.

Web Site Addresses

AT&T (http://www.att.com/)

Altavista (http://www.altavista.digital.com/)

Amazon.com (http://www.amazon.com/)

American Express (http://www.americanexpress.com/)

America Online (http://www.aol.com/)

Barron's (http://www.barrons.com/)

Business Week (http://www.businessweek.com/)

Bloomberg Financial (http://www.bloomberg.com/)

Bonds-Online (http://www.bonds-online.com/)

Computer Associates (http://www.cai.com/)

Consolidated Edison (http://www.coned.com/)

Disclosure (http://www.disclosure-investor.com/)

Dell (http://www.dell.com)

Elliott Wave Chart Page (http://www.wavechart.com/)

EntreMed (http://www.entremed.com/)

Excite (http://www.excite.com/)

Federal Reserve Board of Governors (http://www.bog.frb.fed.us/
   releases/H15/update/)
First Call (http://www1.firstcall.com/)
Hoover's (http://www.hoovers.com/)
Hot Bot (http://www.search.hotbot.com/)
IBES (http://www.ibes.com/)
Infoseek (http://www.guide-p.infoseek.com/)
Intel (http://www.intel.com/)
Investor's Business Daily (http://www.investors.com/)
Lycos (http://www.lycos.com/)
Market Guide (http://www.marketguide.com/)
McDonald's (http://www.mcdonalds.com/)
McGraw-Hill (http://www.mcgraw-hill.com/)
Microsoft Corporation (http://www.microsoft.com/)
Microsoft Network (http://www.msn.com/)
Morningstar (http://www.morningstar.com/)
Motley Fool (http://www.fool.com/)
Netscape (http://www.netscape.com/)
Securities and Exchange Commission (http://www.sec.gov/)
Short-Term Stock Selector (http://www.flash.net/~hesler/)
S&P Comstock (http://www.spcomstock.com/)
Stock Valuation with Sense (http://www.stocksense.com/)
The New York Times (http://www.nytimes.com/)
The Wall Street Journal (http://www.wsj.com/)
Value Investing (http://www.cyberramp.net/~investor/)
Value Line (http://www.valueline.com/)
ValuePro (http://www.valuepro.net/)
Wall Street City (http://www.wallstreetcity.com/)
Wal-Mart (http://www.wal-mart.com/)
Warner-Lambert (http://www.warner-lambert.com/)
Yahoo (http://www.yahoo.com/)
Zacks (http://www.zacks.com/)

Stock Market Efficiency

tock market efficiency has been the most tested proposition in finance and economics over the past 30 years. Stated simply, stock market efficiency implies that a stock's price is its fair value. In other words, if McDonald's sells for $60 per share, then that is what the stock is worth.

Eugene Fama of the University of Chicago first introduced the term "efficient market" in a 1965 paper where he defined it as

A market where there are large numbers of rational, profit-maximizers actively competing with each other, trying to predict future market values of individual securities, and where important current information is almost freely available to all participants. In an efficient market, on the average, competition will cause the full effects of new information on intrinsic values to be reflected "instantaneously" in actual prices.[1]

In the notion of stock market efficiency, information is critical. In this age of the Internet and CNBC, we are constantly bombarded with new information that affects stock prices. Each day, stock prices react to announcements affecting the economy (housing starts, money supply, unemployment figures), industries (new products/services, technology developments, new competition), and individual firms (earnings reports, dividend announcements, new ventures). According to the notion of stock market efficiency, since this information is free and publicly available, it should be reflected very quickly (*instantaneously*) in stock prices.

Empirical tests of stock market efficiency evaluate whether stock prices reflect information about securities. These information tests fall into three categories:

The Information in Past Stock Prices and Trading.   The first type of test is aimed at determining if trends exist in day-to-day stock price changes or if daily stock price movements are independent. This is the well-known *random walk hypothesis.*

Public Information and Stock Prices.   A second test of market efficiency asks whether stock prices reflect public information. One way this proposition is assessed is to see how quickly public information disclosures—such as earnings reports or takeover announcements—are reflected in stock prices. Another method of evaluating public information and stock prices is to examine whether future stock returns are associated with available public information such as stock price/earnings (P/E) ratios.

All Information and Stock Prices.   A final type of test of market efficiency involves assessing whether stock prices reflect nonpublic information—that is, information not available to the investment community. Examples of such information are the trades of corporate managers and directors who clearly know more about a firm's prospects than the investing public.

If the stock market is efficient in pricing stocks, the implications are rather ominous for stock investors. If there are no trends in daily stock price movements (i.e., daily stock price changes are independent), then technical trading rules such 200-day moving averages and point-and-figure charts are of no use to investors. If stock prices react so quickly to corporate news announcements that this information cannot be used to earn abnormal stock returns, then buying on news of good earnings or a takeover offer will not be beneficial to investors.

Likewise, the recommendations of stock market analysts who appear nightly on CNN and CNBC are fruitless, since their stock opinions are based on the same public information that other investors have. Finally, if the stock trades of corporate officers and directors do not yield abnormally good results, then we may presume that the stock market is exceptional in its ability to use information to price securities.

Tests of Stock Market Efficiency

Weak-Form Efficiency

Weak-form efficiency implies that stock prices reflect the information contained in the history of past stock prices and trading. According to this notion, daily stock price changes are independent; thus it is useless for investors to try to detect and exploit trends in stock prices. This is the random walk hypothesis, according to which stock prices are random and unpredictable.

Why might we expect stock prices to follow a random walk? The reason is that the stock market is full of knowledgeable and aggressive investors who attempt to find simple schemes to make money in the market. If a particular trend were to prove successful in predicting future prices, then other investors would attempt to exploit the scheme. Yet such activity would be self-defeating, since it would cause stock prices to reflect the scheme, thereby eliminating the trend.

Consider the coin toss experiment highlighted in the well-known MBA corporate finance textbook by Richard Brealey and Stewart Meyers.[2] Now examine the two graphs in Exhibit B-1. One represents the movement of the S&P 500 over a 60-month period and the other is the result of 60 repeated coin tosses where the index increases by 5% on a head and declines 4.5% on a tail. Which is the S&P 500? If you think it is the top graph, you are correct. Nonetheless, it is not an obvious choice.

Semistrong-Form Efficiency

Semistrong-form efficiency indicates that stock prices should reflect all publicly available information. This includes economic information such as inflation and GNP growth, industry information such as growth and prospects, and company-specific information such as the balance sheet and earnings, management, and product/service prospects.

According to this proposition, stock prices react very, very quickly to new economic, industrial, and company disclosures. Suppose that Exxon announces that it has made a major oil find in China. On the

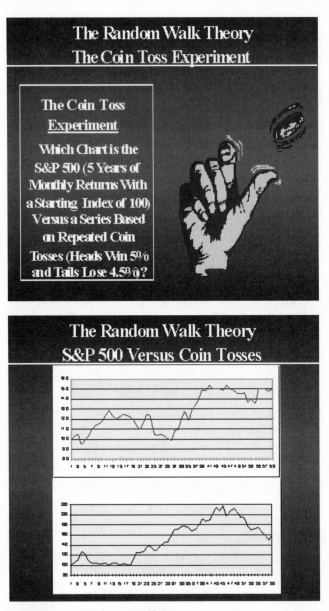

EXHIBIT B-1   Weak-Form Efficiency

basis of information in the report, stock analysts indicate that the oil find will add $10 to Exxon's stock price.

Exhibit B-2 provides two alternative ways the stock price may adjust to the new information. According to scenario 1, the price adjusts instantly to $80 and then goes back to a random walk. Under scenario 2, the stock price adjusts to the new equilibrium price of $80 over a period of time, allowing investors to profit from buying at the announcement. In a semistrong-form efficient market, the stock price follows scenario 1 and adjusts very quickly to the news announcement, thereby prohibiting investors from earning abnormal returns.

Strong-Form Efficiency

According to strong-form efficiency, stock prices reflect all information, including information not available to the investment community. This idea is usually tested by examining the returns earned by corporate managers and directors, who clearly have information not available to investors, on trades in their own company shares. Although these corporate insiders are presumed to have a fiduciary responsibility to shareholders, their privileged position provides them with the potential to profit at shareholders' expense. Rule 10b-5 of the Securities Exchange Act of 1934 limits the trading activities of corpo-

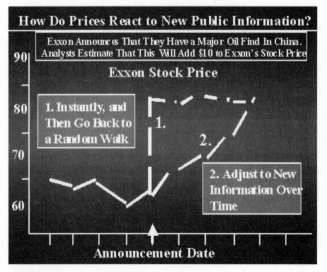

EXHIBIT B-2   Semistrong-Form Efficiency

rate officials and directors in their own stock and requires these insiders to report all trades.

Evidence on Market Efficiency

Tests of stock market efficiency involve assessing returns from a stock selection strategy relative to the returns from a benchmark. Most commonly, the benchmark consists of the returns from either (1) the market index adjusted for the risk of the stock selected or (2) stocks with similar risk characteristics (industry, size, market/book ratios). If returns from the strategy outperform returns from the benchmark in a statistically significant way (better than if by chance), then it can be presumed that the strategy generated abnormal returns (implying that the stock price did not reflect the information being tested). Such a result suggests that the market is not efficient with respect to the information being tested.

Weak-Form Efficiency

Given the ease of obtaining stock price data, there have been many tests of the random walk hypothesis and weak-form efficiency. These include the following:

1. *Tests of runs.*   Evaluate a sequence of consecutive increases or decreases.

2. *Filter rules.*   Buy/sell if a stock rises/falls by some percent, such as 1%.

3. *Market overreaction.*   Stock market psychologists believe that markets as well as individual stocks have a tendency to overreact to news.

4. *Technical trading patterns and charts.*   Consider Dow Theory, moving averages, and head-and-shoulders, inverted V, fulcrum, and point-and-figure charts.

5. *Stock and market indicators.*   Evaluate market breadth, short interest, relative strength, and the confidence index.

Most tests support the notion that (1) successive stock price changes do not exhibit runs and are independent over time, and (2) abnormal returns (above the benchmark) are not associated with alternative technical trading rules or stock and market indicators. Hence, most studies support the idea that the stock market is weak-form efficient.

Semistrong-Form Efficiency

Tests of semistrong-form efficiency fall along two different lines: (1) event studies that examine how fast the stock market or individual stock prices adjust to events such as earnings announcements, and (2) studies of the predictability of stock returns that evaluate whether such returns are associated with available public information, such as stock market capitalization, stock price/earnings (P/E) ratios, and stock price/book value (P/B) ratios as well as seasonal returns, such as the January effect. In an efficient market, stock prices react very quickly to new information and future stock returns are not predictable from attributes like P/E ratios.

Event Studies. Event studies have evaluated stock price movements around many different types of corporate and economic announcements. These include company-specific disclosures of earnings, dividends, tender offers, accounting changes, restructurings, and stock split announcements as well as economic events, such as money supply, inflation, and discount rate announcements. In these studies, stock returns around the event date are adjusted by the benchmark return and cumulated for a period of time, beginning months or days before the event until a similar period after the event.

Most event studies use daily and even trade-to-trade data to assess how quickly stock prices react to different events. For example, one study by Kevin Womack (1996) looked at the adjusted return performance for stocks receiving buy or sell recommendations by analysts from 14 Wall Street investment firms.[3] These results are presented in Exhibit B-3. On the event day, there is +5% abnormal return for buys and −9.5% return for sells. The postrecommendation returns are small in magnitude relative to the event day return. Over the following 12 months, there is an additional +2% return for buys and a 0% return for sells. These results indicate that most of the stock price reaction to analysts' recommendations occurs on the day the recommendations are made.

As noted, event studies have been performed on many different types of corporate as well as economic events. The results indicate that

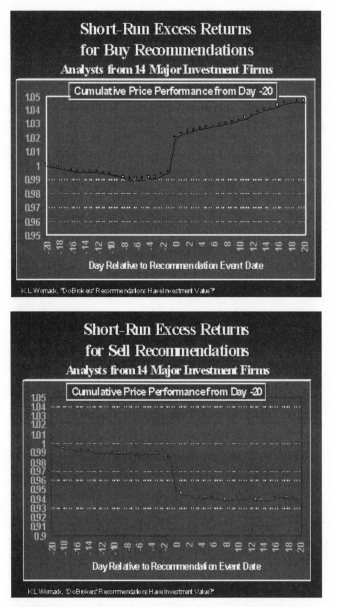

EXHIBIT B-3   Event Study of Buy/Sell Recommendations

stock prices react very quickly to corporate and economic events, with little opportunity for investors to profit abnormally after the event.

The Predictability of Stock Returns. A major body of financial research in recent years has attempted to determine if abnormal stock returns are associated with various stock attributes and/or are evident at specific points in calendar time. The stock attributes have included P/E ratios, market/book ratios, dividend yield, small firm size (defined as market capitalization), and neglected firm status (lack of analyst following). On the seasonal nature of returns, abnormal stock returns have been discovered at certain cusps in time—the turn of the year (January), the month, the week, and the day.

Most of the studies focusing on stock attributes use the following methodology:

1. Stocks are ordinally ranked on the attribute in question (i.e., lowest to highest P/E ratio) at a point in time.

2. The universe of stocks is segmented into portfolios (usually 10) based on the lowest to highest ordinal rankings on the attribute under examination.

3. The risk-adjusted return performance for the groups, or portfolios, is computed over a period of time (monthly, quarterly, or yearly).

4. The stocks are again ordinally ranked on the attribute and steps 2 through 4 are repeated.

   Most studies rerank stocks on a monthly basis, are carried out over a period of at least 20 years, and use beta and market returns to risk-adjust raw returns.

James P. O'Shaughnessy, in his popular investment book *What Works on Wall Street,* evaluates the investment returns associated with many of these stock attributes. He studies stocks over the 1951–1994 period, and compares the returns for the 50 stocks with the highest and lowest attribute measure as well as for stocks in general. The results, along with references to academic studies addressing these issues, are discussed below.[4]

Market capitalization. The small cap effect can be traced in the academic literature to two different 1981 studies by Banz and Reinganum.[5] In each case, the researchers discovered that, using the methodology described above, small cap firms have provided abnormal returns over time. As shown in Exhibit B-4, O'Shaughnessy's results indicate that over the 1951–1994 period, small cap stocks earned 13.4% compared with 11.8% for midcap stocks and 12% for large cap stocks.

P/E ratios. In 1977, S. Basu published the first of his studies on the relationship between P/E ratios and stock returns.[6] Using the standard methodology, he found that low P/E stocks tend to outperform high P/E stocks. As shown in Exhibit B-5, over the 1951–1994 period, O'Shaugh-

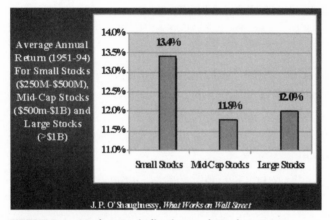

EXHIBIT B-4 Market Capitalization and Stock Returns

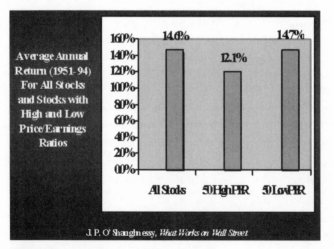

EXHIBIT B-5 P/E Ratios and Stock Returns

nessy found that stocks with low P/E ratios (14.7%) outperformed stocks with high P/E ratios (12.2%) and stocks in general (14.6%).

Market/Book ratios. Rosenberg, Reid, and Lanstein (1985) first published results indicating that low market/book (M/B) stocks tend to earn higher returns than high M/B stocks.[7] Fama and French (1992), in a landmark study, found that the M/B effect was stronger than other stock attributes and even persisted after controlling for other attributes such as risk (beta) and small capitalization.[8] In a follow-up study, Fama and French (1995) found that the M/B effect was closely related to earnings changes. Specifically, low (high) M/B stocks had low (high) returns on equity, which subsequently improved (declined), thereby generating superior (inferior) stock price performance. As shown in Exhibit B-6, O'Shaughnessy also discovered that the M/B effect is very strong, with low M/B stocks earning 17.5%, compared with 11.9% for high M/B stocks and 14.6% for stocks in general.

Semistrong-Form Efficiency: Market Summary. Whereas event studies support the notion of semistrong-form efficient markets, the studies on return predictability cast some doubt. In particular, the evidence on market capitalization and M/B ratios is viewed as being the most serious. In addition to the studies cited above, others have associated predictable returns with dividend yields, earnings surprises, and seasonal patterns. The results cannot, however, be interpreted as

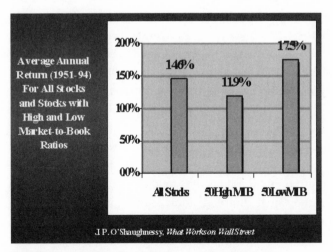

EXHIBIT B-6 Market/Book Ratios and Stock Returns

strictly refuting the efficient market hypothesis, for two reasons. First, the studies use historic and not expected returns. If these relationships are temporary and do not hold in the future, the market cannot be deemed inefficient. Second, since beta is used to risk-adjust returns in most studies, these tests are actually joint tests of market efficiency and the capital asset pricing model.

Strong-Form Efficiency

Strong-form efficient market tests assess whether stock prices reflect all information. These tests have followed two different routes. The first set of studies have evaluated the performance of mutual funds, pension funds, endowments, and bank trust departments. The notion is that these professional money managers have access to information (such as CEO interviews) not generally available to typical investors. The second set of tests have evaluated the performance of the stock trades of corporate insiders. These individuals clearly have information not available to investors and can trade in their own shares as long as this trading is not done around important corporate events such as earnings announcements.

The Performance of Professional Money Managers.   The performance of professional money managers has been studied for more than three decades. These studies have provided almost uniform results—professional money managers tend to underperform the market by 2% to 3% per year. Indicative of these results, Exhibit B-7 shows the percentage of equity mutual fund managers that beat the S&P 500 over the past 30 years. In an average year, only one-third beat the S&P 500, and the recent results have been very poor. Only two times in the past 15 years have more than 50% beaten the S&P 500, and only 7% of the equity mutual fund managers beat the S&P 500 in 1997! These results clearly support the notion of strong-form efficiency.

Returns to Insiders.   Corporate insiders include company officers and directors who must report their trades monthly to the SEC. Jaffe (1974) first reported that these insiders tend to earn excess returns on their trades in their own common stock.[9] Subsequent tests have not been as conclusive. In particular, Seyhun (1986) showed that the returns to insiders are insignificant when the costs of trading are taken into account.[10] Other recent studies have confirmed Seyhun's results.

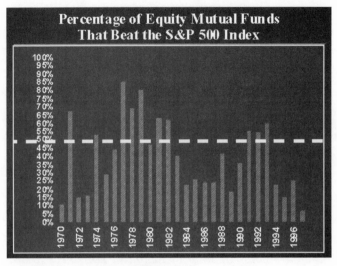

EXHIBIT B-7 Strong-Form Efficiency

Thus, the belief that insiders have access to, and trade on, information that is not reflected in stock prices is not valid.

Efficient Capital Markets Summary

The debate over the pricing efficiency of the stock market is alive and well. Most studies to date suggest that the market is efficient with respect to most types of information. Certainly, the idea that stock prices follow a random walk (successive price changes are independent) has support and is accepted by finance academicians. This indicates that the stock market is weak-form efficient and that trading based on past price trends is not likely to produce superior results. Most studies support the notion that stock prices react quickly to corporate news announcements; hence "chasing" the hot new stories off the wire will not probably pan out. In this sense, the stock market is semistrong-form efficient. In addition, the fact that corporate insiders and professional money managers do not appear to "beat the market" supports the proposition that stock prices reflect all information and thus are strong-form efficient.

The main line of research that goes against the efficient markets hypothesis involves the association of superior stock returns with various stock attributes such as low M/B ratios and small capitalization.

Notes

1. Eugene Fama, "Random Walks in Stock Market Prices," *Financial Analysts Journal* (September–October, 1965), p. 4.

2. Richard Brealey and Stewart Meyers, *Principles of Corporate Finance*, McGraw-Hill, New York, 1996.

3. Kevin Womack, "Do Brokerage Analysts' Recommendations Have Investment Value?" *Journal of Finance* 51 (March 1996), pp. 137–67.

4. James P. O'Shaughnessy, *What Works on Wall Street*, McGraw Hill, New York, 1997.

5. Rolf Banz, "The Relationship between Return and Market Value of Common Stocks," *Journal of Financial Economics* (March 1981), pp. 3–18; and Marc Reinganum, "Misspecification of Capital Asset Pricing: Empirical Anomalies Based on Earnings Yield and Market Value," *Journal of Financial Economics* (March 1981), pp. 19–46.

6. S. Basu, "The Relationship between Earnings Yield, Market Value, and Return for NYSE Common Stocks," *Journal of Financial Economics* (June 1983), pp. 129–151.

7. Barr Rosenburg, Kenneth Reid, and Ronald Lanstein, "Persuasive Evidence of Market Efficiency," *Journal of Portfolio Management* (Spring 1985), pp. 9–17.

8. Eugene Fama and Kenneth French, "The Cross-Section of Expected Return," *Journal of Finance* (June 1992), pp. 427–465.

9. Jeffrey Jaffe, "Special Information and Insider Trading," *Journal of Business* (April 1974), pp. 410–426.

10. Nejat Seyhun, "Insider's Profits, Costs of Trading, and Market Efficiency," *Journal of Financial Economics* (June 1986), pp. 189–212.

Investors' Required Return on Stocks

One of the primary issues in valuing a company is estimating its weighted average cost of capital (WACC). As shown in Exhibit C-1, the WACC is a function of the costs of debt and equity, which in turn represent investors' required return on debt and equity in the marketplace.

The cost of debt is relatively easy to determine—it is simply the current yield to maturity on the company's bonds. This market yield is primarily determined by the issuer's default risk, which is reflected in its bond "rating" as provided by Moody's or Standard & Poor's.

Assessing the cost of stock (or equity) is not as simple as calculating the cost of debt. As discussed in Chapter 5, the most common method of measuring a company's cost of equity capital is the capital asset pricing model (CAPM). The CAPM recognizes that investors' required return is a function of two factors: a risk-free rate of interest and a risk premium. Exhibit C-2 shows the historic relationship, where risk is measured by volatility of annual return. Low-risk securities like Treasury Bills have provided relatively low returns but with little volatility of

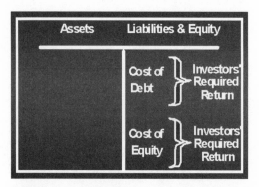

EXHIBIT C-1   Risk/Return and the Cost of Capital

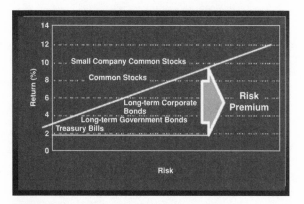

EXHIBIT C-2   The Notion of a Risk Premium

return. Higher-risk securities like common stocks have given higher returns but with greater risk.

Given that the risk-free interest rate is readily observable (you can find the rate on Treasuries in the business section of any newspaper), the key issue is measuring the risk premium. This is where the CAPM comes in. An alternative way of measuring the risk premium involves the arbitrage pricing model, discussed at the end of this appendix.

The CAPM

According to the CAPM, the expected (or required) return ($E(R_s)$) is equal to the return on the risk-free asset (R_f) plus a risk premium. In equation form, it looks like this:

Expected Return	=	Risk-Free Rate	+	Risk Premium
$E(R_s)$	=	R_f	+	$B \times [E(R_m - R_f)]$

The risk-free rate (R_f) is the rate on long-term Treasury securities, which have no credit risk. The risk premium is a function of two factors: a stock's beta (B) and the market or equity risk premium, which is the expected return on the overall stock market (R_m) minus the risk-free interest rate $[E(R_m - R_f)]$.

The theory behind the CAPM presumes several things:

1. Investors are risk-averse and therefore prefer less risk to more.

2. Because of their risk aversion, investors diversify their holdings and seek the highest expected return for their chosen level of risk (as measured by volatility of expected return).

3. Given points 1 and 2, the appropriate measure of risk for a stock is the risk that this stock adds to a diversified portfolio of securities.

4. This risk is measured by beta.

According to the CAPM, the relationship between expected return and risk (beta) is specified by the security market line (SML), as shown in Exhibit C-3. The expected return on the market is indicated where beta equals 1.0. The *slope* of the SML is the market risk premium $[E(R_m - R_f)]$.

The SML changes as market conditions change. As shown in Exhibit C-4, the SLM shifts up or down in a parallel fashion in response to increases or decreases in interest rates. When interest rates go down,

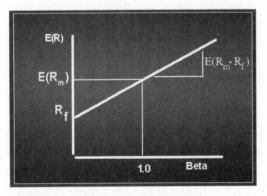

EXHIBIT C-3 The Security Market Line

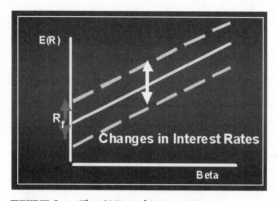

EXHIBIT C-4   The SML and Interest Rates

expected or required returns decrease. All else equal, an increase in stock prices will result. That's why the market tends to go up when the Federal Reserve takes action to lower interest rates. Of course, interest rate increases have the opposite effect. Higher expected or required rates of return, all else equal, lead to lower stock prices.

The slope of the SML changes in response to changes in the degree of risk aversion in the market, as shown in Exhibit C-5. Risk aversion in the market tends to go down during periods of sustained economic growth and low inflation. As investors become less risk-averse, they require less return for every level of risk; hence the slope of the SML declines. As a result of decreased risk aversion, the expected or required rate of return on all securities goes down, leading to higher stock prices.

Increases in the degree of investor risk aversion are reflected in an increase in the slope of the SML. This leads to higher expected or

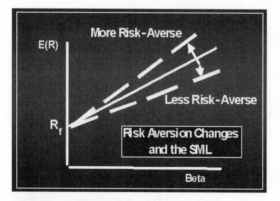

EXHIBIT C-5   The SML and Risk Aversion

required returns and, all else equal, lower stock prices. Risk aversion in the market tends to go up when concerns over recession and inflation are aroused. Stock market crashes, which often are associated with economic events like currency devaluations, also may be attributed to a sudden increase in the degree of risk aversion in the market.

Let us turn now to the two key elements of expected or required return in the CAPM: beta and the market or equity risk premium.

Beta

Beta is a measure of the risk that a security adds to a diversified portfolio of stocks. The concept of beta is actually quite simple. It is the volatility of a stock relative to the market. Consider the following examples:

1. The beta of the overall market is 1.0.

2. A stock with a beta greater than 1.0 is considered more risky than the overall market. A stock with a beta below 1.0 is considered less risky than the overall market.

3. Cisco Systems has a beta of 1.50. If the stock market increases by 10%, Cisco stock would be expected to increase by 15%. On the other hand, if the market declines by 10%, Cisco stock would be expected to decline by 15%.

Betas are usually estimated from historic stock and market returns. The most common approach is to perform a linear regression of the excess monthly return on a stock (the stock return in excess of the risk-free rate) on the excess monthly return on the overall market (the market return in excess of the risk-free rate). Usually 5 years of data (60 monthly observations) are used. This relationship, called the *characteristic line,* is shown in Exhibit C-6.

Exhibit C-7 shows a sample of industry betas. The exhibit demonstrates that betas are related to fundamental economic factors. Stocks in capital-intensive industries that are sensitive to the economy (cyclical industries) tend to have high betas, while stocks in industries whose revenues are relatively insensitive to the economy tend to have low betas.

The Equity Risk Premium

Historic Equity Risk Premium Measures. The equity risk premium (also called the market risk premium) is defined as the expected return

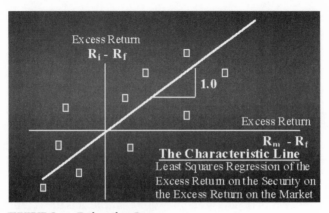

EXHIBIT C-6 Estimating Betas

Industry	Beta
Building materials	1.9
Electrical equipment	1.8
Air transport	1.7
Restaurants	1.5
Software	1.4
Hotels	1.3
Durables	1.2
Beverages	1.0
Food processing	0.9
Electric utilities	0.7
Liquor	0.6

EXHIBIT C-7 Industry Betas

on the stock market minus the risk-free rate of interest. In effect, it is the return that investors require to buy a stock of average risk as opposed to a risk-free Treasury Bond. The most common approach to estimating the equity risk premium is to assess the historic relationship between the average returns on stocks and bonds. Exhibit C-8 shows historic returns on Treasury Bills and Bonds, corporate bonds, and common stocks since 1926, as published by Ibbotson Associates. The exhibit also shows the volatility of returns as measured by the standard deviation.

EXHIBIT C-8   Historic Market Returns, Stocks, Bonds, and Bills 1926–1997

	Arithmetic Mean	Geometric Mean	Standard Deviation
Treasury bills	3.8%	3.8%	3.2%
Long-term treasury bonds	5.6%	5.2%	9.2%
Long-term corporate bonds	6.1%	5.7%	8.7%
Common stocks	12.7%	11.0%	20.3%
Small common stocks	17.7%	12.7%	33.9%

Source: 1998 SBBI Yearbook, Ibbotson Associates.

Arithmetic Versus Geometric Means.   One debate in estimating the equity risk premium from historic returns is whether to use the arithmetic or geometric mean return. The arithmetic mean return is the average annual return over the time period, while the geometric mean return is the compounded annual return.

To illustrate the difference, consider the following example: A stock that paid $0 in dividends cost $100. After the first year, the price increased to $200, for a return of 100%. In the second year, the market tanked and the stock returned to $100, yielding a second-year return of –50%. What would be your average return?

The arithmetic mean return over the 2 years is $(100\% - 50\%)/2 = 25\%$. Yet the investor still only has a stock selling for $100. The geometric mean return for the 2-year period is $[(^{100}\!/_{100})^{\wedge}(^{1}\!/_{2}) - 1.0] = 0\%$, which obviously provides a better measure of the actual return experienced over the time period. Geometric means will be below arithmetic means when a series of returns contains at least one negative number. The geometric mean return provides a better measure of the actual compounded return experience of the investor and is preferred as a measure of historic returns.

The Premium over Short-Term Versus Long-Term Treasuries. Another issue in estimating the market risk premium from historic data is whether it should be computed as the stock return in excess of (1) the return on short-term Treasury Bills or (2) the return on long-term Treasury Bonds. As shown in Exhibit C-8, the geometric mean stock return is 11%. This indicates an equity risk premium of 7.2% in excess of the return on Treasury Bills (3.8%) and a premium of 5.8% in excess of the return on Treasury Bonds (5.2%).

In practice, it is more common to use the risk premium in excess of the return on Treasury Bonds. There are two reasons for this. First, in DCF valuation, there is a presumption of a long-term horizon in determining the value of a company's shares. Computing the equity cost rate as the yield on the long-term Treasury Bond, plus the equity risk premium over that rate, is more consistent with this long-term valuation horizon. Second, because of its sensitivity to short-term economic factors, the yield on Treasury Bills tends to vary much more than the yield on Treasury Bonds. This short-term sensitivity is not consistent with the long-term focus of DCF valuation.

Expected Equity Risk Premium Measures. Expected equity risk premiums involve forecasting the expected market return over some future period (usually 5 or 10 years) and subtracting the risk-free interest rate. Many investment firms perform such analyses and, in recent years, have come to the conclusion that the historic equity risk premium significantly overstates the premium that investors require today. The lowering of the equity risk premium in the United States is due to a number of fundamental changes in the economy, the securities markets, and corporate management methods. Some analysts argue that the lower equity risk premium has been a primary driver of the stock market in the 1990s.

Goldman, Sachs & Co. published a report entitled *The Brave New Business Cycle,* describing the implications of new economic trends for corporate profitability and stock market valuation.[1] The brave new business cycle of the 1990s features longer periods of business expansion with low inflation.

The thesis goes this way. In the United States, companies have faced heightened competition as a result of globalization and trade, deregulation, and technology and have thus lost their ability to boost earnings by increasing prices. To meet investors' requirements in this environment, managers have had to become better at cutting and managing costs. Managers have thus adopted just-in-time inventory, capital spending, and labor management practices—and they have been successful, as gauged by the relevant statistics.[2] The trend has had a very significant impact on corporate profits in the 1990s. Corporate profits have grown for 7 consecutive years (an all-time record) and at the same time have become less volatile and more predictable by Wall Street analysts.

Among the implications of these developments are higher stock valuation levels (higher P/E ratios) due to a lower equity risk premium. According to the report:

Signs of a reduced equity risk premium.　In theory, by stabilizing the growth of the earnings stream, the Brave New Business Cycle should reduce the premium that investors require for equity investments. This premium is nothing more than the difference in expected total return between investing in equities and investing in "safe" fixed-income assets with similar duration, such as intermediate- to long-term government bonds. However, although the equity risk premium is easy to define conceptually, it is difficult to measure because ex post returns are not the same as ex ante expectations, even for periods of several years. Even so, support for the notion that the equity risk premium has declined can be found in two related facts. First, the P/E multiple for the S&P 500 has been trending up for more than a decade, whereas it should normally rise in recessions and early expansions and then fall progressively during expansions, as the excess slack in the economy is exhausted. Second, this increase has far outstripped the modest decline in real yields on 10-year government bonds that has occurred since the early 1980s. These disparate trends strongly suggest that the equity risk premium is probably moving down.[3]

An article in *The Economist* shares the view that equity risk premiums have declined significantly in the 1990s. Among the evidence cited is that fact that share prices in the United States have continued to go up while the growth in corporate earnings has slowed.[4] From a valuation perspective, a lower equity risk premium means a lower discount rate on stocks—which, all else being equal, leads to higher stock prices.

To support the notion that the historic equity risk premium has been too high, the article cites the fact that bonds are almost as volatile as stocks these days. Exhibit C-9 plots the annual volatility of monthly stock and bond returns using the Ibbotson data. The plot shows that, whereas stock returns were three to four (or more) times as volatile as bond returns through the 1960s, over the past decade stock and bond returns have been almost equally volatile. Since volatility is an indication of the relative riskiness of stocks and bonds, this plot suggests that the premium investors require to buy stocks as opposed to bonds has declined.

One argument for using a historic equity risk premium is simplicity. Historic measures are easily computed and readily available (e.g., from the annual Ibbotson study). But the market realities suggest that the relative risk of stocks and bonds has changed and that the equity

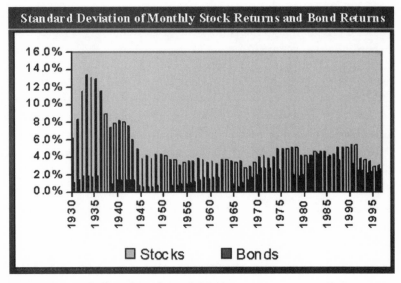

EXHIBIT C-9   Volatility of Stocks and Bonds

risk premium has declined from previous levels. An expected equity risk premium is more difficult to derive and is not readily available. However, most commentators on the topic indicate that, during the 1990s, the expected equity risk premium (over the yield on long-term Treasuries) has declined to the 2% to 4% range.

The Arbitrage Pricing Model

The main competitor to the CAPM as a model of expected return is the arbitrage pricing model (APM). The APM is similar to the CAPM in that expected or required return is measured as a function of the risk-free interest rate plus a risk premium. The main difference is that whereas there is only one risk premium factor in the CAPM (the overall market), there are multiple factors in the APM.

According to the APM, the expected return on a stock is a function of the risk-free rate plus the sensitivity of the stock to several economic factors. These factors are determined using historic returns. The APM appears as follows:

$$
\begin{array}{ccccccc}
\text{Expected} & = & \text{Risk-Free} & + & \text{Risk} & + & \text{Risk} & + \cdots & \text{Risk} \\
\text{Return} & & \text{Rate} & & \text{Premium}_1 & & \text{Premium}_2 & & \text{Premium}_n
\end{array}
$$

$$
E(R_s) \;=\; R_f \;+\; B_1 \times [E(R_1 - R_f)] + B_2 \times [E(R_2 - R_f)] + \cdots \; B_n \times [E(R_n - R_f)]
$$

The $[E(R_n - R_f)]$ term represents the risk premiums for the different factors (1 through n), and the B_n term represents the sensitivity (beta) of the stock to the risk premium factor. In using APM, these different risk premium factors are determined using a factor analysis of the stock's historic returns. Whereas these factors may go unidentified, it is presumed that one predominant risk premium factor driving all stocks is the overall stock market (which is the only factor in the CAPM). The other factors may be general or stock-specific in nature, and may include gross national product (GNP), interest rates (especially for financial stocks), commodity prices (energy stocks), or currency values (multinational firms).

The CAPM is a specialized case of the APM. It presumes that there is only one risk premium factor influencing stocks—the overall stock market. The APM is a more complete specification of expected return and is potentially a better measure. However, two problems persist with APM and have limited its use: (1) the failure to identify the specific factors affecting returns, and (2) the resulting problems with measuring and interpreting the sensitivity of a company's stock to unidentified factors.

Notes

1. Edward F. McKelvey, *The Brave New Business Cycle: Its Implications for Corporate Profitability,* U.S. Economic Research, Goldman, Sachs & Co., New York, 1997.

2. For example, the inventory/sales ratio in the United States hit an all-time low in 1998. In addition, the delivery time for capital equipment had declined to less than 3 months, and U.S. firms were employing a record number of part-time employees.

3. Edward F. McKelvey, *The Brave New Business Cycle: Its Implications for Corporate Profitability,* U.S. Economic Research, Goldman, Sachs & Co, New York, 1997, p. 4.

4. "Welcome to Bull Country," *The Economist,* July 18, 1998, pp. 21–23.

Glossary

accounts payable   The amount owed to suppliers for goods and services purchased on credit; payment obligations usually range between 30 and 90 days.

accounts receivable   The amount due from customers for goods and services sold on credit; discounts are often given for timely payment (e.g., within 10 days).

alpha   The rate of return on an investment in excess of the expected rate of return as forecast by a pricing model (e.g., CAPM).

after-tax cost of debt   The tax-adjusted cost of debt; the nominal interest rate adjusted for the tax benefits of interest payments. The equation is $(1 - \text{tax rate}) \times (\text{nominal interest rate})$.

arbitrage pricing model (APM)   An asset pricing model that predicts expected returns on a security on the basis of a correlation between the security and multiple input variables.

average-risk stock   A stock with a *beta* equal to 1; an issue that moves with the market.

bear market   A long-term downward trend in security prices. Recently this has been defined as a decline of 10% or more over an extended time period. The worst bear market in the last 50 years occurred between 1973 and 1974.

beta   The measure of *systematic risk* of a security. The beta of the market is defined as 1. If a security's beta is greater than 1, it is expected to exceed market changes (e.g., when the market increases by 5%, the security increases by 10%). If a security's beta is less than 1, it is expected to lag behind market changes (e.g., when the market increases by 10%, the security increases by 5%).

bonds   A security issued by a borrower that establishes a contractual obligation to repay a specified amount at a future date, usually with periodic interest payments.

book value   The accounting value of a corporate security.

book value per share (BVPS)   Common stockholder equity divided by the number of shares outstanding. This is an estimate of the equity stake in an organization that each share represents.

bottom-line growth   A company's growth in net income.

bull market   An extended period of increasing security prices.

capital asset pricing model (CAPM)   An asset pricing model that determines the required rate of return on securities on the basis of a *market risk premium* and a *risk-free rate.*

capital markets   Financial markets in which securities are bought and sold.

cash flow   An exchange of cash, either inflow or outflow, as a result of a transaction.

cash inflow   The net cash amount flowing into a firm (e.g., revenues) as a result of the ongoing operations of a business.

cash outflow   The net cash amount flowing out of a firm (e.g., expenses) from the ongoing operations of a business.

clientele effect   The tendency of investors to purchase stock of a company based on its dividend policy. Investors who desire predictable current income buy stock with higher dividends (e.g., ConEd), while those who desire growth buy stock that pay little or no dividends (e.g., Intel).

common stock   Equity ownership in a corporation. Two important characteristics of common stock are that its owners have a residual claim on corporate assets (behind bondholders and preferred stockholders) and are subject to limited liability.

common stock equivalents   Common stock plus securities convertible into common stock of a company.

compound   The process of accumulating the time value of money over time. For example, compounding interest payments means that an investor who earns interest in one period will earn additional interest in the following period because of the reinvestment of interest in each period.

compound annual growth rate (CAGR) A rate that assumes annual compounding of growth.

contingent claim A claim whose value is based on the value of another asset or the outcome of a specific event.

corporate value The estimated total dollar value of an enterprise, usually determined by models and appraisals.

current stock price The most recent price level at which an equity investment traded as determined by the financial market where that security trades.

cyclical stocks Companies or industries whose financial performance (revenues and earnings) is tied to business cycle fluctuations. The automotive, steel, and cement industries are examples.

debt/equity ratio The total amount of debt financing the firm has in its capital structure divided by the dollar amount invested by shareholders.

defensive stocks Stocks that provide necessary services, such as electric utilities and gas; essentials, such as food; or staples, such as soft drinks. Because of the nature of these products, the stocks provide a degree of stability during periods of economic decline.

depreciation The periodic allocation of the cost of property, plant, and equipment over the useful revenue-generating life of the asset. Depreciation is a noncash expense and is not a cash outflow.

depreciation rate Annual depreciation divided by annual revenues.

diluted earnings per share Earnings per share adjusted for all potential equity claims on earnings. Diluted EPS is lower than basic EPS because it accounts for potential dilutive common shares from complex securities like convertible bonds and stock options.

discount The process of calculating the present value of expected cash flows. To discount means to multiply a number by less than 1.0.

discount factor The multiplier used to convert an expected future cash flow into current dollars.

discount rate The rate of return used to measure the time value of money. The discount rate varies with risk of the cash flows being discounted.

discounted cash flow approach A valuation model based on the present value of expected cash flows.

dividend   A payment of cash or stock by the company to its stock-holders.

diversification   Spreading investment holdings across multiple industries, strategies, or firms to reduce the company-specific risk associated with an investment portfolio.

Dow Jones Industrial Average (DJIA)   A price-weighted equity index of 30 blue-chip New York Stock Exchange companies.

earnings   Net income.

earnings before interest and taxes (EBIT)   Income generated by the company before the payment of interest on debt and income taxes.

earnings before interest but after taxes (EBIAT).   Same as EBIT minus the payment of income taxes.

earnings per share (EPS)   Corporate earnings divided by shares outstanding.

efficient capital market   A market in which information asymmetries do not provide profit opportunities and new information is quickly interpreted and reflected in the value of shares.

excess marketable securities   Marketable securities held by the firm for investment purposes. Marketable securities do not include treasury stock of the issuing firm.

excess return period   The number of years that a company is expected to earn a return on incremental investment in excess its weighted average cost of capital.

expected return   The return an investor expects to earn at a specific level of risk.

expected return of the market (R_m) The expected return on a market benchmark index (e.g., S&P 500) for a specific period. Historic data are often used to estimate this variable.

fairly valued stock   A stock's price that is equal to its intrinsic stock value.

Financial Accounting Standards Board (FASB)   The primary rule-making body that establishes, interprets, and publishes financial accounting principles for public and private firms.

fiscal year (FY)   The accounting year consistent with the operating cycle for which a firm reports its periodic financial statements.

free cash flow (FCF)   Equal to cash inflows minus cash outflows.

free cash flow to equity (FCFE)   Equal to free cash flow minus interest expense.

free cash flow to firm (FCFF)   The free cash flow available to all share-holders and stakeholders after capital expenditure obligations are fulfilled.

fully valued stock   A stock with a price that is generally considered to be at the high end of its intrinsic value. High-growth firms eventually become fully valued when all future growth expectations and opportunities are priced into the shares and there is limited additional upside.

fundamental analysis   Security analysis that incorporates all available public information relating to a particular company, including historic prices, industry data, and overall market performance.

greater fool theory   A theory based on the belief that anyone who makes an investment will be able to sell it to a less informed investor for a profit in the future.

growth stocks   Stocks of companies in expanding industries where the growth in earnings on revenues is expected to be significantly greater (e.g., 15% or more) than the economy in general.

incremental working capital expenditure   The change in *working capital* from period to period.

initial public offering (IPO)   The first publicly traded issue of a corporation's common stock.

intrinsic stock value   The perceived value of a security as opposed to the market value or book value. It is defined as the present value of the expected future cash flows of the firm.

inventory   The firm's raw material, work in process, and finished goods surplus that has not been used or sold in the normal operating process.

investment rate   Investment in property, plant, and equipment divided by annual revenues.

leverage   The use of debt financing in a firm's capital structure.

leveraged buyout (LBO)   The purchase that is financed with a large percentage of debt and is secured by the firm's assets.

long Treasury rate   The yield on long-term U.S. Treasury securities—typically the benchmark 30-year Treasury Bond.

market capitalization   The total market value of the outstanding debt and equity of a firm.

market risk premium   The difference between the expected return on the market portfolio (usually the historic return on the S&P 500) and the *risk-free rate of return.*

merger A combination of two firms in which one firm absorbs the assets and liabilities of the other firm in their entirety.

momentum trading strategy A technical trading technique that involves buying a stock because the trend in a stock's price has been up, and selling a stock because its stock price trend has been down.

net change in working capital The difference in working capital from one period to another.

net investment New investment minus depreciation.

net operating income (NOI) Earnings from continuing operations before paying interest on debt or income taxes.

net operating profit (NOP) See *net operating income.*

net operating profit after taxes (NOPAT) Operating income before interest payments on debt and income taxes. Used to calculate cash flows to the firm, the measurement seeks to exclude the tax benefits of debt financing in the profit measurement.

net operating profit margin (NOPM) Net operating profit per dollar of sales (NOP divided by revenues).

net present value (NPV) The present value of future cash flows minus the initial cost of the venture or project.

operating income Income from continuing operations before paying income tax and interest expense.

overvalued stock A stock whose price is greater than its intrinsic value.

par value The nominal dollar amount assigned to a security by the issuing firm. Par value for stock is generally 1 cent or $1 and has nothing to do with the ultimate market price or book value of the issue. Par value for bonds is generally $1,000.

period of competitive advantage See *excess return period.*

pretax cost of debt The nominal rate of interest on a debt issue; the figure does not incorporate the tax benefits of debt interest expense.

preferred stock An ownership claim on corporate assets senior to that of common stock but junior to debt. It is technically an equity security, but has features similar to both debt and equity. Preferred stock pays shareholders a periodic dividend payment.

However, unlike bond payments, preferred dividend payments are not legally binding and the board of directors can withhold dividends during hard times.

premium The amount by which a security sells above its *par value.*

present value (PV) The value of future payments discounted to today's value to incorporate risk and the time value of money.

price/book value (P/BV) ratio The market price per share of stock divided by the book value per share.

price/cash flow (P/CF) ratio The market price of stock per share divided by the cash flow per share. Cash flow per share is roughly estimated by using earnings before interest, taxes, depreciation, and amortization on a per share basis.

price/earnings (P/E) ratio The relationship between earnings per share and the market price of common stock. Generally speaking, a high P/E multiple relative to other companies in the same industry implies that investors have confidence in a company's ability to generate higher future profits.

price/earnings/growth (PEG) ratio The P/E ratio divided by the projected earnings growth rate. It measures the price that one pays for expected future growth. This measurement was popularized by the Motley Fool.

price/sales (P/S) ratio The market value of a firm divided by its annual revenues. Companies with high profit margins usually have higher P/S ratios.

price volatility The relative rate at which the price of a security moves up or down, as determined by the annualized standard deviation of daily changes in price.

pro forma Projections of what a company's financial performance will be in the future.

random walk hypothesis The theory that investment price movements do not follow any pattern or trend over time and that past price movements have no impact on future price movements.

relative value approach Valuing a firm relative to other firms in the industry on the basis of size, earnings, and similar characteristics. Common relative value measurements include market/book, price/earnings, price/cash flow, and price/sales.

residual value The terminal value of a company beyond the *excess return period.* Calculated by dividing NOPAT by WACC.

return to stockholder   A shareholder-realized return in the form of capital appreciation and dividends over the holding period.

revenues   Net sales generated by firm operations.

revenue growth rate   An annualized growth rate of sales over a specified time period, usually 5–10 years.

risk   Unanticipated change in investment returns over an extended period of time, as measured by the volatility of returns.

risk-free rate of return(R_f)   The rate of return on the 30-year U.S. Treasury bond.

secondary market   The markets in which securities are traded after their initial issuance. The NYSE, AMEX, and NASDAQ are secondary markets.

senior claims   The highest level of financial claims issued by a company. The level of seniority is used to determine claims on assets upon liquidation. Senior debt claims are paid prior to any payments of junior claims. Debt and preferred stock have claims that are senior to common stock.

share repurchase program   A program under which a firm purchases shares of its own stock via the secondary market.

shares outstanding   The total number of shares issued by a firm that have not been retired or repurchased.

short sale   Borrowing a security from a broker and selling it at the current market price, with the understanding that it must later be bought back (hopefully at a lower price) and returned to the lending agent.

short squeeze   A situation where a rise in stock prices forces investors who sold stock short to purchase shares to cover their short position and cut their losses. As the price of the shares continues to rise, more short sellers feel compelled to cover their positions.

spread to Treasuries   The difference between security yields and the yield on 30-year Treasury Bonds. High yield, emerging debt, corporate debt, and dividend yield are often measured as a spread to Treasury Bonds.

standard deviation   A statistical measurement equal to the square root of the variance; a measurement of dispersion of a data sample around the average. A security with a high standard deviation of returns is risky because of the large range of potential returns that the investor can expect.

Standard & Poor's 500   A market value weighted index of 500 stocks that represents more than $8 trillion in *market capitalization* in the U.S. equity markets.

systematic risk   Risk that cannot be diversified away by holding a portfolio of securities. Measured by a stock's beta.

takeover   The act of acquiring control of an organization through a cash or stock bid.

tax rate   The ratio equal to the corporation's provision for income taxes divided by income before taxes.

technical analysis   Analysis of market data (stock prices, volume, correlations, etc.) in an attempt to predict future price movements of a security on the basis of historic market trends. Technical analysis includes chart analysis, moving averages, support and resistance measurement, and numerous other measures of historic relationships.

top-line growth   Revenue growth of a company.

undervalued stock   A stock whose market price is below its intrinsic value.

unsystematic risk   Any risk attached to a security that can be diversified away by holding a portfolio of securities.

value to common equity   Equal to total corporate value minus senior claims. The current market value of all common stock.

ValuePro 2000   Easy-to-use stock valuation software that applies the *discounted cash flow approach.*

volatility   The relative rate at which the price of a security or index moves up or down, as determined by the annualized *standard deviation* of daily change in price.

weighted average cost of capital (WACC)   The weighted average cost of financing for a firm.

working capital   Accounts receivable plus inventories minus accounts payable. Working capital is required to support the revenue-generating activities of a firm.

yield   The annual percentage rate earned on a particular security or investment asset.

List of Acronyms

AMEX	American Stock Exchange
APM	arbitrage pricing model
BV	book value
BVPS	book value per share
CAPM	capital asset pricing model
CAGR	compound annual growth rate
CGS	cost of goods sold
CEO	chief executive officer
CFO	chief financial officer
DCF	discounted cash flow
DJIA	Dow Jones Industrial Average
DOS	disk operating system
EBIAT	earnings before interest and after taxes
EBIT	earnings before interest and taxes
EDGAR	electronic data gathering analysis and research (SEC data service)
EPS	earnings per share
FCF	free cash flow
FCFE	free cash flow to equity
FCFF	free cash flow to the firm
IPO	initial public offering
LBO	leveraged buyout
M&A	mergers and acquisition

M/B	market/book ratio
MBA	Master of Business Administration
NASDAQ	National Association of Securities Dealers Automated Quotations
NOI	net operating income
NOP	net operating profit
NOPAT	net operating profit after taxes
NOPM	net operating profit margin
NPV	net present value
NYSE	New York Stock Exchange
P/BV	price/book value ratio
PC	personal computer
P/E	price/earnings ratio
PEG	price/earnings/growth ratio
P/S	price/sales ratio
PV	present value
R&D	research and development
SEC	Securities and Exchange Commission
SGA	sales, general, and administrative expenses
S&P500	Standard & Poor's 500 Index
URL	uniform resource locator
WACC	weighted average cost of capital

Index

About the Authors

Gary Gray, Ph.D., is a Visiting Professor of Finance at The Pennsylvania State University and is a consultant to several Wall Street investment banks. Previously he was a Managing Director with Lehman Brothers and was with Shearson Lehman Brothers and E. F. Hutton. Dr. Gray has been an investment banker/financial engineer since 1972, specializing in new product development in municipal bonds and preferred stock. He has been responsible for a number of innovative financial products, including tax-exempt zero coupon bonds and capital appreciation bonds; tender option crossover refunding bonds; residual interest bonds (RIBs)/select auction variable rate securities (SAVRs); municipal call hedging option programs (Muni CHOPs); bond payment obligations (BPOs); agricultural revenue bonds; secondary market programs for tax-exempts and preferred stock, including multiple option municipal securities, and a variety of unit investment trust products and leveraged limited partnership structures.

Dr. Gray attended Penn State on a football scholarship, where he played inside linebacker, and was a graduate assistant coach under Joe Paterno. He has published articles in numerous periodicals, including *Harvard Business Review* and *Municipal Finance Journal.* He is coauthor, along with Pat Cusatis, of *Municipal Derivative Securities: Uses and Valuation,* which was published by Irwin Professional Publishing in October 1994. He is an avid fly fisherman and runs the Encierro each July in Pamplona, Spain.

Patrick J. Cusatis, Ph.D., is a Visiting Associate Professor of Finance at The Pennsylvania State University and is a Director at First Union National Bank. Previously Dr. Cusatis was a Vice President with Lehman Brothers and specialized in new product development, computer modeling, quantitative techniques, and hedging strategies. He was responsible for the financial modeling and implementation of Muni CHOPs, BPOs, RIBs/SAVRs; and a secondary market program using levered RIBs/SAVRs. Dr. Cusatis also was responsible for developing a call valuation strategy model for issuers with multiple series of municipal bonds outstanding. He currently is responsible for the tender option bond program at First Union National Bank.

Dr. Cusatis has published numerous articles in books and journals, including the *Journal of Financial Economics, Journal of Applied Corporate Finance,* and *Municipal Finance Journal.* He is coauthor, along with Gary Gray, of *Municipal Derivative Securities: Uses and Valuation.* He is an avid fly fisherman, hunter, and antiques collector.

J. Randall Woolridge, Ph.D., is the Goldman, Sachs & Co. and Frank P. Smeal Endowed University Professor of Finance at The Pennsylvania State University. His teaching and research interests are in corporate finance with an emphasis on the valuation consequences of corporate strategic investment and financial decisions. He has won the Excellence in Teaching Award at the Penn State MBA Program. Dr. Woolridge has also participated in over 300 executive development programs in more than 20 countries in North and South America, Europe, Asia, and Africa. His specialty areas in executive programs include corporate financial management and strategy, financial engineering, security analysis, and creating shareholder value. He has consulted for numerous corporate clients—among them AT&T, Merrill Lynch, Goldman Sachs, Morgan Stanley, Bankers Trust, Paine Webber, Bank of Boston, and Knight Ridder.

Dr. Woolridge has published over 25 articles in leading academic and professional journals, including the *Journal of Finance, Journal of Financial Economics,* and *Journal of Applied Corporate Finance.* His research has been highlighted extensively on the financial pages of: *The New York Times, The Wall Street Journal, Barron's, Fortune, Forbes,* and *Business Week.* He has appeared on CNN's *Money Line* and CNBC's *Business Today.* Dr. Woolridge is an avid marathon runner and he hates fly fishing.